The Art of the Filmmaker

The Art of the Filmmaker

The Practical Aesthetics of the Screen

Peter Markham

OXFORD
UNIVERSITY PRESS

OXFORD
UNIVERSITY PRESS

Oxford University Press is a department of the University of Oxford. It furthers
the University's objective of excellence in research, scholarship, and education
by publishing worldwide. Oxford is a registered trade mark of Oxford University
Press in the UK and certain other countries.

Published in the United States of America by Oxford University Press
198 Madison Avenue, New York, NY 10016, United States of America.

Library of Congress Control Number: 2023944341

ISBN 978–0–19–763153–9 (pbk.)
ISBN 978–0–19–763152–2 (hbk.)

DOI: 10.1093/oso/9780197631522.001.0001

Paperback printed by Marquis Book Printing, Canada
Hardback printed by Bridgeport National Bindery, Inc., United States of America

For my mother Jean Scott, who taught me more about story and storytelling in cinema than anyone.

Contents

Acknowledgments

I would like to give my thanks to the following, without whose inspiration, insights, guidance, and encouragement, whether they realize it or not, I could not have written this book.

Eli Arenson, Dubois Ashong, Tessa Blake, Martin Bostock, Clive Boutle, Emma Burge, Tomas Gomez Bustillo, Lee Citron, Paul Cronin, R. J. Dawson, Will Dickerson, Aihui Dong, Sabrina Doyle, Gareth Dunnet-Alcocer, Ryan Farzad, John Patton Ford, David Henry Gerson, Brady Hallongren, Julian Higgins, Bruce Isaacs, Al Kalyk, Ka'ramuu Kush, Moya Lee, Alexa Sascha-Lewin, Jeremy Merrifield, Chloe Okuno, Joe Petricca, Asaph Polonsky, Philip Rakesh, Josema Roig, Ashley Rowe, Barry Sabath, Omer Ben Shachar, Anthony Sneed, Angel Soto, Matthew Specktor, Courtney Stephens, Kat Street, the Sundance Collab, Justin Tipping, Brian Udovich, Patty West, Zoé Wittock, Oran Zegman, Dr. Mahlet Zimeta, others whom with my apologies I have no doubt omitted to mention, the Directing Fellows and those of other disciplines I was fortunate to know during my career at AFI Conservatory, and those I have taught since—all of whom *teach me*.

My special thanks go to Suzanne Regan for her wise and invaluable guidance during the book's final stages.

My deep gratitude goes also to my wife Barbara Tfank, whose wisdom, counsel, and constant support I hold immeasurably precious.

Finally, I am indebted to screenwriter and mentor Gill Dennis (1941–2015), who taught me the art of teaching and the inescapability of truth.

Introduction

*The formal control, the precision of the framing and the movement within
the frame, the pacing of the action, the sound—it was all there, immediately
evident.*

—**Martin Scorsese on Ari Aster's *Hereditary***

How do we understand the filmmaker's art? Of what is it comprised? What are its
principles, its methods, the spectrum of its approaches—across the generations,
across cultures, across sensibilities? What factors form its foundations? What are its
facets, its imperatives, its functions and purposes? Does it adhere to hard and fast
rules, or is it more supple, an agile art—an amalgam of arts—adapting to the different
challenges each film presents its filmmaker? Or might it perhaps derive its genius
from both polarities? Is it informed by intuition, by recognized technique, or again by
something of the two seemingly incongruous wellsprings?

In considering these questions, this book makes use of particular shots, scenes, and
sequences from three films in particular (those providing the case study sequences)
among many others—not as exercises in film theory but as resources for close exploration of the filmmaker's art. This approach harkens back to the means by which past
filmmakers learned their craft, when making films to learn how to make films was
nowhere near as practical an enterprise as it is now. There were no smartphones, no
digital cameras, not so much as an analogue camera. When an aspiring filmmaker
couldn't get hold of a 16 mm film camera, they would shoot on 8 mm. Then would
come the editing, by hand, laborious and a very different proposition from processes
readily and thankfully available today. In those predigital times therefore, "learning
by doing" was not so easy. Directors had to learn how to learn the art of the filmmaker
by *watching* films. Orson Welles watched John Ford's *Stagecoach*. Martin Scorsese
watched the films of Orson Welles, Federico Fellini, Michelangelo Antonioni, Alfred
Hitchcock and many, many more. (This book demonstrates how the filmmaking art
of notable contemporary exponents Ari Aster, Barry Jenkins, and Chloe Zhao can be
as enlightening as those of established masters, several of whom are also referenced.)

In listening to many of the commentaries provided on Blu-ray "extras" and online,
and in engaging in class discussion both at film school and in my own sessions, it's
become apparent to me that many commentators simply theorize or tell the story of
the film they have watched rather than discussing it as cinema. Filmmaking students

The Art of the Filmmaker. Peter Markham, Oxford University Press. © Oxford University Press 2023.
DOI: 10.1093/oso/9780197631522.003.0001

often confuse and conflate critical theory; political, social, and cultural perspectives; and simple opinion with insight into the art of visual storytelling. The notion of *practical aesthetics*—neither the simple "coverage" of dramatic action nor what is often considered the affectation of style but is instead the means of creating the world, modulating space and time, conveying information, generating emotion and sensation, and engaging audiences by telling a story effectively—rarely occurs to many students, even to some working filmmakers, until it has been pointed out.

The Art of the Filmmaker: The Practical Aesthetics of the Screen provides specific criteria through which the reader might more fully appreciate the layered understanding that Martin Scorsese reveals to us in his appreciation of Ari Aster's *Hereditary*. Filmmaker or not, through the approach of the book the reader will, I hope, attain a more acute insight into the mind, practice, and art of the director and other creative filmmakers: the cinematographer, the production designer, the costume designer, and the editor.

The book's reader might be a student filmmaker, a practicing filmmaker, a student or scholar of film studies, theory, or history; might be a student of media studies or scholar of arts programs encompassing broader, more eclectic concerns; or might be an informed, committed cinephile eager for further substantial exploration of the art to which they are drawn. The student of filmmaking will gain both foundational and advanced insights into the practical aesthetics of the cinematic address that will stand them in good stead as they progress through their career, while the more experienced practitioner may refresh and renew their understanding, using the precepts and new perspectives explored in the book to both challenge and develop a grasp perhaps already comprehensive. Students and scholars of film studies, like those of film theory and history, will find a great deal of pragmatic information on the decision-making processes of filmmakers—and by inference all media creators—historically and, most importantly, in present practice. The lover of movies, meanwhile, whether relative newcomer to their art or its sophisticated devotee, will acquire resources by which to enrich their appreciation, deepening their awareness of the multiple and interconnected levels at which the cinematic address functions.

Whatever the nature of the reader, they need to be aware that throughout this book, its concerns are the intention, method, and practice of the filmmaker in the creation and capture of the fiction on the screen and on the formulation of the elements of the screen as a designed address to the audience. This is not a work about the *reading* of films, in the sense that a film as a *text* might be considered an entity independent of its creator, the interpretation of which takes precedence over any intended "messaging" of the filmmaker. It is, in contrast, a work about the design and what might be figuratively described as the *writing* of the film's address to its audience, in terms of its dramaturgy—the representation of its dramatic narrative on the screen—and of the qualities of this visual (and sonic) address that bring about elements of filmic discourse that words on the page of a screenplay, no matter how expertly written by the most proficient practitioners of this complex craft, cannot by themselves realize, can only describe or hint at, or even lack adequate formulation of altogether.

Indeed, the scope of what audiences—in a global multiplicity of cultures, subcultures, sensibilities, preconceptions, and mindsets of one kind or another, from one day to another in the plethora of news and social media, and in the changing currents of social mores and agendas—might *infer* from a film cannot lie within the already capacious province of the effective filmmaker who, rather than second-guessing the permutations of interpretation, of the *reading* of their film, will rigorously formulate their practical aesthetics so as to ensure their movie takes its audiences on a preconceived, designed journey common to all in which even the ambiguities of its narrative—in terms of meaning, possibility, emotion, and ethical complexity—can be understood as intended across the cultural and generational spectrum constituted by its viewers. Telling the story in a way that prevents audience members from constructing their own narratives (as they *read* a film) broadly independent of that designated by the filmmaker is a prime aspect of the cinematic art—unless the filmmaker seeks, deliberately, to open up precise, alternative possibilities without settling conclusively on any one.

What viewers around the world, of different ages, at different times will bring to any movie will be legion. The filmmaker who attempts to anticipate, then accommodate, the magnitude of this range of possibility dilutes their address and weakens their movie's authority. Where, by contrast, there is specificity, there is authenticity—and where there is authenticity, there is universality. It is the local that is rendered global while the posited global finds itself nebulous. (The universal appeal of America mainstream cinema over the decades has not been due to any broad reaching out to world cultures so much as to the distillation of the American psyche and its manifestation in the tropes of American onscreen myth.)

In exploring the filmmaker's art formulated by the practical aesthetics of the screen, the chapters in this book include the following:

- A brief examination of various modes of appreciating cinema.
- A structured, detailed exploration and delineation of specific criteria to be usefully employed in understanding the filmmaker's art.
- A forensic analysis of sequences and aspects of this art from three feature films by notable filmmakers.

The first section of the book also provides insights essential for the reader to consider as they go forward to reflect on the nature and interfunctionality of the filmmaker's art:

- The "five domains" in which a film comes to life.
- The "five tasks" of the filmmaker and the "two vectors' of the filmmaker's process.

What is meant by the term *filmmaker*?

The medium of the novelist is prose. While this may be immeasurably complex and the skills of the writer multifaceted, the words on the page, the sentences and paragraphs, are the author's vehicle for storytelling. There is one mind at work, one craft, one address, no matter how eclectic.

The screen is an altogether different medium. While the director orchestrates the elements that constitute its discourse with the intention of telling a story, the creative team are storytellers also. The screenwriter self-evidently writes for the screen, while the cinematographer, production designer, costume designer, editor, and accomplished film actor do not merely embellish how the story is shown but bring their crafts into the service of its telling, creating a world, evoking emotions, revealing character, delivering information, prompting visceral sensation, fostering wonder or dread, and even conveying a creative vision: a thematic question, a paradox, an insight into the human condition. Their skills are not cosmetic (or if that's all they are, the "filmmaker" is failing in their tasks). On the contrary, their contributions are integral to a film's storytelling. Their individual crafts must work not only within their own terms but in conjunction with each other—we might use the term *interfunctionality* to describe this mutual dependence. All the artists listed here, in addition to the director, are filmmakers. Not only must they master their own disciplines, but they need to develop an understanding of those of their colleagues, too, and of how they meld to form the language and art of the moving image.

This book is therefore intended for all creative contributors to cinema as well as students of film studies and theory and informed viewers. If at times it appears to address the director alone, there is an open invitation, and indeed a request, to all filmmakers and other readers to listen in—and intently too.

The Term *Practical Aesthetics*

The common assumption that substance and style are antithetical, that there can be substance without its representation, communication, and perception, that style must always be in some way or other an interchangeable veneer laid on top of some narrative independent of it, suggests that the choice of aesthetics has, as a matter of course, to be purely subjective. That it may be determined very precisely by the practicalities of storytelling might therefore come as a surprise to many. This crucial aspect becomes especially apparent in the three case studies. Ari Aster with *Hereditary*, Barry Jenkins with *Moonlight*, and Chloe Zhao with *Nomadland* each in their own remarkable fashions, clearly demonstrates it. To fully appreciate the unity of substance and style in their work and how this is encapsulated in their practical aesthetics, the reader is advised to watch and know each film in its entirety in addition to the sequences described in each chapter, in conjunction with their reading of the book.

Another frequent association made is a connection between the concepts of aesthetics and either beauty or perfection of form or both. It is not the intention of this book to advance any such assumption. By *practical aesthetics*, I mean the language of the screen in all the aspects discussed, from composition and mise en scène to the "flow of energy" to the elements of shape and line—units of visual articulation I call the *ikones* of screen rhetoric. An image on the screen may indeed be beautiful, may incorporate perfect symmetry, but it may also be ugly, messy, florid, even grotesque. What is important is not that it's pleasing to the eye, painterly, or picturesque— although it may have those qualities if that is appropriate to a film's visual discourse— but how it functions in relation to the material it depicts, how it relates to the language of the film as a whole and to the filmmaker's address to their audience—one that conveys emotion, cognition, visceral sensation perhaps, and suggests (and often dictates) the fears, wishes, and questions the viewer experiences in the process of watching a movie.

Far from being the manifestation of any sense of decorum, these aesthetics have a practical purpose and constitute the resources of the visual storyteller.

Analysis, Intuition, and Practicality

No amount of forensic examination can uncover the magic, mischief, and mystery that distinguish the best cinema. Such qualities cannot be reduced to the foundations of any schema. If much of what this book explores might lie within the realms of Aristotle's *techné*, this is not to deny what Plato referred to as "the voice of the god"— that element of the creative act spurred by inspiration. Irrational, mysterious, yet quintessentially human, it is this, for all their mastery of craft, that marks the art of the very best filmmakers and makes for the best films of others.

The filmmaker, however, cannot and does not rely on intuition alone, nor should the practicality of the cinematic mind be an obstacle to its inspirational aspect. On the contrary, diligent practice can be seen as the conduit to, enabler of, and catalyst for that unknowable genius. If this book can navigate a stretch of that path only, its reach aims to be substantial and invaluable—without this conscious path there can be little subsequent voyaging. The rest is for the reader to travel in their own personal way.

How to Best Use This Book

Screenshots are provided for immediate reference. On second reading, the reader should have access to the case study films themselves. They will need to pause the frame as the book breaks down the scenes and sequences. This takes time and focus, since the mind of the audience moves more quickly than information on a page and frequently works subliminally. Digging into that complex, rapid, and fluid process is fundamental to the success of the book but requires a degree of application on the part of the reader.

PART I
PERSPECTIVES

1
Appreciating the Art of the Filmmaker

In attempting to analyze the art of the filmmaker, many of us offer comments drawing on disciplines and fields of study other than cinema. To differentiate the understanding explored in the chapters that follow from those approaches so the reader might benefit fully from this book's focus, it will help first to consider some of the various perspectives offered across this compass.

Understanding the engagement of the audience member with a movie is essential both to the reader seeking to explore the filmmaker's art and to the filmmaker in their practicing of it. A movie audience engages with a film cognitively, emotionally, viscerally, even neurally as it follows its story and characters, eager to know what is going to happen next. In a darkened auditorium dominated by a big screen, not only does the audience absorb the messages a movie conveys, but its members also mirror the reactions of those around them, most of whom they are unlikely to know. Audiences range from the aficionados of what is termed *arthouse cinema* on the one hand to passive consumers on the other, those who may arrive at a movie theater without foreknowledge of the film they are to watch, selecting a movie from whatever they might find on offer.

Most moviegoers tend to assume that watching a story is easier than reading one, as in some senses it indeed is; all that is required, at the most basic level at least, is simply to sit back and take in whatever the film offers, which some may regard as disposable as the concessions consumed during its screening. Indeed, watching a film on the big screen is not only a perceptual but an *experiential* activity—the eye aware of nothing outside the frame before it. What audience members do not generally understand, however, is the complexity and organization of the messaging they are taking in. To many of us, the art of the filmmaker, even when declamatory, flamboyant, or openly self-aware is a largely invisible art. On close inspection, however, its intricacies and connective tissue become apparent, enriching and deepening in the process the experience of the viewer.

In exploring the art of the filmmaker, the reader cannot afford to ignore the nature of audience engagement. Nothing more of the discourse of cinema can be understood without an acute awareness of this: the journey through the individual scenes, sequences, and movements of a film and the sense of its totality this affords. As Krżystof Kieślowski commented: *The film doesn't exist without a viewer. And the viewer is most important.*

Even if less pertinent to the essence of this book, the film critic's perspective also bears consideration. Critics offer opinions generally more informed than those of the

The Art of the Filmmaker. Peter Markham, Oxford University Press. © Oxford University Press 2023.
DOI: 10.1093/oso/9780197631522.003.0002

average audience member, assessing the merit of a film based on a range of criteria, drawing comparisons to other examples of a filmmaker's work and other relevant films. They tend not to comment on the specifics of visual language, as their address is to the public, not the categories of dedicated viewer for whom this book is written. In considering the art of the filmmaker, the reader should distinguish between on the one hand the critic's perspective of a film as a completed artifact and on the other the sense of one—presented here—as an entity founded on the decision-making of the filmmaker during its evolution as a work in progress.

Also bringing informed takes to their deliberations, the film studies scholar and the theorist will incorporate traditional and contemporary theories of which many filmmakers might be barely aware, even ignorant. Even if the cineaste happens to be familiar with them, they are unlikely to employ such concepts as central motivating and informing criteria in their approach to their filmmaking, whether in general or in the context of any specific film.

Film historians may in some instances examine and deconstruct a director's *style*— their mode(s) of cinematic address. Many highly film-literate directors also offer historical perspectives on movies, on their practitioners and approaches, that will be of eminent interest to those exploring the art of the filmmaker. Such practitioners write from the standpoint of mastery in their art—Paul Schrader and Martin Scorsese are examples—their insights invariably profound.

Philosophers concerned with theories of mind will engage with questions of emotions, perception, imagination, and motivation that are relevant to the nature of fiction, of the screen as a means of its capture, and of the screen's language—the means of the filmmaker's address to their audience. "Continental" philosophers discussing existentialism and phenomenology have tended to have more to say about film than their "analytic" or Anglo-American counterparts. Filmmakers though, like novelists and poets, are unlikely to *think* or *work* as philosophers while going about their business, as they formulate their visual and sonic storytelling, their staging, shooting, and editing—even if in certain cases they may hold in mind concepts expounded by particular thinkers.

Sigmund Freud's reputed words *The poets and philosophers before me discovered the unconscious,* true or not, reveal not only the psychologist's appreciation of the insights of the poet into the human psyche but also their insights into the narrative arts and their complex natures. The notion of character as mimetic of the human psyche, for example, and the filmmaker's concern for the authenticity of a character founded in some truthful aspect of our motivation and behavior, indicate a psychologist's shared interest with the student of the filmmaker's art—as does the response of the audience. Story and drama are not alone in the arts as providing a playground for the psyche, as the term *entertainment business* indicates. Such purported "escapism," though, can reveal the deepest paradoxes and truths of the human condition.

In regarding the filmmaker's creation of the human and social world of their film, the reader might consider the perspectives of the sociologist, related either to the authenticity of "real" worlds or to invented worlds and their parallels and contrasts with those we know. Film as social commentary may indeed serve to educate, publicize, and campaign, but the proselytizing filmmaker who ignores human contradictions, like the moralizer and commentator more concerned with "correct" agendas than with the filmmaker's art—and what might be thought of as the transgressions and heresies of that art—offers the reader little in the way of its appreciation.

One may not "like" a film, may not care for its characters, their milieu, or their actions. One may not appreciate its genre, may not approve of it as regards its mores and assumptions, especially when it is an "old" film made in the past at a time of sensibilities now regarded as unacceptable. None of this means, however, that the reader (filmmaker or not), cannot learn from such a film about the art and practical aesthetics articulated by its filmmaker—especially when seen in the context of cinema's adaptive language, its imperatives, constants, currents, and generational totality. It is from this perspective—central to any understanding of the *practice* of cinema—that the reader can best appreciate the insights this book offers.

2
Language and Cinema

What Is the Language of Film?

Does cinema have a language? Could the visual discourse of the screen be described as such? What, to come to the point, is meant by *language*, and how might this apply to cinematic representation and address?

Merriam-Webster defines language as *a systematic means of communicating ideas or feelings by the use of conventionalized signs, sounds, gestures, or marks having understood meanings.*

Note the following words and phrases:

- *Systematic*, which implies deliberate organization.
- *Communicating*, which suggests the transfer of information as being a function of language.
- *Ideas or feelings*, which suggests this communication may be either cognitive or emotional in nature.
- *Conventionalized signs, sounds, gestures, or marks*, which relate to the earlier *systematic* and which, in each instance, might be applied to the language of the screen.
- *Understood meanings*, which imply a listener, reader, or viewer already acculturated in the language. This is pertinent to the nature of cinematic discourse, which on the one hand might express meaning inherent in its form (geometry, line, shape, color, contrast, etc.) and on the other might be derived from usage (context, emphasis, dissonance, mischief, tonality, narrative point of view [POV], etc.). See Chapter 7 for an investigation of these alternative modes.

Merriam-Webster also includes the following definition: *the suggestion by objects, actions, or conditions of associated ideas or feelings.*

Here, language is understood also as an *indirect* means of communication, but one that prompts particular thoughts or emotions. These will either be familiar to the listener, the reader, or the viewer from the course of their lives, or understood by them from previous usage—in the case of cinema, through the subculture the filmmaker sets up during the course of their film; through the viewer's familiarity with genre, its tropes and conventions; and through their awareness of other films and broader filmic contexts.

The Art of the Filmmaker. Peter Markham, Oxford University Press. © Oxford University Press 2023.
DOI: 10.1093/oso/9780197631522.003.0003

Merriam Webster then adds this: *the form or manner of verbal expression.*

This relates to *style*, understood not as a veneer of elegance or beauty, merely decorative or decorous, but as integral to language and its communicative function. The frequently accepted notion of style and content as separate, antithetical elements assumes style, and indeed the aesthetics constituting it, to be independent of language and meaning, a solely ornamental resource. In certain circumstances, this might be true: In *On Film-making: An Introduction to the Craft of the Director*, Alexander Mackendrick notes the difference between the *pictorial* and the *visual*. The former he sees as the beautifying of the image, the rendering of it as something pleasant or spectacular to observe. The latter, the *visual*, he understands as unrelated to notions of elegance or spectacle but as a resource of communication through the image and its presentation.

The language of film is articulated on the planarity of the screen through visual aesthetics, which if they are to communicate anything to the viewer must be *practical* (thus *visual* in Mackendrick's sense of the word) rather than *pictorial* (i.e., decorative). Composition, mise en scène, framing, geometry and line, shape, color, light, contrast, depth of field, and eye trace, orchestrated within the deliberate design of the filmmaker, form an address to the audience, and rather than being organized simply to please the eye, convey information, emotion, and visceral sensation with deliberate intention.

Merriam-Webster's next definition is this: *The vocabulary and phraseology belonging to an art or a department of knowledge.*

The language of cinema—in terms not literally of *vocabulary and phraseology* but of their visual equivalents—both as *an art* and a *department of knowledge*, has developed and shifted from Louis Le Prince's 20-frame *Roundhay Garden* footage of 1888, on through the silent era to the "talkies," to the impact of television, of documentary, and then more recently of music videos and contemporary visual media. Fluid and agile, while continuing to draw on film's earliest compositional and editorial foundations the language and aesthetics of film might be seen to an extent as esoteric—their tropes, shorthand, subtexts, and complex discourse comprehended by viewers in consequence of an extensive engagement with the medium.

Also mentioned in Merriam-Webster is the meaning of language as an idiom that expresses profanity. The dictionary quotes Ring Lardner's words: *shouldn't of blamed the fellers if they'd cut loose with some language.* This concept is pertinent to a cinema that constantly and irreverently seeks to subvert accepted norms. Handheld camera work, jump cuts, extreme angles and close-ups (CUs), willfully perverse framing, singular camera placement, rapid and dizzying camera movement, lens distortion, the theft of visual elements from digital media, tonal dissonance through the incongruous juxtaposition of one image with another, contrasts of the emotion of an event with its accompanying sound or music, and extreme manipulation of time in a shot (whether speeded-up or slowed down) offer examples of film's perennial striving for a transgressive and viscerally unsettling discourse that profanes tradition and decorum.

Cinematic Language as Theft

Another critical facet of the evolution of the language of film has been its significant degree of theft from other forms. Most evident of these thefts, perhaps, are the elements it shares with theater. Dramatic narrative, its dynamics of conflict, its structures, stagecraft, and mise en scène are obvious aspects. Cinema's concerns for composition are shared with painting and photography also. Parallels in narrative can be found in the short story and the novel—the articulation of narrative POV in film, for example, might be considered as being more closely related to its counterpart in prose fiction than to that in the theater. While American mainstream movies tend to adopt the three-act structure, others may incorporate "chapters" or work within their individual structural forms (as is the case with much of literary fiction). The long sequence shot perhaps bears a similarity to the run-on sentence, while the short, single static shot might be compared to one of brevity. (Unrelated to formal or visually "linguistic" concerns meanwhile, the auto-fictive canvases of filmmakers such as Truffaut [*The 400 Blows*], Fellini [*I Vitelloni*, *Amarcord*], and more recently Almodóvar [*Pain and Glory*] and Spielberg [*The Fabelmans*], might invite comparison to literary autofiction.)

Sequential images that tell a story are the discourse of graphic novels and comics—the *panel* and the shot self-evidently having much in common. Sound design in film and the ways in which it conjures images in the mind through effects invite parallels to the radio play and current fictional podcasts. Music, meanwhile, is not only an element of the language of cinema—whether as accompaniment, means of support or emphasis, critical comment, or mischievous juxtaposition—but its tonality and rhythm inform the flow of tone and narrative momentum of the musically aware filmmaker's work.

Cinema, like any art, steals also from itself, its 130-year-long history constantly mined for references and inspiration by the film-literate filmmaker. Conscientious creative teams will refer to examples of work from contemporaries, from masters, and from the wealth of cinema of varying merit from past decades as they seek to form and define the language of their films.

In recent years, the evolution of new visual media, and of the devices and platforms on which they are viewed (and on which movies themselves are often watched), has given fresh forms of discourse. From text messages to smartphone videos and "selfies" (new manifestations of the 8 mm "home movie"), to online conferencing, the cinema screen has incorporated these contemporary forms into its language.

3

The Five Domains in Which a Film "Comes to Life"

In order to develop the structured approach necessary for productive insights into the art of the filmmaker and the practical aesthetics central to its realization, the reader might do well to consider the domains in which a film *comes to life*. These five domains cover the aspects of a film's fictionality, address, and response:

(i)   The fiction that plays out in the domain "beyond" the screen: the story, characters, emotions, and world of the film.
(ii) The planarity of the screen.
(iii) The "screen of the mind."
(iv) The hearts, minds, and guts of the audience.
(v)   The memory of the audience.

Although most of these categories could be applied to other narrative forms, only cinema, together with TV and other visual media, includes the second category: a physical screen. While this bears some parallels to the theater stage and to a page of the graphic novel's "panels," it is in many respects, particularly in regard to its kinetic nature, profoundly different.

The Fiction That Plays Out in the Domain "beyond" the Screen

This is the fictional realm we imagine existing beyond the screen: story and plot, events, situations and scenarios, actions, characters, their emotions, the stakes, pitch and register of the drama, the physical world, and the human world. The reader might consider these elements in the way that a child might imagine them, as having their own reality on the "other side" of the screen—the illusion cinema offers as it prompts our suspension of disbelief.

The domain of the fiction beyond the screen requires authority if it is to come to life. It may not offer an accurate impression of any actual physical place or space and may be created by the filmmakers through camera placement, lensing, and cutting, but it must appear credible within its genre and universe. If we the audience cannot

The Art of the Filmmaker. Peter Markham, Oxford University Press. © Oxford University Press 2023.
DOI: 10.1093/oso/9780197631522.003.0004

accept it, none of the other domains in which a film should come to life will compensate for our disbelief.

Discussed in detail in Chapter 5 on dramatic narrative, this filmmaker-created sphere with its constituents is the province of the screenwriter, the actor, the production designer, the cinematographer, and the director.

The Planarity of the Screen

The screen is not only the means of capturing the action of the fictional domain beyond it but is also the conduit between that realm and the audience. It is not neutral, not a mere window into that world through which we peer—although a filmmaker might have it seem to adopt that function—but serves to both create and modulate it. It is selective in what it shows us and what it doesn't, in what is included within its framing and what isn't. It can modulate dimension and distance, manipulate space, articulate narrative POV, and orchestrate the flow of energy. It projects information, emotion, and visceral sensation. It conjures tone, which may or may not be the tone of the events it depicts. The fundamental realm in which cinema comes to life, it can enchant, mesmerize, shock, inform, conceal, reveal, reduce, seduce, repel, deceive, flatten, heighten, demean, or transcend.

The resources of storytelling on the planarity of the screen, where the practical aesthetics of cinema are manifested (explored in depth in Chapters 7 to 10), constitute the core and focus of this book.

This domain is the province of the screenwriter (who self-evidently writes for the screen), the cinematographer, the editor, and the director. The accomplished film actor also understands the address made by the screen.

The "Screen of the Mind"

Whatever you can get away with not showing should be omitted.
—Abbas Kiarostami

At this point it will be useful to consider the concept of the *screen of the mind*— referred to throughout this book—at some length, particularly as it constitutes such a compelling means by which a film comes to life.

As in our everyday existence, there are in our experience of cinema two canvases on which we witness images: one offers what we see, the other is formed by what we imagine. In a darkened movie theater, we see the physical screen while we see another screen prompted by its images and sounds—the mind's eye, or what we might call the screen of the mind. What the filmmaker does not show, we conjure. What we see on this internal screen may be as potent—often is *more* potent—than what we see on the physical screen. (This is why the radio play of the past and its current manifestation in the form of the fictional podcast have proved and continue to prove so *visually* engaging.) When we read a novel or short story, or when we are told a story, we of course also witness images on the screen of the mind, but unlike our experience as we watch a screen, these are the sole images we see—there is no physical screen. The symbiosis of two screens is fundamental to how we engage with a film.

The reader might consider instances of when, with a film, what we see on screen is not necessarily what we get—when what we see there might actually be *less* than what we get.

Perhaps the most basic way in which we the audience might witness unseen events is when a character becomes a narrator, telling of events they have lived through or heard of. Such is the case with Chloe Zhao's 2020 *Nomadland*, in which nonfictional people tell of their personal experiences. In Barry Jenkins's 2016 *Moonlight*, Juan tells Little of his own boyhood in Cuba, and Kevin later boasts to Chiron of a sexual escapade, whether real or fabricated. (This is shown later, in Chiron's nightmare, on the physical screen.) In the diner in the last act, meanwhile, Kevin relates to Black the events of his life after high school. In these instances, the filmmaker leaves us to imagine their narratives. Such is also the case in Ari Aster's 2018 *Hereditary* when Annie reveals her family history to the grief counseling group. In none of these instances do the filmmakers make use of flashbacks, so we do not see these stories play out on the physical screen.

Not everything any character describes, every anecdote, item of gossip, vignette, object, or sight needs to be shown on the physical screen. Were that the case, the plethora of visual storytelling would be overwhelming. How could we know which images were significant and which weren't, and what might be their hierarchy of importance? The selection of what is shown on the physical screen and what is left to the imagination is thus a significant aspect of the filmmaker's craft.

Another means by which the screen of the mind can be stimulated is when a character mentions an event we have previously witnessed on the physical screen. Such is the case toward the end of *Moonlight* when the adult Kevin reminds Black of the last time they met—after Chiron's assault on Terrell when he was arrested—and we ourselves recall the moment visually. When, also, we return to a setting we have seen previously, and particularly when we see that setting from the same angle and within a similar framing, that incident may briefly spring to life once again on the screen of the mind. In *Moonlight*, at the start of the scene in which Juan confronts Paula, even though this occurs at night, we are reminded of the film's opening episode. (See the case study in Part III.) Set during the day, this shows Juan's confident control over his neighborhood drug trade—a contrast to his powerlessness in the face of Paula's accusations. The shots that introduce both scenes are similar: in each Juan drives up, steps out of his car, and makes for Terrence on the other side of the street. As we see the later image, we recall, subliminally, the earlier one, shot from the same angle. (This the filmmaker knows. This he implements in his film's address to his audience.)

The selective framing out from a shot of someone or something can induce us to conjure that missing visual element in our minds. We may also see only a part of a thing—in an image similar to what is known in literary terms as a *synecdoche*—which prompts us to imagine the entire entity.

The camera may not have visual access to an event or may be pointed in another direction so that we do not see, but only hear, what is happening. Indeed, sound and its design are a potent means of stimulating the screen of the mind. Whether distant or apparently adjacent, sounds prompt the imagining of their cause. As Robert Bresson wrote in his *Notes on the Cinematograph*: *When a sound can replace an image, cut the image or neutralize it. The ear goes more toward the within, the eye toward the outer.* A sound, he suggests, evokes an image, while an image never evokes a sound.

The reader might consider how images and events thus conjured may be central to the storytelling. The message in *Hereditary*, when we find Peter awake in his bedroom the morning after the death of his sister Charlie and we hear the screams of Annie as she discovers her decapitated corpse, is direct and powerful. As we watch Peter's frozen expression on the physical screen, we see his mother's anguished features on the screen of the mind (rendering her reaction all the more shocking). As Bresson would have it, the image of Peter is external to us, that of Annie and the horror she discovers internal—both to Peter and to us. How might we react, by contrast, to a direct depiction of Annie in her state of shock, and how might this change our perception of the register and nature of the event? Doesn't Peter's emotional drama draw us into the moment, whereas the sight of Annie's extreme trauma might prompt us to avert our eyes?

Suspense is a potent prompter of internal images. Hitchcock talked of the "bomb under the table," seen by the audience but not by the characters, and gave this as an example of suspense as opposed to surprise—which would be the case if a bomb were to explode without our foreknowledge of its presence. How does this suspense work? We anticipate the bomb exploding but are uncertain when, or whether it might be discovered in time for the characters to escape to safety. What we anticipate we see internally, our anticipation manifested through images on the screen of the mind. When, in *Moonlight*, Terrell circles Chiron in the school playground, coming to settle by Kevin, and we know that Terrell has coerced Kevin into beating up his friend, we anticipate the violence—the "bomb" exploding—before it occurs. What we see on the screen of the mind is in this instance confirmed by what we subsequently see on the physical screen.

The play of possibility that we experience when following a story is another source of inner images. What will happen next? we wonder, as alternative scenarios flash across our minds. Rapid, fleeting as the visual representations of these permutations are, they are vital to our experience. (When the film delivers an unexpected outcome, the contrast to what we have anticipated/imagined induces us to have to catch up with the storytelling—which can render the moment all the more compelling.) The filmmaker may not consider this consciously—they and we accept the way the mind works without giving it a second thought—but they are constantly exploiting it by misdirecting us, by hinting at possibilities that never transpire, or that eventually do so only after intervening incidents have delayed them.

Images may suggest other images, as in visual metaphors, *images of absence*, and *images of tonal dissonance*. A metaphorical image suggests a different image. Early in Krzysztof Kieślowski's 1993 *Three Colors Blue* there is a car accident, after which we see a beach ball fall from the wrecked vehicle to roll across a field. One of the passengers in the car is a young girl, so that when we see the ball on the screen, we see the child on our inner screen.

(1) Anna in the car in *Three Colors Blue*. (2) Later, a beach ball falls out of the wrecked car. The ball is a metaphor for the child. When see it we think of Anna and recall her earlier CU.

What we might describe as an image of absence is one in which a presence is used to suggest an absence. When, in *Nomadland*, Fern visits the deserted gypsum factory (see the case study "*Nomadland*: Empire—Opening and Ending" in Part III) and steps into a meeting room, the two empty chairs to the right of frame prompt, on the mind's screen, two amorphous seated people. Similarly, in Akira Kurosawa's 1957 *Throne of Blood*, his version of Shakespeare's *Macbeth*, when we see a row of courtiers on one side of Washizu's court, then an opposite row with two empty mats in the foreground, and we know that Miki has been murdered and his son abducted, we see those absent characters on our interior canvas.

The contrast of the complete row of courtiers on the right with the incomplete row on the left highlights the absence of the murdered Miki and his abducted son, bringing to mind the thought and thus the images of them.

The Hearts, Minds, and Guts of the Audience

What is the most essential domain of cinema, the most vital realm in which a film must come to life? Surely this lies in the experience of its audience? If this is not stimulated, a film consists of little but shadows on the screen. We accumulate, assume, deduce, and guess at information throughout a movie as our emotional engagement builds. Without a successful narrative game of cognition and emotion between storyteller and audience, we remain mystified by, or worse, indifferent to what we are watching.

The emotions in the auditorium, of whatever complexion—agreeable, disagreeable, prompted by what the audience sees and hears up on the screen and on the screen of the mind, and by what it knows, fears, or desires—are at the core of cinema. The fictional emotions of the screen prompt real emotions in us. A movie may be wildly operatic, a vehicle for heightened melodrama, as in *Hereditary* when the possessed Annie chases the doomed Peter up to the attic, or may be subdued, the tension simmering under the surface, as in the opening to the dinner scene in the same film, but the emotions arising in the audience must be keenly felt or the scenes will have failed. We may have empathy for a character, sharing in their emotion, or may know what a character does not know and therefore react emotionally to events on the screen in ways the character doesn't, or may simply have feelings at odds with those of a character. We may experience less emotion than the screen depicts (which, in cases of misjudged melodrama, can be unfortunate, although in instances of fictive trauma might be just as well), or we may experience more than the screen generates. (As Kiarostami commented, *The most effective tear doesn't run down the cheek, it glistens in the eye.*) The filmmaker's chosen tone or tones—their attitude to their material—will modulate the audience-character emotional ratio and relationship.

What are the broad dynamics of our emotional engagement? The emotion generated by film storytelling can be immediate or cumulative. It can be subdued or intense, or can have a timed delay, coming with the hindsight afforded by revelation and realization, while it may be at its most powerful at a story's end. Aristotle's *katharsis*, mentioned just once in his *Poetics*, is generally understood to be a purgation and purification of dangerous instincts and emotions but might also be considered the clarification of a profound understanding derived from emotional epiphany—on the part of both character and audience.

An audience also needs to be involved *cognitively* with a movie, knowing and not knowing what characters know and do not know, knowing more or less than they do. The reader might reflect on the game the filmmaker as storyteller plays with the *hierarchy of knowledge* that their film sets up—who knows what and when, among characters and viewer—and how this stimulates the minds of audiences eager to understand what is happening and what it might mean. (Little's ignorance of Juan's business, in contrast to other characters' and our awareness, is a case in point.) An audience's knowledge usually grows throughout a film, although late revelations may disabuse it of mistaken interpretations. This engagement preoccupies the viewer, in whose mind fresh permutations of possibility continually spring to life.

Visceral sensation, feelings in the gut, neural senses, and the physical reactions to events in a movie may be confused with emotions but are more primal. Cinema, especially on the big screen, is an experiential medium, one that invites expectations on the part of audiences regarding a heightened engagement with "the movies" and their preconceptions of how a film comes to life.

This domain is the province of the screenwriter, director, cinematographer, actor, editor, and sound designer.

The Memory of the Audience

As the reader will no doubt know from personal experience, when story, character, and visual language reverberate with sufficient power, a film lives on in the mind, inviting subsequent viewings, new insights, and deepening appreciation. Such a film may later become a "classic," achieving longevity. Among the contributing factors to this are the resonance of emotional engagement, and endings that pose unanswerable questions, that yield paradoxes in our sense of meaning or convey universal, timeless truth in a fresh, singular manner. Stories that attain mythical reach and deliver subversive insight, memorable imagery, and charismatic characters stay with us.

This is the domain filmmakers hope to reach.

A Note on Screenplays

Some might maintain that a film comes to life in the screenplay, but a screenplay is not a film. Audiences do not in general read a film's screenplay. The screenplay is a means to an end—the film. Usually—although not always—it is a crucial, indispensable means. The screenplay is the formative DNA and RNA of the movie, but like those nucleic acids, is not the creature itself.

4
The Five Tasks of the Filmmaker

Having considered the five domains in which a film comes to life, the reader will find it invaluable to note the five tasks of the filmmaker. Scrutiny of these categories, which are closely related to, and indeed bring about, those delineated in the previous chapter, will inform the reader's insight into the perspectives of the filmmaker and their decision-making processes, which is indispensable to the understanding of the practical aesthetics of the screen. These tasks may be defined as follows:

(i)   The communication of information.
(ii) The evocation of emotion.
(iii) The stimulation of visceral/tactile/neural sensation.
(iv) The expression of a creative vision (not necessarily conscious).
(v)   Telling the story.

The telling of the story is the fundamental duty of the filmmaker—but it takes the effective functioning of the previously listed tasks to render it successful.

The Communication of Information

How can an audience lacking sufficient information or receiving information that is vague or confusing follow a story without having to infer its steps? In such a hit-and-miss process they may misconstrue the narrative or fail to understand it altogether.

When, however, a filmmaker gives out too much information, repeats information unnecessarily, conveys it through redundant means, provides an excess of explanation, or conveys a surfeit of clarity rather than crediting the audience with the intelligence to connect the dots, audiences are likely to become bored and to disengage.

A fundamental aspect of the filmmaker's art is the following of the path between these polarities of lack and surfeit that best serves their storytelling.

Information can be direct, implied, ambiguous, concealed, revealed, portioned out, or delivered in a single instant. It can be shown visually; indicated sonically; or conveyed in dialogue, in a voice-over, or through a caption. The novice filmmaker often tends to shy away from offering direct information, believing it to be too obvious, too "on the nose," which they see as a failing. They may even avoid communicating it altogether, or may not even know it themselves. They mistake vagueness for ambiguity or dereliction of duty for cleverness, or believe they are being sophisticated

The Art of the Filmmaker. Peter Markham, Oxford University Press. © Oxford University Press 2023.
DOI: 10.1093/oso/9780197631522.003.0005

in giving out arbitrary clues rather than the purposefully selected increments of information vital to an audience's gathering of understanding.

If spoon-feeding the audience results in leaden storytelling, that audience should not have to work out every element of a story for itself. The filmmaker must understand the information that needs to be communicated simply and directly, that is best offered incrementally or might be suggested or implied in one fashion or another. In their 1946 *Notorious*, for example, Alfred Hitchcock and screenwriter Ben Hecht have main characters' names repeated, clearly in the dialogue, *three times*—both in the case of Devlin, when he attends to the hungover Alicia, and in the case of Nazi scientist Dr. Anderson, when Alicia first enters the conspirators' mansion. There's no shame on the part of such a masterly director and writer in ensuring the audience knows who's who as they are introduced. Indeed, the information is planted so deftly that we the audience remain unaware of its methodical repetition.

Hereditary begins with a caption that reads as an obituary in a local newspaper. It supplies the names of each member of the Graham family and sets down their relationships. The death of Ellen, Annie Graham's mother, is stated first, setting the scene for the start of the story. Given the limited time the caption remains up on the screen, we have just enough time to read it, retaining only a certain amount of the information crowded into its lines. This, however, is sufficient to inform subsequent scenes. The prelude that follows clearly conveys the nature of each of the main characters and suggests the state of their relationships. The precise *significance* of some informational increments, however—such as Ellen's sigil, or Charlie's habit of sleeping in the tree house—is not yet revealed. (See the case study in Part III for a detailed analysis of the film's prelude.)

In *Nomadland* also, filmmaker Chloe Zhao sets the scene with a first caption telling of the gypsum plant in the town of Empire shutting down after "88 years," then a second informing us that the town's zip code was shut down in the same year. Fern's actions as we first see her—packing some plates, holding close to her face a man's work jacket, bidding the storage unit's owner farewell—convey as much backstory as we need in order for us to connect with her as she begins her journey. Interestingly, we don't learn her name until a lunch scene at the warehouse some six minutes in, when in the course of the conversation it is mentioned *three times*—in contrast to the names of others around the table, mentioned once only.

In *Moonlight*, Barry Jenkins concludes each of the film's three preludes with a caption giving one of the protagonist's three names. He has us wait until the scene of the dinner with Juan and Teresa before we first hear Little's name spoken (by the character himself, who also gives his real name, Chiron), but the facets of his character and the predicament in which he finds himself are clearly conveyed when he takes refuge from pursuing bullies in a condemned apartment. His second manifestation as Chiron is clearly marked when the teacher calls him out by name in class in the middle section's first scene. His adult self, Black, is revealed immediately when the film's third movement starts by the nightmare he has of verbal abuse from his mother (the filmmaker repeats shots used in Little's earlier episode). Jenkins is studious also in making clear the natures of other main characters, such as the avuncular, drug-dealing Juan, the supportive Teresa, the needy Paula, the bullying Terrell, and the flawed but well-meaning Kevin.

The filmmaker might also leave us to our own devices, to connect one increment of knowledge to another as a means of arriving at a third, two plus two leading to four—or even five, as might be the case, particularly in crime and "whodunit" movies.

No filmmaker can afford to ignore the imperative of communicating the information necessary to the telling of their story. Far from being a menial task, this necessity might be thought of as a game the filmmaker plays with their audience, one inviting both well-tried and innovative approaches.

The Evocation of Emotion

If information is communicated in order to tell the story, why is a story told if not in order to evoke emotion? Discussed in the previous chapter, emotion is the most important aspect of an audience's multifaceted engagement with a film, and one the filmmaker must elicit.

Stanley Kubrick said: *People react primarily to direct experience and not to abstractions; it is very rare to find anyone who can become emotionally involved with an abstraction.* Modulating the flow of emotion, as the audience is kept in a state of constant apprehension, even anxiety, is an imperative for the filmmaker.

The contrasting emotional flow of the three films discussed in the case studies shows how it is not necessarily the *register* of emotion a movie yields that indicates its worth so much as its *orchestration*. The quiet emotions of Yazujiro Ozu's *Tokyo Story* (1953) are no less compelling than the disturbing cruelties of Michael Haneke's *Funny Games* (1997). The devastating horrors of Elem Klimov's *Come and See* (1985), while distressingly powerful and delivered with consummate mastery, are no more valid than less traumatic feelings of movies such as Mike Leigh's *Another Year* (2010) or Lulu Wang's *The Farewell* (2019). With emotion, it is not volume, not how much it soothes or perturbs us, nor how relentless or by contrast how restrained it might prove, so much as its modulation, that makes it count. Emotion will often be at its most powerful when subdued, suppressed, or even denied by a character unable to cope with it—when a character holds back their tears, we may find them welling in our own eyes.

Evoked by story; by incident, character, performance, staging, camera, and cutting; by sound and music; by the filmmaker's control of tone and energy; and by the perspectives they offer in what they show or do not—emotion and its spectrum of fear, shame, sadness, love, longing, grief, and joy is the filmmaker's most profound currency.

The Stimulation of Visceral/Tactile/ Neural Sensation

Conveyed by the filmmaker and experienced by the audience (and considered briefly in the previous chapter among the domains in which a film comes to life), the raw humanity that cinema can reveal, its prompting of our tactile, enteric, neural, and sexual sensations, renders our engagement the more complete. It is an undeniable and often illicit currency of cinema's discourse through which, under cover of the movie theater's darkness, the filmmaker renders their address primordial in its force-fulness, subverting both our rationality and emotions with its stimulation of our common physicality and taboo impulses, and with the adrenalin rush that accompanies a quickening pulse.

The instant of Charlie's death in *Hereditary*, for example, marked by the dull thud of her head hitting a pole, precipitates our immediate, involuntary gut response, a re-action that precedes the emotional shock running through the following moments. In *Moonlight*, the loud crash of a chair over Terrell's head when Chiron assaults him jolts us viscerally—a deliberate shock on the part of Jenkins's intentions, and one resulting from an act of violent revenge on the bully that we cannot help but take primal satis-faction in even as we may be appalled by it. Even *Nomadland*, its calmly meditative currents notwithstanding, evokes our physical senses. There's the crackling fire, for example, around which the encamped narrators tell their stories, their faces illumi-nated by a warm glow that we too feel. The same movie's vignette of Fern's fingers wip-ing dust off a table top (see the case study in Part III) prompts a mirrored tactile sense in us as we witness it, while *Hereditary*'s moment of Annie's shivering as she experi-ences a sudden draft during Joan's séance elicits our shared subcutaneous response.

In action movies, by contrast, the filmmaker prompts our visceral reactions through the mayhem of visual dynamics complete with screeching vehicle tires and frequent impacts, minute-by-minute, life-and-death stakes, and loud, immersive sound design. Such factors are common to much of mainstream cinema, from thrill-ers and horror movies to superhero outings. Not only does the filmmaker bring their movie to life in this way, but they also render it "larger than life" by means of the often adrenalin-inducing festive spectacle widely regarded as intrinsic to "the movies."

Eroticism has similarly long proved a potent current in cinema. If violence—conflict in its most visually dynamic manifestation—excites and draws audiences, sex remains its perennial partner, tethered or not. Given that filmmaking has been male dominated throughout the decades, its perspective on the erotic has largely fol-lowed suit. With *The Piano* (1993), Jane Campion challenged that orthodoxy. Andrea Arnold, Céline Sciamma, and Julia Ducournau are among filmmakers who also give contrasting, more comprehensive, astute insights. LGBTQ+ filmmakers such as Terence Davies and Gus Van Sant have also shifted the previous imbalance. The gaze of the movies, challenged in past decades only by the few female filmmakers able to work, is now no longer exclusively male, no longer straight male.

The Expression of a Creative Vision

If *creative vision* sounds a fanciful, rather vague term, too general, too nebulous to de-fine, the reader's consideration of its several aspects can bring invaluable insights into the breadth and depth of the art of the filmmaker. Theme, thematic question, tone, and voice—all aspects of a filmmaker's vision—are complex concepts worthy of scrutiny. *Theme*, for example, might be understood as the abstract noun that underlies the nature of the film's story (war, romance, revenge, grief, intrigue, ambition, survival, etc.) or might be a combination, perhaps the opposition of two such words. Theme might also be seen as an issue, such as cybercrime, climate change, people trafficking, corruption in politics, or the environment. None of these considerations seems particularly helpful in understanding the notion of creative vision, however. Theme might be more usefully understood as a concept such as "transference of guilt"—common to much of Hitchcock's work. (*Hereditary*'s theme might in this respect be thought of as the passing down of psychic disturbance through the generations.) Such a concept might be construed as a vision of the human condition, a definition one might see as central to any concept of creative vision.

Theme might further be considered as "warning": "Do *that* and *this* will be the consequence." So *Hereditary* might be construed as saying that when we fight against the past, that past will destroy us. *Moonlight* might be thought to suggest that when we go to violent extremes to defend ourselves, we render ourselves *more* vulnerable.

Paradox is another useful approach to the meaning of theme. "Permanence of home is to be found in transience of home," might be considered *Nomadland*'s theme. "Strength resides in vulnerability" might be *Moonlight*'s.

This connects with the concept of the thematic question, one that is in general unanswerable and related to the "cost" of a story's conclusion. "Can personal freedom compensate for lost love?" might apply to *Nomadland*, at the end of which Fern sets out for a life on the road with the grief of her husband's loss and the demise of Empire as the cost of her transformation.

Voice might be thought of as the sense of a filmmaker's vision not only in one film but over their body of work. *Tone*, the attitude of the filmmaker to their material, informs this but does not constitute voice in its entirety. Preferred genre, dramatic register, world and milieu, and nature of the chosen characters all play a part. Some philosophical understanding on the part of the filmmaker also contributes to voice, but then so do the subconscious dynamics of their psyche. Voice may be thought of as the nature of the material to which a filmmaker gravitates, to the timbre, style, or general nature of their storytelling. Zhao, in both *The Rider* (2017) and *Nomadland*, reveals the journey of characters previously on the inside of a community finding themselves on the outside and learning how to embrace this. Jenkins, in both *Moonlight* and *If Beale Street Could Talk* (2018), follows characters who find authentic relationships through the throes of adversity. Ari Aster, in *Hereditary* and *Midsommar* (2019), dramatizes the passage of an estranged youth toward exaltation from a diabolical community—and the sacrifice that comes of this.

Susan Sontag suggested that voice comes of limitation. The artist does what they can do and avoids what they can't. Voice might also derive from a filmmaker's background, the interaction of their personal circumstances and culture, their fears and phobias, the degree of their fearlessness; from their sense of themselves, their gender, sexual orientation, ethnicity, and history; and from their failures in life rather than their successes.

Filmmakers cannot take classes in voice. Voice cannot be taught or learned and is difficult, perhaps impossible, to adopt. It can be hard to define and perhaps should be. It is usually, however, sensed by audiences. The three filmmakers in the case studies distinguish themselves thus, and at early stages in their careers.

Vision, indeed, rarely seems an aspect of the filmmaker's decision-making process, instead coming about through the choice and development of their material, both in granular part (scenes, sequences, characters, etc.) and architectural whole (a film, a body of work). Significantly, some notable filmmakers dismiss the concept altogether—even if their cinema exemplifies it! Why, after all, make something conscious and subject to analysis when for the practitioner its tacit functioning is in little need of assistance, when too much self-awareness might actually prove counterproductive?

Telling the Story

Paramount among the tasks of the filmmaker, storytelling is the craft that all other skills serve—unless we consider creative vision to be the ultimate goal (if one perhaps not pre-designed). When we cannot follow a film's story, the filmmaker leaves us frustrated and confused. If we can, they have performed their primary obligation. For this to happen, the filmmaker needs to understand both their story and how to tell it—the mechanics of dramatic narrative and the practical aesthetics of the movie image, as well as how one informs, interacts with, and supports the other. There is a notion that the screen is merely the slave to story, that the director's work is solely about directing the actors and "covering" the action in preparation for editing, that this is all there is to storytelling. But this is to misunderstand the inevitably selective nature of "coverage" and the effect of the choices the filmmaker makes in this regard on tone; on the emotional engagement of the audience; on narrative POV (who we are "with" in a story, who is our conduit into the drama); on the visual structure of a film; on the flow of energy, the punctuation of a scene or a sequence; on breath and resonance; on action and imagery; on the modulation of tension; and above all on the relationship of the audience to the film.

The "Two Vectors" of the Filmmaker

In considering the filmmaker's tasks, the reader might also find it useful to reflect on the two vectors of their art:

1. The screen as window into the fiction.
2. The screen as address to the audience.

Whether looking in or looking out, the screen and the dynamics of its practical aesthetics (along with sound from the speakers) constitute the filmmaker's conduit between the two realms of fiction and audience.

PART II

CRITERIA

5

Dramatic Narrative

Before further examining the practical aesthetics of the screen, the reader should understand the foundation on which, by and large, its canvas is predicated—namely dramatic narrative. The nexus of this narrative *and its representation on screen*—namely the film's *dramaturgy*—and the filmmakers' success in realizing the interaction of these two fundamental elements is a central consideration in assessing the success of the filmmaker's art. Indeed, without an understanding of dramatic narrative, the analysis of film's practical aesthetics will at best be incomplete. The latter are not merely cosmetic, seeking to add elegance, beauty, ugliness, grittiness, or pictorial embellishment, but when effective are functioning resources rooted in dramatic narrative. Even when regarded within the context of the visual conventions of a film's genre or the references from which the director and cinematographer might have drawn inspiration, the aesthetics of a film should not be arbitrary but integral to its story, its storytelling, and the emotions its filmmaker seeks to convey.

By *dramatic narrative* we mean the narrative constituted by the world, the characters and their configuration, and above all, the *story* of the film—all of the elements that comprise the aforementioned and discussed domain that lies "beyond the screen." In the context of this book, we can take this narrative to be fictional, although the term might also be applied to nonfiction; *Nomadland*, indeed, incorporates such components from the nonfiction book from which it is drawn. The dramatic narrative is the fundamental stratum of a film, usually expressed through the screenplay, that the actors realize through performance and the director, cinematographer, production designer, and editor realize through the practical aesthetics of the screen—to which should be added sound design and soundscape.

Dramatic narrative encompasses not only story, characters, and world—both physical and human—but also the stakes and register of the drama, premise, theme, genre, structure, tone, and passage of time. It tends to eschew the discursive, the descriptive, and the meditative, but may on notable occasions allow for, or indeed prompt, such aspects—as it does in the hands of Chloe Zhao in *Nomadland*.

Story: The Spine of Dramatic Narrative

By *story*, specifically in dramatic narrative, we mean a series of connected events instilled with tension (often founded on suspense) and friction (often, although not exclusively, in the form of conflict between characters). These events build

The Art of the Filmmaker. Peter Markham, Oxford University Press. © Oxford University Press 2023.
DOI: 10.1093/oso/9780197631522.003.0006

cumulatively in terms of emotion and the *significance* of their stakes toward an ending that, in the light of all that has come before, resonates emotionally—whether happy or sad, uplifting or disconcerting—with a sense of meaning.

The nature of story—a vast and venerable topic—is the subject of much scholarship that could fill not only this book but many others besides. Suffice it to say that story is the predominant means by which most of us come to understand our world. Story is intrinsic to our everyday interlocution. Without a second thought, we tell each other anecdotes and tales, recount incidents, and shape experiences to exchange information as we engage with one another. Story is the currency of our interaction, the canvas by which we relate to and view each other, society, our lives, and the world. Story proves more persuasive than evidence, more compelling than reasoned argument, more engaging than facts, and more seductive than dispassionate observation.

Audiences expect a film to deliver a story. A story is not an arbitrary sequence of events but a succession of related episodes that build upon each other to offer the listener/reader/viewer an experience of cumulative gratification. A story that is weak, does not hang together, or does not work cannot be rescued by the art of the storyteller, no matter how proficient. A story that is strong may survive poor storytelling craft—or it may not.

A film's story may be slight, epic, gentle or savage, realistic (*Moonlight, Nomadland*) or fantastical (*Hereditary*—in some, though not all respects), or familiar or strange, but whether we the audience like it or not, thrill to it or loathe it, if we find its narrative logic somehow *undeniable* and cannot pull it apart, it takes on an autonomy, a life of its own—as a mimesis of human existence that to us in some way makes sense of our own lives.

A cineaste or cinephile with no sense of story, without the constant wish to know *what is going to happen next*, fails to understand the filmmaker's art. No amount of esoteric insight into lenses, camera mounts, visual effects, or technicalities of one kind or another on the one hand, or of film theory or cultural context on the other, can substitute for a need to understand a film's story. A story may be all that a film delivers, be a vehicle for a filmmaker's vision, or prove a combination of the two—a singular tale, a distinctive voice. A viewer may appreciate much more about a movie than its story, but without the basic desire—the imperative—to follow the course of events and anticipate to where they might be leading, the reader, no matter how informed, is unlikely to progress to further understanding of a film's practical aesthetics.

There are conflicting interpretations of the term *plot* and of what constitutes plot and what story. For the purposes of this breakdown, the reader might consider plot the mechanism by which the story moves forward—how the writer makes happen what needs to happen. We tend to say not "Tell me a plot" but "Tell me a story." Story is what compels us emotionally. *Events, situations, scenarios,* and *actions* are components of story and plot. Functioning both as stand-alone and interdependent entities, they offer moments that come alive in this fictional universe.

Crucial to story are its *stakes*—how much the characters have to gain and to lose. The term *rising stakes*, often heard, while helpful in some respects can be misleading, tending to suggest that any final reckoning has literally to be between life and death—of the individual, of a group or community, or even of humanity in its totality. That might work well for melodramas, for "genre" outings, but for other cinema it might be more helpful for us to think of increasingly *significant* stakes, in which it is *meaning* that is at risk for a character. Meaning, perhaps, is all to us, or to most of us. A sense of meaning determines our sense of identity. Without meaning, we feel empty. So when a character in film faces a moral dilemma that threatens the loss of their sense of meaning, when whichever path they choose, it will be lost, the tension in a story is at its greatest—greater even than when their physical survival is threatened. When this happens, the *soul*—that indefinable, elusive, yet recognizable entity, a character's inner essence or self—comes to dramatic life, and with it, the film.

In *Hereditary* we learn that in the face of his demonic antagonists, Peter's soul is at stake. As we find that he has little ultimate agency in the matter, the horror of the film's malevolent, deterministic universe takes its full effect. In *Moonlight*, Chiron must choose between on the one hand power over others as a means of self-defense, and on the other his vulnerability in the face of Kevin's welcoming love. The stakes of his physical safety are thus trumped by those of his inner self, to which he discovers he must stay true. Fern, in *Nomadland*, faces the choice between a permanent home and a transient existence and opts for the latter, which she finds fulfills the needs of her inner being.

Structure in Film: The Architecture of Dramatic Narrative

Structure is the framework of dramatic flow, its sections and their linear proportions as they relate to each other. Films might adopt conventional structures such as those of three and five acts. A climax in three-act structure will occur as the story meets its conclusion, while in other structures—such as that of five acts or more—this may occur earlier. A movie might, on the other hand, incorporate its own form, perhaps proceeding in a "chapter" or episodic fashion. *Acts* might also be described as *movements*, a word with more musical implications, and one the reader might helpfully regard as affording a measure of distance between cinema and theater.

Structure may be reflected on the screen when the filmmaker chooses to shift stylistic approaches for each movement to give visual modulation to the journeys of story and character. The filmmaker may also mark the stanchions of the structure that underlies a film's story by changes of tension, rhythm, tone, light, place, and the visual dynamics of shot size (opting perhaps for wider shots such as vistas), as well as shifts in the flow of screen energy. Such articulation can be seen, for instance, at the end of *Hereditary*'s prelude and the beginning of its first movement, when the Graham family return home and Ari Aster gives wide shots of their car arriving and of their lobby, empty in the brief moments before their entry. (See the case study in Part III.)

Scenes and sequences have their own structures, reflected in the nature of the shots, camera, and cutting the filmmaker employs in order to articulate their individual sections.

Narrative Units: The Building Blocks of Dramatic Narrative

Scenes, sequence, vignettes, and acts or movements—what might in general be thought of collectively as narrative units—will generally have been included only when fulfilling a purpose or function. Not always evident when considering an episode within its own parameters, this becomes apparent when explored in the broader context of an act/movement or of a film in its entirety. The reader might attend to this wider perspective in order to understand the workings of an episode not only in terms of its granular construction but also in its connectivity to the narrative as a whole.

In much of filmmaking education the mantra is propounded that scenes must always move the story forward. We might, however, question this imperative of consistent momentum, of always "cutting to the chase." A constant, onward flow of story would allow little space for either the complexity of dramatic narrative or the totality of a movie's address (examined in Chapters 7 to 10). Storytelling, indeed, is about much more than propelling a story forward at every step of the way. *Suspense*, to give a fundamental example of the storyteller's resources, would be hard to elicit if scenes were always progressing.

Quentin Tarantino is a filmmaker known for stretching out the tension in a scene to a point that audiences can find hard to bear but that nevertheless *intensifies* their engagement. This can be seen in his *Once Upon a Time in Hollywood* (2019), when Cliff Booth, visiting the Spahn ranch and its hippy residents, enters the bedroom of George Spahn only to find him in bed and turned to the wall. *Is he asleep?* we wonder. *Is he awake? Is he dead? If he wakes, how will he react to the intruder? Will he prove hostile? Will he be accommodating? And what, we wonder, does he even look like? Innocuous or imposing? And how long will Booth, and indeed we the audience, have to wait before finding out?*

The scene arrests the story's momentum while heightening our anticipation and uncertainty. It plants images on the *screen of the mind*, the putative images of a character we have not yet seen and those of his possible actions on encountering Booth. Only in the subsequent scene, when Booth discovers a tire slashed on his car and exacts revenge, does the story move forward—although it could be argued that even here, the event sets up later episodes, sowing seeds of suspense rather than merely providing onward flow. The sequence at the ranch tautens the tension of the narrative, stretching it so that when it is finally released, the story springs forward with a pent-up energy stored hitherto.

Returning to consideration of the case studies, the sequences analyzed from *Hereditary* and *Moonlight* list the information, emotion, visceral sensation, and creative vision each communicates. Such elements are integral to any deliberation on the function or (several) functions of an episode or narrative unit. There are other categories of function too, many of which can be found in Chloe Zhao's singular approach to *Nomadland*. Wonder, for example, has long been a resource of the big screen—perennially the conveyor of spectacle. It can be found both in Zhao's use of landscape and in her inserts of the natural world and its detail. Such visual poetry is not supplementary to the dramatic narrative, not spectacle for its own sake, but integral to her film's vision.

Her depictions of frozen time in the rooms of the abandoned gypsum plant and of the everyday items left behind there (see the case study in Part III) serve to move the story *backward*! It is through this retrogression that the filmmaker enables her protagonist to move her personal journey forward. In Zhao's intimate vignettes of Fern, in her van at night for example—again, intrinsic to a dramatic narrative encompassing both the cosmic and the personal—the filmmaker has us invest more fully in her travails. Such vignettes—and this is also true of those of the film's canvas of the natural world—allow for the *resonance* of emotion, revelation, and new knowledge, which we the audience need time to reflect upon.

To insist that not all scenes need to progress the story is not, however, to maintain that many, perhaps most, shouldn't be doing just that. Narrative momentum plays to the desire of audiences to escape the confines of their lives—to be *entertained* for two hours or so. Just how that drive is achieved, maintained, accelerated, and rendered immersive to the viewer makes for invaluable analysis on the part of those seeking to understand the filmmaker's art. If it is the modulation of narrative momentum that matters—of its rhythm and flow of energy—rather than its speed, momentum there has to be. In dramatic narrative, situations change; energize the story; and generate fresh directions, new perspectives for characters and audience, and shifts of emotion. In these respects, it builds our engagement.

Characters: The Action and Emotion of Dramatic Narrative

Characters seem to us mimeses of people. No matter what their function in a story might be—whether as protagonist, antagonist, secondary character or tertiary one appearing in passing only, and whether they have the multiple, contradictory traits of the fully dimensioned protagonist or serve a specific purpose at one point of the story and present a single trait—we as an audience want them to "ring true." They may be "larger than life," they may present the slightest of vignettes, but they must be credible, at least within the world and genre of the film—vital elements of that life "beyond" the screen. We may be taken into their narrative POV, know what they know, feel what they feel; we may observe them objectively, from more of a distance; or we may shift in our connection to them. We may believe we are aware of the emotions of characters but subsequently discover our understanding to have been misplaced. We may find ourselves at odds with a character, critical of them, appalled by them even, but when they demonstrate an autonomy, a quality we are powerless to deny, we follow their journey as it brings a movie to life.

Character, as manifested in dramatic narrative, is a complex amalgam of (a) fictional being, imbued with truthful, at least believable, human traits, and (b) functional building block of the story. It isn't always easy to see beneath this illusion of a person. We are too immersed in the flow of emotion and energy, and in the simple desire to know what is going to happen next, to deconstruct the nature of a character's aspects and their interaction with others. To those with a basic grounding in dramatic narrative, however, the main characters will immediately be evident—namely the protagonist(s), or primary character(s), and the antagonist(s), who function as their adversary (or adversaries). The former seeks an objective while the latter stands in their way, or the antagonist works toward a goal and the protagonist takes action to prevent their success in attaining it.

The primary characters, the protagonists in *Hereditary*, are the four members of the Graham family. The unseen, demonic King Paimon is the antagonist, acting through the proxies of Joan and, in the backstory, Ellen.

The protagonist of *Moonlight* is Chiron, known initially as Little and later as Black. Another primary character, who appears in each of the film's three movements or acts, is Kevin. Mentor at times, companion at others, antagonist at one point, Kevin is instrumental in precipitating Chiron's ultimate salvation.

Fern is the protagonist of *Nomadland*. Dave, the film's other main character, enters the narrative as her companion and mentor, finally becoming a foil to her inclinations toward a life on the road—the one she eventually adopts.

Secondary and minor characters may also act as catalysts for the main characters' journeys. Terrell, in *Moonlight*, functions as Chiron's antagonist in the film's second movement but also serves as a force of *triangulation* to move the Chiron-Kevin relationship forward (or perhaps backward). Without the bully coercing Kevin into punching his friend, there would be no betrayal, no nadir in Chiron's companionship with him, and nothing for the putative lovers to push against that might lead to their eventual rapprochement.

Joan, in *Hereditary*, is an indispensable secondary character, since with Ellen, the grandmother, being deceased, and Paimon's presence invisible, the story would have to rely on largely unseen supernatural forces as antagonists to the Graham family. That Joan appears first as Annie's ally, before being revealed as an agent of demonic forces, marks her as a *shapeshifter*—a protean, multifunctional character ideal for moving a story forward at key points. Peter's classmate Bridget, meanwhile, is more of a tertiary or minor character. Attracted to her, Peter divests himself of Charlie by tempting his sister with the chocolate cake that causes her allergic reaction and leads to fatal consequences. Main character Charlie's death raises the stakes and prompts the guilt that roils the Graham family and unleashes their mutual bitterness. She is the film's first sacrifice, Steve the second, Annie the third, and the benighted Peter the fourth and final—his soul the last bastion of personal agency in the movie's determinist universe.

Characters may embody or represent a force intrinsic to a film's conflict. *Hereditary's* Steve, a main character, one with whom we share intimate time, functions as the story's proponent of harmony. The manager of the family constantly working to keep everyone together, he provides an important building block in the film's dramatic narrative, representing reason in the conflict with Paimon's demonic conspiracy, an abstraction that proves inadequate in the face of the forces of fate. His all too human, fearful, controlling instincts, meanwhile, reveal him as not entirely altruistic and lend authority to his characterization.

The nature and function of characters in *Nomadland* reveal the notable powers of invention of writer-director Zhao in combining nonfiction and fiction. Fern, Dave, Fern's sister's family, and Dave's son are fictional. (Although *Fern* sounds like *Fran*—Frances McDormand plays her—while *Dave* is played by David Strathearn.) Other "characters" are nonfictional.

Without the fictional characters in the film, there could be no dramatic narrative. Fern, in part, takes the place of the author/narrator of the book on which the film is based and provides Zhao with the vehicle for character and story development her film needs—the spine around which its other elements find cohesion. The book traces the nonfictional Linda May's journey throughout, but illuminating as this is in human terms, other elements would be required to render it the viable dramatic thread of a main character.

The *configuration* of characters—how they might be grouped, related, and opposed to each other in order to drive the narrative and bring about its denouement—constitutes another vital consideration. Is it the case that in a film there are characters who are simply morally good or bad? Is there perhaps one evil figure, a master criminal, a psychopath, such as the willful villain of a James Bond movie, who precipitates the drama? Might all the characters, on the other hand, act essentially in good faith—as they do in *Nomadland*—in which case the circumstances in which the characters find themselves, rather than any antagonist they face, prompt the drama? Or are the characters each a mixture of good and bad, supporting and antagonizing one another in different episodes? (Think Chiron and Kevin in *Moonlight*.) Perhaps they are all morally dubious, as might be the case in a noir or a black comedy such as Bong Joon-ho's 2019 *Parasite*. How, in other words, does the friction, the tension, the conflict, the drama of the film come about?

In *Moonlight*, there are the adversaries and there are the mentors. Chiron's adversaries comprise the bullies who initially chase him, his mother Paula, and Terrell. He has his mentors, too: Juan in the first movement (for both good and bad); nobody in the second, in which he goes adrift; and Kevin in the third. Terrell is an example of the willful villain who lacks any apparent redeeming features. Chiron, while defeating him through a resort to violence, loses out to him in the sense that Terrell drives him to later adopt the false persona of Black, by which he himself becomes at one point a bully (to Travis). Black briefly becomes a mentor to his mother Paula before he can in turn be mentored by Kevin.

Hereditary offers the steadying, organizing Steve; the febrile, impulsive Annie; the obsessive loner Charlie; the vulnerable, emotionally troubled Peter; and the machinating adversary and shapeshifter Joan (another character who lacks redeeming features). The configuration is kindling, in Steve's case literally, for the malevolent possession that devastates the family.

Nomadland's Fern has her enablers: the unhoused, nonfictional travelers who tell their stories—and she has her tempters: her sister and Dave, who offer the path of family and security. She also has her sage Bob Wells, who not only sings the virtues of a life on the road, but in revealing his grief over his deceased son enables her to engage with and accept her own loss. She even has her gatekeeper to personal freedom—the storage unit manager, who by accepting payment for storing her belongings facilitates her first voyage out into the world, then by taking possession of them enables her final embrace of a peripatetic lifestyle.

Moonlight, especially, presents its characters without the judgment that can render dramatic narrative a vehicle for moralizing. We are left to interpret the nature of Juan, for example, according to our perspectives—those of us familiar with neighborhoods like his, and dealers like him, will perhaps perceive him differently from those of us who are not. Barry Jenkins's attention to the detail and dimensionality of his character and to Little's regard for him, however, leads us, wherever we are coming from, to a *shared* sense of this contradictory figure—recruiter of youths in his criminal business yet parental mentor to and protector of the bullied child who reveals, ultimately, shame in his activities.

The nature and significance of individual characters and their configuration in a film will have an impact not only on a film's casting and the making of its story and episodes but also on its visual storytelling, its staging, shooting, and cutting—in short, on the filmmaker's art. When *Hereditary*'s Annie is with Joan, for example, she is invariably trapped in some way—in her car as the latter approaches, at the table having tea, in the parking lot where Joan accosts her and the fluid sequence shot holds them both in the frame (which tightens as the scene progresses), and in the first séance. Charlie is generally alone or isolated in the frame (unless at the party, when she's overwhelmed by the crowd). Peter is frequently similarly alone, in his bedroom, wandering through the house, or preoccupied in class and oblivious to the lesson. Steve visits one family member after another, the sole character who makes the effort—although his caregiving strikes us as perhaps not entirely altruistic.

Moonlight's Juan is seen at the film's opening with Terrence and Azu in a long sequence shot of wide framing—instrumental in revealing his status in the neighborhood. He doesn't step forward into a single until the end of the shot and in so doing stabilizes a previously unstable camera. Little is by contrast shown alone, fleeing and then hiding from his pursuers. In the rough and tumble of the soccer mêlée, Little keeps his distance, before finding Kevin emerging from the group to befriend him. Later, when Chiron, as Black, has Travis deal drugs, Jenkins has him watch from his car, keeping him in a single rather than having him enter the fray himself as Juan did. Throughout the film, indeed, Little/Chiron/Black is isolated in both predicament and visual language before his mentors step out of their milieu to join him. Only when

Black leans toward his mother at the rehab center, offering her his love, does he himself take on the role of mentor.

Loner Fern, in *Nomadland*, when joining groups at different stages of her story is depicted in varying degrees of integration—at lunch with fellow warehouse workers when she's shown sitting at a crowded table, at RTR gatherings where she appears largely in single shots, at a social evening when she dances with Dave and is shown among the crowd, at a barbecue with her sister's family when she's again barely glimpsed in a group shot, and then at a Thanksgiving dinner with Dave's family. At the film's ending she's alone in the frames—in the abandoned gypsum plant, then in her empty home, where she at last finds the means to accept her grief before setting out on the life true to her.

World in Film: The Environment of Dramatic Narrative

This may seem "real," or it may be fantastical. It may exist in a context of war or violent crime or in the subdued ambience of everyday existence, but in any context it must above all seem *truthful*. We the audience must find it credible, whether the setting is a neighborhood in contemporary Los Angeles or a mountaintop castle in some purely concocted mythical, medieval kingdom. This applies not just to the immediate physical vicinity of the episodes described in the screenplay and represented on the screen but also to their broader environment.

No world in a film is real. Even if it seems so, it cannot be—it is fictional. (This is to forego discussion of documentary or nonfictional cinema—topics outside the scope of this book.) What matters to us is truthfulness. *Hereditary* is set in the recognizable world of a well-heeled American family subject to everyday pressures. If it transpires that its universe rests on supernatural, demonic foundations, the dynamics of a family's psychology are tellingly portrayed. The predicament in which the Graham family find themselves may be supernatural, but the emotional interactions of the characters are authentic. Their horror realm may be abnormal, but even this has a consistent logic we cannot pick apart. *Moonlight* and *Nomadland* by contrast reveal broadly "naturalistic" worlds. Even so, they are vividly evoked by their filmmakers, who create a comprehensive sense of their environments, their workings, and their rules—in the bedrock of their dramatic narratives and in the images this prompts on the screen. Each creates an authenticity, a sense of reality built on thorough research, but both offer far more than slavish reproduction, coming alive in their fictionality in the way that other, purely invented worlds also might—*truthfulness* being their common factor.

The world of the dramatic narrative and its manifestation on screen might be divided into the *physical* and the *human* or *cultural*. Physical aspects of a world might include its natural elements (geography, terrain, climate) and its human-made environment (settlement, urban or otherwise, architecture). The multifarious cultural components of a film's world might include the period in which it is set; the nature and composition of its social milieu; its economic circumstances; its shared preconceptions of meaning, morality, and status and what these depend on; its behavioral norms; its attitudes to love, death, sex, violence, money, youth, age, or beauty; whether it is a new or old society, central or peripheral, controlling or oppressed; whether it places the individual over society or vice versa; and whether it demands loyalty at all costs or encourages transgression—or combines aspects of both attitudes. Unfamiliar or purely invented human worlds require particular care on the part of the filmmaker in formulation and presentation. Inconsistencies, aspects weakly conceived or ignored, and rules unclear or confusing undermine a purely fabricated world's authenticity.

Whether a film's world has been successfully created or by contrast reproduced from an original, the reader might reflect on whether it is a backdrop to the narrative or is integral to it: Might the story happen anywhere, or does it require the specific world in which it is set?

In the three case study films, the world of the dramatic narratives, economically described on the page, is consummately represented on the screen.

The Grahams' home in *Hereditary*—with its many rooms, corridors, attic, Annie's models, Charlie's odd miniature figures, and accompanying treehouse—is entirely appropriate to the story traced within its compartmentalized environment. Aster's world is given added authenticity by his film's sorties into a less concocted, "real" world outside—Ellen's memorial, the premises in which the grief-counseling session takes place, Charlie's and Peter's classrooms, the spacious home that's the setting for the party the siblings attend, Joan's street and apartment block, an art store's parking lot, and Steve's office. This eminently everyday world lends credibility to the exaggerations of the family's house while accentuating its disconcerting qualities.

Little and Juan's neighborhood of seemingly innocuous housing, condemned apartments, and diners in *Moonlight* is conjured in the film's opening sequences, while Chiron's high school in the film's second movement seems typical enough. Even if the story could take place in many parts of the United States, the comprehensive realism of the environments Jenkins evokes infuses its world with a specificity and authenticity that complements the fiction of Chiron's emotional journey.

While considering *Moonlight*'s apparent realism, the reader might find it enlightening to reflect on the film's scenes set on the beach and in the ocean. Here we see the *four elements* come into play—the earth (sand), water (ocean), air (the ocean breeze), and fire (literally in Kevin's blunt, metaphorically in the friends' sexual encounter). This primal aspect of the film's world affords the film's dramatic narrative a mythical dimension that is effortlessly realized by Jenkins on the screen.

Nomadland's world is by no means lacking in mythical foundation either—a world of death as the film starts, characterized by the closed gypsum plant and the loss of Fern's husband, her journey through an environment of rejuvenating nature also replete with the four elements, the rooted settings of the family homes she visits, her return to the dead human-made world of Empire that has been frozen in time, and then finally the open road through the natural landscape to which she commits herself.

A Note on Dramatic Narrative Modified through Process

Although this book is not concerned with the practices of film *production*, the reader should understand that no matter how deliberate the filmmaker's intentions, how comprehensive their planning, how consummate their vision, it is rare that all eventualities of production can be anticipated—particularly when it comes to shooting on location. Weather, unexpected circumstances of one kind or another, and the pressures of schedule and time may prompt the reconceptualization of elements of the dramatic narrative.

Actors, meanwhile, may offer contributions the filmmaker might find preferable to their preconceived intentions; although usually this will not go so far as to change the foundations of narrative, on occasion it might. Should this occur before a shoot—perhaps when a writer-director sees some quality in an actor that might usefully inform the nature, even the prominence of their character—the dramatic narrative itself might in part be revised. The nature of the production; its budget, schedule, and genre; and the status of the filmmaker will of course have a bearing on whether such an option might be possible.

A film is continually re-explored in its editorial stage. Cutting a film is not a process of duplicating the detail of a screenplay but of realizing the dramatic narrative that underlies it. Editing a story on screen may reveal aspects of that substratum that no longer work. Maybe the order of episodes needs revision, or the function of a scene changes, or its meaning shifts. Perhaps what was seen as essential no longer appears necessary. Perhaps what was a minor embellishment now demands heightened prominence, or what was shot by chance—a moment, a look, an action—is incorporated into the flow of the narrative.

The success of practical and creative filmmaking rests in part on a filmmaker's intentions, to which they need to remain faithful throughout the vicissitudes of production, but also—paradoxically—on their ability to embrace the questions and challenges that arise along the path to a film's completion. Such unpredictable factors may prove invaluable in the successful evolution of a movie.

The study of a film's screenplay (so long, of course, as this is not merely a transcript taken from the finished movie) may reveal variations and differences in the completed film that are the result of these processes.

6
The Elements in Front of the Lens

The fictional world that we the audience are led to believe in is created in part from the physical reality of the set and/or location; by action and performance before the camera; and by how these elements are formed, depicted, connected, modulated and manipulated by the filmmaker. When this combination of captured actuality and aesthetic works successfully, even the most informed reader can find it hard to make out the precise nature of the physical and practical components involved in the creation of a film's fictional world. They won't know the exact configuration of a set, the number of takes required to achieve the shot, the length of each take, or what was shot and did not make the final cut—although they might count the number of setups used. What we see on the screen is, at least in general, not so much the recording and transferring of physical and temporal actuality—indeed, it may not be that at all—as the representation on the screen (and from the speakers) of the fiction the dramatic narrative elicits.

The reality of the set or location, and the action played out upon it, can never be identical to the "reality" fabricated by camera and cutting, a world that comes to exist within the framing of successive shots and the shifting placement of the camera, and which, moreover, exists not in three but two dimensions on the planarity of the screen. Space can be expanded or contracted by lensing and editing, while time can be manipulated by editing, or on occasion by the slowing down, speeding up, or "ramping" of an individual shot. The flow of energy is created and modulated—as well as by performances and actions captured on camera—by selective lensing and camera movement, and by editing. The nature of what is depicted within a shot is determined not just by what is captured by the camera in the moment—although this may be profound, especially in respect of performance, but by *how* it is captured—the framing, lensing, angle, and lighting—and by its context. Factors affecting its significance, nuance, and register include its placement within the dramatic narrative/story/world, the reverberations of what has preceded it, connections to other moments/scenes/images, any images it conjures "on the screen of the mind," and sound design and music.

Even when a scene is shot in a single take or in postproduction made to look as though it has been, the framings selected by the filmmaker determine what we see and what we don't, which angle we see this from, and what lens we see it through—a long lens that compresses perspective, a wide that exaggerates it, a neutral option that approximates human perception.

The Art of the Filmmaker. Peter Markham, Oxford University Press. © Oxford University Press 2023.
DOI: 10.1093/oso/9780197631522.003.0007

Sets and Locations

The precise design of a set, either constructed on a soundstage or found (and probably adapted) on location, may or may not be what is presented on screen. Constructed sets, in particular, may in actuality be larger than their fictional representations, especially when the spaces involved are constricted. There needs to be room for cameras, dollies, and lights, and for the crew to work. When the filmmakers preplan camera angles rigorously, they may discover that one or more walls may not need to be built, so that a set, as constructed, may be incomplete and open to its soundstage:

> It's better to know which set walls need to be removable before you build, and why invest thought, resources, and time into a corner of a room that ultimately won't be on screen?
>
> —Ari Aster, *Hereditary* screenplay (A24 Films, 2020)

The dimensions of what might *appear* as a constricted space may need to be enlarged in physical actuality so that the lenses utilized convey an impression of narrower confines. When wide-angle lenses are used for a wide shot (WS) in a cramped space, the result may give the impression of a space larger than it actually is (while perhaps distorting horizontals and verticals). Less-constricted dimensions shot on neutral or longer lenses, with the camera placed at a greater distance from what it shoots, may yield the illusion of a more contained area (while avoiding unwanted lens distortion). On the other hand, a filmmaker shooting a socio-realist drama might decide to sacrifice their options and work in tighter spaces. Although this might render any wider view of a room hard to capture, they will settle for more restricted shooting possibilities, adopting a visual language attuned to the modest dimensions in which they have chosen to work. They may also feel that the actors will benefit from the dimensional reality of surroundings that might help them elicit the authentic performances more generous space might hinder.

The hard realities of genre and budget will often determine such choices. In larger-budget productions, especially those in less realistic genres, actors may perform on a soundstage in front of a green screen, their settings created in digital postproduction. On lower budget "indies" and socio-realist dramas, on the contrary, the cast may work in the very location in which a story is set or somewhere closely resembling it.

Chloe Zhao's actors and nonactors in *Nomadland* worked in environments close to, if not the same as, their real-world counterparts. Barry Jenkins's sets for *Moonlight* were often found in the actual locations in which his story is set—such as the Liberty City projects of Miami—and adapted to the needs of its world by production designer Hannah Beachler. The Grace Yun–designed interior of Ari Aster's Graham family house for *Hereditary*, meanwhile, was designed and constructed precisely. Its dimensions were spacious enough to suggest the family's powerlessness in the face of the forces of supernatural malevolence but also facilitated the camera placement, lensing, and movement orchestrated by Aster and cinematographer Pawel Pogorzelski. At other times they seem deliberately convoluted and constricted, an inescapable maze to echo the narrative in which the characters are trapped.

The Grahams' home is an instance of a fictional setting being created from separate physical sets. The downstairs lobby and sitting room and the upstairs corridors were separate. Individual rooms were separate. The interior of the house was built, while its exterior existed on location. The composite result is eminently credible.

The reader may wish to research production details to examine a film's transitions from one discrete component of a setting to another and to reflect on the visual language, particularly the editing, utilized to render spatial continuity credible when in actuality there was none.

Actors and Staging

From the "method"-inspired work of Marlon Brando in Elia Kazan's *On the Waterfront* (1954) to the uninflected actions of nonactor Martin LaSalle in Robert Bresson's *Pickpocket* (1959), there are perhaps almost as many approaches to acting as there are actors, even if there are fewer distinct philosophies of the craft. One factor in particular affects the filmmaker's visual storytelling, however—namely the difference between performers who are camera aware and those who are not. When that awareness is based not on vanity but on the actor's understanding of their craft as a component of the language of the screen, the symbiosis of film staging and camera can be highly effective. The flow and vectors of energy and drama, the relationship between camera and action, will prove agile and compelling.

Actors either unaware of the camera or choosing to hold the filmmaker's craft as subservient to their own (as though the sole task of the director, cinematographer, and editor was to record performance) may prompt the filmmaker's use of a more "passive" camera. Nonactors and children, meanwhile, are unlikely to prove capable of collaborating with the camera (although trained child actors may be more skilled). This may not necessarily invalidate the input of any of these groups, as the filmmaker might consider the authenticity of a performance to override the limitations of its presentation on the screen.

An experienced film actor knows to follow precise staging, how to hit their "marks" and move in coordination with the camera, with its framing and movement, while appearing oblivious of any constraints this imposes on their performance. Elaborate sequence shots involving complex action and interaction between characters and intricate camera moves become achievable that with less skillful and cinematically aware performers would be difficult to bring about. An actor's ability to coordinate their own movements with the camera's, their sense of timing, and their ability to take cues at specific moments (even while delivering an authentic performance) can make for masterly visual discourse. When this happens, what takes place in front of the lens is what takes place on screen—although it is of course *a realm of fiction contained within the frame*—while other activity occurring outside of the frame, such as the placing or replacing of props, or actors awaiting their cues to enter a shot, is not shown.

Jenkins and actor Mahershala Ali demonstrate such a collaboration in the opening sequence of *Moonlight* analyzed in the case studies chapters. *Hereditary*'s family séance, also explored, shows Toni Collette, Gabriel Byrne, and Alex Wolff working in tandem with Aster's fluid camera during the scene's initial long takes, in order to achieve an interaction of staging with shifting framing and composition.

Looking to other movies, we might consider the scene in Krzysztof Kieślowski's *Three Colors Red* (1994) in which Irene Jacob's Valentine enters Josef's home for the first time. Here, within a single shot, and in collaboration with Jacob, the camera functions at one moment as her POV and at another as the observer of her hesitant path through the house as she comes to discover Jean-Louis Trintignant's initially oblivious Josef.

(1) Valentine opens Josef's front door.   (2a) Her POV pushing through the hallway.

(2b) The camera pans left . . .   (2c) then right as the POV shot continues.

(2d) Valentine enters her own POV R-L profile.   (2e) Valentine motivates the camera move.

(2f) Valentine turns into L-R profile.   (2g) Her cross motivates the dolly forward …

(2h) to a single of Josef. Cut to   (3) Valentine settles in the doorway.

Some way into this developing shot, we see Irene Jacob stepping into frame at the desired point, hitting her mark to give a right to left profile (as the subjective shot changes to a third-person POV), then pacing her subsequent moves in coordination with camera movement and framing—pausing again to give a second profile, this time left to right, before crossing to camera right. She then motivates the camera's forward move as it discovers Josef and then passes her so that she falls out of frame. The energy of that dolly forward is picked up in the reverse on Valentine, as she moves toward a static camera—an example of how the energy of the camera (the perceiver), and what it shows (the perceived) can connect to sustain an orchestration of flow across a cut.

When a filmmaker works with a cast consisting largely of nonactors, intricate editing in camera achieved by complicated camera moves and shifting framing is unlikely to prove practical. A simpler approach to shooting will be in order. (See Zhao's approach in *Nomadland*.) More extensive coverage of the action may then be needed, and thus more cuts—Nadine Labaki's 2018 *Capernaum*, for example, was apparently reduced from an initial assembly of over twelve hours in length to its running time of 126 minutes. A scene that with trained film actors might be achievable in one or two developing shots—as the actors enter and leave the frame as appropriate, crossing at orchestrated moments—will instead need to be assembled from individual singles. Here, the looks the nonactors give to each other will prove essential to the effectiveness of the cuts between them. With more footage, the filmmaker can be more selective in finding moments of telling performance, bringing their movie to successful fruition through editing—*Capernaum*'s emotional power is testament to this.

Staging, in such circumstances, is likely to be simple; unversed actors can be inhibited by having to hit their marks throughout a long take and will lack a professional's sense of timing. On the other hand, nonactors, asked to perform tasks they carry out regularly in real life, might prove oblivious to the camera. The filmmaker may then capture a "performance" that appears natural, simply because it is. This strategy can prove helpful when orchestrating background action using extras familiar with their activity. The authenticity of Zhao's "RTR" people presents an impression truthful to a world that is their own, their milieu convincingly portrayed through simple coverage.

Performance

An actor's performance on screen can be, and indeed often is, the consequence of the capture of what has occurred in front of the camera. This may be the case in a single shot, whether brief or lasting longer, but also when a performance has been consistent over several takes and setups throughout a scene. Performances, however, will often vary between sizes, angles, and takes, in which case consistency and dramatic modulation may be realized only in the editing. In such an instance, the performance we see on screen will have been created, never having happened continuously on set. This may be intentional, the director having elicited alternative performances from the actor with a view to choosing the most useful in the cutting room. The actor also might have requested further takes to try different approaches or give a better rendering. There may even be a measure of improvisation, the actor giving spontaneous alternative performances under the director's auspices. Actors aware of shot size and framing, meanwhile, might temper their performance accordingly, adjusting the rendering in a WS for a big close-up (BCU), for example. Here, actor and camera work symbiotically.

In relation to these considerations, it is important for the non-filmmaking reader to have some sense of the shooting process familiar to its practitioners:

The filmmaker may shoot a *master*—usually a wider or group shot—that covers most or much of a scene and the action in it. This provides the foundation for the additional setups required for the scene to come together in the edit. Such an approach, however, is not adopted by all filmmakers in all circumstances. Others will design the flow of shots within a scene with deliberation as to exactly how and when they connect. With either approach, though, what appears on screen as a continuous event will have been created by the joining of a number of separate shots.

A scene that might have taken many hours to shoot, involving numerous shots and several takes of each, may flow seamlessly on the screen for only a few minutes. Moments and actions may have been shot from different angles, while individual takes generally overlap the action covered in others to give a number of options for cutting points and so facilitate smooth and effective editing. The events of an episode may never have been continuously realized on set, existing in their fictional realm only, the character's journey of action and emotion an amalgam of the actor's fragmented performances. The filmmaker, however, may support the actor by shooting at least a continuous section of a scene, if not the whole, to help them realize a consistent, organic flow of emotion and rhythm within the episode.

The filmmaker may utilize the persona and energy of a character or milieu to inform their camera and/or cutting. In such an instance, the *charge* of *what* we the audience see comes to determine *how* we see it. Barry Jenkins makes use of the watchful authority of Juan in *Moonlight*'s opening sequence to prompt fluid camerawork both precise in its internal editing and free in the restlessness of its swirling background, then allows the character to stabilize the shot as he brings control to the episode. A filmmaker may on the other hand choose to contrast the nature of a character or milieu by adopting an incongruous mode of visual discourse, so as either to offer a critical, satirical, or distancing comment on it or, on the contrary, to dignify whoever lacks any measure of poise in the narrative.

A further aspect of the interaction between performer and camera is the phenomenon of the actor who is the subject of a shot, particularly a single, vesting control of the frame. Here, the power of an actor's or nonactor's performance at a particular moment leads to their command of the shot. "Beats" of intense reflection, of the telling of a personal backstory, of emotional realization, or of a dramatic shift in a character's perception may facilitate the performer's authority over the camera. Angle, lensing, and lighting will not of course be determined by the actor/nonactor, but the emotional truthfulness they convey may demand either a simple static frame or at most a slow move into or around them. In these instances, their eyeline will often cleave to the axis of the lens, so that without quite *breaking the fourth wall* (looking directly into the lens), a character seems to address us, the audience. Without cuts, without noticeable camera movement, we cannot escape the intensity of these moments. Here, the performance on set is shown on the screen with little mediation from the filmmaker (lens and lighting apart), unless the score or source music either reinforces it or offers a comment on it.

At its most straightforward, this aspect can be seen in *Nomadland*'s vignettes of Linda May, Swankie, Bob Jones, and others as they tell their actual life stories. Their authenticity brooks no intervening artifice. Annie, in *Hereditary*, tells the story of her relationship with her mother, arresting camera movement and cutting for the thirty seconds of the shot's duration, in which we feel as trapped in her predicament as she does.

Toni Collette's performance as Annie in *Hereditary*'s grief counseling scene possesses the frame.

Chiron's moment of reflection, shortly after his beating at the hands of Kevin in *Moonlight*, may last only fifteen seconds or so, but it feels like an eternity, and again, the actor's performance demands the camera's undivided attention. With no dialogue, with a flickering light, with a low, slowly building chord and sparse, deep percussion, Chiron's moment of decision captivates us.

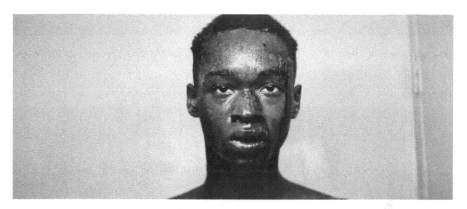

Ashton Sanders as Chiron in *Moonlight* commands the shot.

Props and Equipment

The counterparts of things that seem real or functional within the fictional world beyond the screen are often themselves nonfunctioning, not practical, and often constructed from alternative materials. Firearms invariably fall into this category, as do other weapons. The chair that *Moonlight*'s Chiron brings down on the head of Terrell was surely of lightweight construction, flimsily built so as to fragment on impact. In *Hereditary*, the glass of the window through which the stuntperson substituting for actor Alex Wolff dives was not glass, which would have seriously injured them, but the safer sugar glass. The fabrication of an event through the crafts of special effects exemplifies the actuality that is made to look dramatic on screen. The cutting together of numerous camera angles to create a fictional collision or explosion, by manipulating time and modulating the flow of energy, by placing us at the heart of the impact then taking us out of it perhaps, to find waves of debris hurtling toward us, exemplifies the method of filmmaking craft in the service of fictional mayhem.

When it comes to explaining how something such as a piece of equipment works—what needs to be shown and what need be only suggested—the filmmaker, aware that the art of storytelling is not about the simple recording and broadcasting of raw narrative, selects the elements that will create a credible impression. In Anthony Minghella's 1996 *The English Patient*, there is a scene set in a church (not shot on an actual location but in a set on a soundstage) in which Kip secures Hana to a rope that at its other end is attached, through a system of pulleys and counterweights, to Kip himself. As Kip drops on the rope from a tall pile of sandbags, Hana rises at the other end. Kip lowers himself to the church floor, then hauls on the rope to lift Hana higher

(1a) Kip lowers himself.

(1b) Attached to the other end of Kip's rope, Hana rises.

(1c) Now on the floor, Kip hauls Hana higher, then in

(1d) draws her to the opposite wall.

so she can inspect frescoes above. He proceeds to ease her across to the frescoes on the opposite wall by gently drawing his rope over.

The setup for these actions was designed and operated by a special effects crew, who lowered Kip and raised Hana independently. The author, as second unit director, was deputized to shoot inserts depicting the mechanism Kip was supposed to have set up, in order that the audience might understand and so believe in it. That material, however, was never shot, as it proved unnecessary. We see Kip descend. We see Hana ascend. The connection is all, and we never think to question the precise nature of the mechanism by which the sapper could haul Hana higher with such apparent ease, or how he might swing her from one side of the church to the other. Minghella and editor Walter Murch could see that any detail of the supposed mechanics involved would interrupt and slow the story while distracting from the mischievous charm of the event. The world beyond the screen revealed to the filmmakers in the cutting room that all that was needed for its successful evocation had already been captured.

This scene is an instance of an event "cheated" on the set but convincing on the screen. The chosen raking angles, the framings, and the cutting tell the simple story without need of explanatory illustration of the fictional mechanics behind the action.

7
Screen Language

Following a well-told story on the screen is not a purely passive activity. When we watch a film, we are not only "connecting the dots" of the dramatic narrative, becoming detectives of the subtext, imagining what has been hidden, and weighing what might happen next—as we do when reading or listening—but actively engaging with a visual discourse that in its own ways imparts information, emotion, and visceral sensation; poses questions; invites interpretation; challenges us; and shocks or surprises us by turns. This we do generally without consciously thinking about it. We understand the language of the moving image but do not in general consciously understand *how* we understand it. Mostly, we follow it tacitly. Even if, for the filmmaker, that understanding may also be in part intuitive, at their best they constantly ask questions of it, challenging, embracing, manipulating, subverting, and reinventing it, and bringing their work to life through its multiplicity of resources. This is not to argue that conscious method should entirely replace the vital contribution of intuition in the creative process, but to assert that the two function best symbiotically.

The reader might find it useful to reflect on the difference between *grammar* and *language*, and how this might apply to film. Shot sizes, for example—extreme wide shot (EWS), wide shot, long shot (LS), medium/mid-shot (MS), medium close-up (MCU), close-up, big close-up (BCU), extreme close-up (ECU), over-the-shoulder (OTS) shot, and others—may indeed be defining terms invaluable to the filmmaker and central to considerations of film grammar, but to what degree do they give us a sense of the purpose or meaning of each? Editing that proceeds on purely grammatical foundations, meanwhile, tends to lead to formulaic visual discourse. One manifestation of this might be the use of "matched cuts" on the assumption that a specific shot size should automatically be followed by a reverse angle of the same size, and that angles must be mirrored in order that they constitute such a reverse. While this may prove effective, it might not be adequate to the visual language a scene may require. It is the dramatic narrative that needs to inform the filmmaker's approach rather than notions that a film must be shot and edited according to any assumed grammatical decorum. Editing might articulate narrative POV, for example, might emphasize the power of one character over another, or on the other hand it might heighten their vulnerability; shift our relationship to the material by taking us from the midst of the action to its periphery or vice versa; or serve any number of purposes not related to grammar but to function, meaning, and emotion. Just as correct grammar on the page does not necessarily lead to effective fictional prose, so "correct" film grammar may not result in the most effective formulation of a film's visual language.

The Art of the Filmmaker. Peter Markham, Oxford University Press. © Oxford University Press 2023.
DOI: 10.1093/oso/9780197631522.003.0008

A film is an address to an audience. The means and manner of that address, how it succeeds, what it communicates and how, and to what degree it anticipates the reactions of the audience and how much on the other hand it leaves those open are the concerns both of filmmakers intent on learning the practice of cinema, or refreshing their skills, and of students, scholars, and readers wishing to delve deeply into its art. When so much of the exploration of the crafts of visual storytelling is rooted, rightly, in looking *into* the story and world of a film and how the screen captures those, it is essential also to understand the opposite vector of engagement—the reaching *out*, by means of image and sound, to the hearts and minds of the audience.

Precisely how the language of the screen speaks to us, complex as this is, is thus essentially two pronged.

Visual Language and Meaning

How might we conceive of the relationship between the language of visual storytelling and the meaning it communicates? In Chapter 2 we saw how the discourse of the screen is indeed a language, but does this differ in any way from the language of written or spoken storytelling? (Each of these at times makes its way into the agile discourse of cinema.)

Stepping aside from cinema, we might find it helpful to refer to the philosopher Ludwig Wittgenstein, who in his *Philosophical Investigations* wrote that *the meaning of a word is its use in the language*. He saw this hypothesis as opposed to the notion of words denoting specific, unchanging meanings—a concept espoused in his earlier *Tractatus*. Wittgenstein discussed the notion of *language-game* that adopt differing formulations according to the situation and activity in which they take place. Might the discourse of the screen be seen as such a language-game, or as many? Might Wittgenstein's tenets be applied also to the language and practical aesthetics of the screen? Might a CU have one meaning in one scene, quite another in another, one in one film, something else in a different film according to use? Might it invite empathy, perhaps bring us into a character's narrative POV in one instance—when revealing their reaction to what they see, for example—while in another maintaining the energy and status, even threat of a character? Might loneliness be conveyed by showing a character alone in the frame in one context (as with Fern in the opening sequence of *Nomadland*—see the case study in Part III) but also by showing someone in a crowded frame in another (as with Chiron, in the hallway after class in *Moonlight*, seen also in the case study in Part III)? In Alfonso Cuaron's 2018 *Roma*, the filmmaker on the one hand shows Cleo outside a movie theater, after boyfriend Fermin has deserted her, but later, as she goes in search of him, on the other hand depicts her as a small figure in a wider vista. The sense of her loneliness is powerfully communicated through both approaches because in each there is a *contrast*—in the first instance between her stillness and silence and the frantic energy of the street sellers around her, and in the second between her tiny human presence in the frame and the setting of decrepitude in which it is placed.

In Cuaron's *Roma*, Cleo's loneliness, after Fermin has deserted her, becomes apparent in the contrast between her stillness and the activity packing the frame around her.

Cleo's companionless search for Fermin, if invariably peopled by the bustle of everyday life, is powerfully shown in the isolating frames prior to an encounter with his friend. Tiny and in a frame devoid of the background action (apart from a couple of dogs) that has hitherto energized the shot, Cuaron's protagonist approaches the man's backyard, a lonely figure in a desolate prospect.

In *Nomadland*, Chloe Zhao shows Fern's loneliness in the context of the frame's emptiness. (See p. 54.)

If the purpose and meaning of a shot or a cut can come from context—within the screen's fluidity of space, within a moment, a scene, a sequence, within the filmmaker's articulation of narrative POV, or perhaps within the context of the structured visual design of the entire film—might there be more to how the language of the moving image functions? Is use all that is at work? Is the filmmaker entirely free to pick and choose which element of visual language to adopt in order to suit their purpose at any point in their movie, or might there be other considerations? Can the filmmaker acculturate the audience to their own designed language completely, or are images— elements of them at least—possessed of inherent meanings we cannot help but react to in specific ways?

With Fern solitary and small in a shot comprised largely of negative space, Zhao evokes her loneliness in *Nomadland*, the bleak setting depicted conveying not only emotion but the sensation of coldness and dampness.

Bruce Block, in his book *The Visual Story: Creating the Visual Structure of Film, TV, and Digital Media*, delineates categories of what we perhaps might consider not so much elements of film *grammar* as visual *rhetoric*, such as space, line, shape, tone (black to gray to white), and color. Since there is no word in general use to encompass these elements of the image, for the purposes of our exploration of visual aesthetics it might be helpful to refer to these units as *ikones*, from the Greek word for image, *ikona* (εικόνα).

In contrast to Wittgenstein's insight into words and their meaning, Block suggests that these *ikones* have qualities not dependent on use but inherent in their individual aspects. Diagonal lines, for example, he maintains are innately more dramatic in their effect than verticals and horizontals, which on the contrary tend to suggest stability—an assertion borne out not only by use of the expressionist "dutched" angles of film noir and horror but by close analysis of usage in specific contexts. Kurosawa's *Throne of Blood* includes a scene in which Toshiro Mifune's Washizu (Macbeth) encounters the ghost of Miki (Banquo)—a character he has secretly had murdered. As the episode progresses, the pronounced horizontals and verticals incorporated into the initial shots of Washizu give way to diagonals that reflect his increasing alarm.

Kurosawa's changing geometry does indeed appear to convey alternative meanings inherent in its nature—stability and instability given contrasting visual representation. Even when other factors are considered—shot size, performance, the progression from stasis to movement (of both actor and camera), and a precise visual modulation of narrative POV that brings us ever closer to Washizu's experience of alarm—the power of *line* as a resource of language is immediately evident.

(1) Horizontals, verticals, and symmetry convey equilibrium.

(2) Heightened performance contrasts with a "stable" composition of horizontal/vertical geometry.

(3a) The shift to diagonals.

(3b) Diagonal connection of Washizu to the ghost of Miki.

(4) Washizu's later POV of Miki.

(5) Diagonals become more pronounced.

Kurosawa contrasts the equilibrium suggested by horizontal and vertical lines—as Washizu attempts to regain composure between appearances of the Miki apparition—with the drama and instability conveyed by diagonal lines.

Another aspect of the language of the screen that might be considered inherent is the opposing properties of left and right of the frame. The left tends to convey stability, the right instability. (This concept is commonly regarded as applying to the theater stage also.) An instance of the phenomenon can be found in *Nomadland*, when Fern must choose between staying in the home of Dave's son and embarking, once and for all, on a life on the road. (See the case study in Part III.) In *Hereditary*, this phenomenon is manifested with graphic horror as Steve immolates to frame right, terrifying Annie, who witnesses the shocking spectacle from frame left.

In *Hereditary* Annie, frame left, is rooted to the spot as Steve perishes in flame to frame right.

Connected with the notion of the opposing properties of either side of the frame is the way in which the left section might tend to suggest the past, the right the future. When Juan, in *Moonlight*, recounts to Little events of his boyhood in Cuba, he looks to the left of frame as he turns to Little, while later, as he tells the boy that *at some point you gotta decide for yourself who you're gonna be*, he turns away from him to look out to frame right—and the future.

Juan looks to frame left as he tells of his Cuban boyhood.

He then looks to frame right as he talks of Little's future (and, subtextually, his own).

Color

The nature of our psychological and emotional reactions to color is complex and contested. Our responses would appear to depend, to greater or lesser extent, on acculturation, although primary colors red and blue would seem to most of us stimulating and restful, respectively. A face flushed with anger turns red, while we talk of "blue" moods, of having "the blues." Given narrative, dramatic, and cultural context, however, even these assumptions might not bear scrutiny. Yellow flowers in a green field might provoke a very different reaction from that to a parched yellow desert.

The color palette chosen by filmmakers—directors, production designers, costume designers, and cinematographers—constitutes a fundamental aspect of the visual language they formulate. Cold colors, hot colors, "dry" colors and the degree of saturation or desaturation of the image will each affect our responses. Rigor of control of the palette can further influence our reactions. World and setting might be considerably more authoritative when conveyed through meticulous color design. Ari Aster's selection of blue, orange, and to some extent yellow, set against the dingy greens and browns of the Graham home, serves to unify and define the world of *Hereditary*. This visual control provides a foundation for our acceptance of the film's world, characters, and emotions. Red, blue, and yellow can similarly be traced throughout *Moonlight*. Blue, for example, might be associated with the ocean in which Juan bathes Little, a warm yellow with the set dressing in the scene in which Chiron visits Teresa for supper. Apart from these examples, the chosen colors would seem a facet of the film's connective tissue rather than messengers prompting primal responses.

The meaning of a color then, and the degree of meaning, are perhaps derived from its use in the games a filmmaker plays with their language. Some filmmakers will exert more deliberate color control than others. Some will embrace vibrant primary colors—Pedro Almodóvar is a masterly exponent—while others will adopt a more subdued spectrum. Some will barely consider color at all, an indication perhaps of less acute visual sensibilities.

Nevertheless, the fact that we talk of *warm* and *cold* colors surely indicates natures inherent in our responses. Whatever the method by which a filmmaker selects the colors of their movie, there seems to be at least a measure of inherent meaning at work in the messages they convey.

Eye Trace

In master editor Walter Murch's seminal *In the Blink of an Eye*, *eye trace* comes fourth in the list of his six criteria for making the cut. (See Chapter 10.) The term refers to the dynamics and sequential flow of our visual engagement within the frame and across frames—the journeys across the screen our eyes take as we watch a film, particularly on a big screen. By making use of our reflexes, the filmmaker directs our focus to a particular point in a shot, moving it across the frame and across a cut or transition to the first frame of the following shot, then over that frame and so on. The phenomenon, a fundamental aspect of our perception of the world around us, is a vital tool in the filmmaker's orchestration of the audience's engagement with their film. Movement within stasis, stasis within movement, a pinprick of light in darkness (Joan's candle, lit at the start of her séance in *Hereditary*), a primary color in a frame of contrasting or muted colors, diagonals that lead the eye to a particular spot, a character in an unpopulated frame or who contrasts in some way to other characters present, emptiness amid fullness, a sound that links to an image, a significant character or object we've seen in a previous frame now repeated in a new one, the place to which the movement of the camera leads us—these are some of the many ways in which the filmmaker guides our look to specific sections of the frame. As Murch explains, our eyes usually enter the frame at the point on which they were directed in the previous shot. If we find our new focus of attention in that same place, this will make for a smooth cut or transition, but when we have to search for a new locus, the cut will be more noticeable, perhaps even jarring.

When Chiron sleeps at Teresa's house in *Moonlight*, Barry Jenkins makes a transition from scene to scene and indeed across time by showing Chiron looking down, then cutting to him asleep later. Our eyes follow his look across the cut, rendering the transition smooth and not obtrusive to our visual engagement.

(1) Chiron looks down. Cut to . . .:

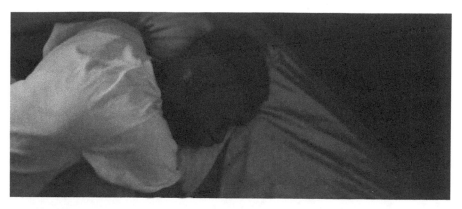

(2) Chiron asleep. His look in (1) guides our eyes smoothly to his sleeping self.

When Annie attends the group therapy session in *Hereditary*, Aster cuts from a single of her to a WS of attendees that includes a chair to the right of frame that, in contrast the others either side of it, is empty. Her look in her single directs our eyes across the cut and into the incoming frame, past the line of seated figures to camera left in the new frame and to the chair on the right. To ensure that our eyes have settled on the empty chair, he has the extra to camera right of it shift slightly. The empty chair, which suggests the presence of Ellen, thus becomes our focus of attention. (This is an example of an *absence*, the empty chair, suggesting a *presence*—that of the deceased Ellen.)

(1) Annie looks to camera right. Cut to . . . :

(2) WS of attendees. Our eyes, following the direction of Annie's look, settle on the empty chair. The man to camera right of it quietly brings his hands together, ensuring that we are looking at this section of the frame.

Eye trace is also a significant resource in the language of visual storytelling within an individual shot, whether the camera is moving or static. In the case of the latter, the filmmaker can induce our eyes to travel across the frame so that elements of it become the increments in our understanding of what we are seeing. We cannot see the image in any other way, cannot take in its components in a different order than that the filmmaker has designed, and that order will determine the meaning we derive from it. In a scene in his 1974 *Chinatown*, Roman Polanski draws our attention back and forth from a foreground conversation to Jack Nicholson's Jake Gittes, sitting by the open doorway listening in, through background movement—either Gittes's or that of various extras crossing in both lateral directions. We cannot help but look from foreground to background at crucial moments as the scene progresses.

In Polanski's *Chinatown*, Jake Gittes, in midground, sits by an open door listening to a foreground conversation. Gittes's movements and those of the extras crossing behind him draw the attention of the audience from Mrs. Mulwray to him at key moments in the scene, even though he is smaller in the frame than the foreground characters and remains silent until he rises and finally joins them.

Contradictory as it may seem then, the language of cinema would appear to incorporate the tenets of both the visionary Wittgenstein and the grounded Block, conveying meaning in substantial part through use and context but in correspondingly significant part through a visual messaging whose meaning is inherent in its nature.

Uninflected versus Inflected Cinematic Language

Before considering further individual elements of the language, it is important to note that the individual approaches of filmmakers may, to greater or lesser degree, be *inflected* or *uninflected*. Robert Bresson was a master of uninflected style, his aesthetic austere to a fault but, consistently realized, telling his stories effortlessly while steering our engagement with precise control.

In *Pickpocket* (1959), Bresson intercuts the expressionless looks down and ahead of the protagonist with his prying open of a woman's purse. The repeated shots remain static. There is no pushing in to heighten emotion or emphasize tension, no high-contrast lighting, no extreme lensing; the visual language remains neutral and uninflected.

Here, a montage of two subjects, thief and purse, creates a tension that the tightening of the shots, whether in camera or editing, would destroy. Bresson's simplicity of approach thus eschews the linguistic devices other filmmakers accept as givens.

Looking at the case studies, *Nomadland* (its foundations in a nonfiction book) tends not to use camera moves or the tightening of shots to project emotional meaning, although camera placement, framing, and cutting thoughtfully modulate our sense of its flow. *Hereditary*, by contrast, uses the camera in agile and contrasting ways, varying camera movement and shifts of size and angle within a shot to denote meaning and significance.

The Image

As can be seen in the example of Bresson, some filmmakers construct their films from everyday images that are in themselves innocuous. The meanings he conveys derive not so much from the images themselves—he deliberately eschews visual poetry within the shot—but from their juxtaposition. Bresson saw a poetry in his work and the meanings he wished it to communicate, arising from the joins he created rather than the unassuming shots themselves. That this master created such an astonishing body of work demonstrates how a consummate and distinctive sense of practical aesthetics can be key to the greatest cinema.

Yet what worked for this master may not work for others with different sensibilities, whose canons adopt broader, eclectic approaches. For these filmmakers, images may indeed resonate with innate dramatic power. Stanley Kubrick's *2001* (1968), for example, is replete with famously extraordinary imagery that ranges from the sun rising behind planet Earth to an embryo in a womb, a black monolith among warring hominids, and the eye-like countenance of Hal, its dissonant amalgam of hinted-at humanity and insentient AI captured in the filmmaker's simple, circular icon.

Hereditary's culminating vignette—the final scene depicted as a miniature model—encapsulates the film's story and themes with disarming yet haunting wit. "Don't take me too seriously" it seems to mischievously suggest, while the striking image marks a memorable conclusion to Aster's demonic tale.

The final image of *Hereditary*, coming after Peter has been fully possessed by King Paimon, depicts the moment as a miniature model much like Annie's vignettes. The diagonal lines echo earlier compositions in the film and suggest a religiosity at odds with the story's demonic conspiracy.

Nomadland's images of landscape and nature possess their own poetry, suggesting a richness to be found outside of humanity's settled existence. The scene in *Moonlight* in which Juan teaches Little to swim, with its elemental power and suggestion of baptism —ocean the foreground, sky the background (air and water elements) to mentor and pupil—conveys a poetry above and beyond its simple action.

The image of Juan teaching Little how to float in and of itself conveys significance. The elements of water and air and the act of mentorship, almost baptismal in nature, yield a frame rich in poetry and suggested meaning.

Images may also suggest other images or themes beyond their immediate depiction. When a part of an object is shown but we see on the screen of the mind the complete thing, we have the visual equivalent of the literary *synecdoche*. The wheel of a car suggests an entire vehicle. A shoe stepping down prompts the image of the complete character. When an image of one thing suggests a different thing, it becomes a visual *metaphor*. (See the example in Chapter 3 from *Three Colors Blue* of the beach ball that suggests the child Anna.) When an image suggests a theme or abstract quality, it becomes a *symbol*. Such images function through the context of a film's particular thematic dimensions. One hand reaching for and clasping another might express love, rain running down a windowpane, grief.

A filmmaker may insist that in their work *what you see is what you get* and that their images are the simple depictions of moments and events. Meaning resides in story and character alone, they might claim, rather than in the language through which they are revealed. Although such an unassuming approach need not necessarily lead to an unassuming film, the interaction of content and its articulation on the screen—in other words *cinematic dramaturgy*—will be absent when a film lacks visual organization, when at no point do the practical aesthetics of the image come into their own. We might regard such a practitioner not as a visual storyteller but as a simple recordist of staging and performance. Indeed, without visual cohesion, elements on screen may become shambolic and distract us.

Visual Language and Style

Well, style is very important. It's what Martin Scorsese says differentiates all filmmakers. Style is the important identifier of someone's personal expression.
—**Jim Jarmusch,** *The Guardian*, **July 2019**

Style comes from the soul.
—**Author, AFI Conservatory directing class, 2012**

As with aesthetics, style is commonly perceived in terms of elegance, beauty, and/or panache. The adjective *stylish* conveys intimations of appealing design, intended to draw and please the eye. Style in cinema, however, runs the gamut from visual decorum to documentary grittiness. As with practical aesthetics, to which it is closely aligned, the term should have no connotation of either correctness or bravura discourse.

Style is frequently considered to be distinct from content; the phrase *style over content* or (worse) *substance* is heard so often that it has become a cliché. This preconception is founded in the notion that there is a consistent objective reality on the one hand and an observer of it on the other. In whichever way the reality is observed, its nature remains the same. This assumption has been challenged in areas other than cinema—in quantum physics, for example, and in the writings of Wittgenstein—and does not withstand scrutiny when regarding the screen as the interface between story and audience. In film at its best, content and style work as symbiotic partners, neither able to exist without the other. The style of a movie may be an expression of its content in terms of aesthetics, culture, energy, and so on, or it might be a comment on those elements, even run counter to them. A rigid world might invite a static camera, linear storytelling, and slow, measured editing to match its nature, or it might suggest to the irreverent filmmaker a fluid camera, jump cuts, a dislocation of time that subverts it. The former might usefully be described as *complementary style*, the latter as *subversive style*. The important consideration is the connection between and interaction of what is shown and how it is shown.

In Lynne Ramsay's 1999 *Ratcatcher*, the filmmaker tells their story both in a documentary (complementary) style that reflects working-class life in Glasgow and in more formal compositions that accord this a subversive elegance counter to such gritty depiction.

A group of boys are captured by Ramsay's unobtrusive camera in the filmmaker's *Ratcatcher*—an example of what might be described as *complementary* style.

Elsewhere in the film, a formal precision of composition marks Ramsay's more *subversive* style—a revelation, perhaps, of the protagonist's inner world.

8

The Shot

Composition and Mise en Scène

Not only are the terms *composition* and *mise en scène* often conflated, but they tend to invite assumptions we might challenge. Given the practical aesthetics we are considering as the foundation of the language of the screen, composition and mise en scène should be understood not as the means of measuring any degree of decorum, as criteria for assessing correctness, but as key to understanding the resources of a film's visual language and the representation of its dramatic narrative on the screen.

Composition is widely understood to refer to the nature of the formation of the frame's canvas from its *abstract* elements—their proportions and shapes, lines, shades, and colors—as they relate to the shot's overall construction and geometry. So far so good. Closely linked in common thought to the concept of aesthetics as harmony, however, and largely understood to relate to what may be pleasing, even beautiful, to the beholder, the term can skew toward the imperative that a shot at its best must through its composition be pleasant to the eye. A shot, an entire movie, may indeed be formally elegant, but if the visual language is not functional, such design may be merely decorative—*pictorial* rather than *visual* as Alexander Mackendrick would have it. (See Chapter 2.) In contemporary culture, elegance is often taken to be less honest than the "grittiness" of *in*elegance, of ugliness even. Either, however, when designed purposefully and as they relate to a film's specific visual storytelling, can be seen to work—or if applied without thorough process, not to work.

Composition connects closely to Bruce Block's categorization of visual rhetoric (even if he includes no section on it) but also to Wittgenstein's notion of meaning in a language afforded by use. For example—and to illustrate Block's perspective—a horizon may be high in the frame, inherently oppressive, or low, an open sky suggestive of freedom and possibility (depending on dramatic circumstances and weather, of course). A figure might be seen walking away from us in a composition with a single point perspective (see Fern in the back shot from *Nomadland* later in the chapter), and we will have the sense of them heading, inevitably, toward their destiny, or we might see characters entrapped in receding corridors (as in *Hereditary*) so that we feel their inability to escape their circumstances. (While we don't necessarily reflect on such responses, they nevertheless take their effect.)

The Art of the Filmmaker. Peter Markham, Oxford University Press. © Oxford University Press 2023.
DOI: 10.1093/oso/9780197631522.003.0009

We tend to remember what is strongly presented visually, so decisive compositions make for effective memes in a movie's discourse. Such a phenomenon can be clearly seen in *Moonlight* when, in identical compositions, Chiron and later Black are shown from above plunging their faces into a washbasin of water and ice cubes. (See case study.)

Mise en scène has two accepted meanings. The first is simply *setting*. The second—more useful to the reader—is the placing of *specific* rather than *abstract* elements within the frame: characters, objects, sections of a setting, as opposed to the compositional arrangement of *ikones* (shape, line, space, perspective, etc.).

Looking at the shot in the case study "*Nomadland:* Empire—Opening and Ending," for example, in the section "Letting Go," we see in frame (1) Fern walking away from camera. We might observe the composition's receding diagonals from all four directions, the vanishing point below the center of the frame, the triangular shapes (of road and snow), and the contrast between light and dark. In considering the shot's mise en scène, on the contrary, we might note the placement of Fern center frame, heading for the vanishing point, the row of dwellings to the right, the one to the left, and placing of the snow and rows of bare trees.

In the forthcoming section on framing, in the screenshot of Kevin phoning Black, the composition reveals what Block would describe as *deep* space to the left of frame, *flat* space to the right, and a thin section of flat space along the bottom edge. The lines are largely vertical and horizontal, while the central figure, on a plane of *mid* space, renders a diagonal. The center of the frame is marked by a horizontal bright light from a fluorescent, which contrasts with the darkness to the left. The shot's mise en scène places Kevin center frame, in right profile, setting a lateral vector to an out-of-focus illustration of what appears to be a loving couple—pertinent to his affectionate ministrations to Black.

When the abstract elements of composition and the specific components of mise en scène work together within the contexts of story, drama, and emotion, the result is telling, the film conveying relevant "messages" to us. The interfunctionality of the two concepts is fundamental to the practical aesthetics the diligent filmmaker employs.

Staging may remain the same from one cut, one angle to another, but fresh composition and mise en scène created on the screen by new angles reveal new vectors of the drama. (See the example in the later section on camera angles from the party scene in *Hereditary* in which, when Peter points out the chocolate cake to Charlie, there's a cut from a lateral profile 2-shot—Charlie frame left, Peter frame right—to a deep shot, cake in foreground, the siblings close to each other, to the center right of frame in midground. Not only does the position of both characters change within the frame, but their placement in relation to each other is rendered closer.)

Considerations of composition and mise en scène (and framing) relate to aspect ratio. The factors governing visual organization in the widescreen format of 2.40:1, for example, differ from those pertaining to Academy ratio of 1.33:1. The former offers greater opportunity for arrangement along the lateral axis, the latter along the vertical. The ratio 1.66:1 also gives more vertical possibilities, while 1.85:1 provides more lateral. the aspect ratio of *Hereditary*, 2:1, offers a degree of both.

Selection

We might benefit from bearing in mind not only the determinants that inform the canvas of shots within themselves but also the degree to which their context—the relationship with and to shots adjacent and elsewhere in the movie—figures in the filmmaker's design of their visual discourse. With this in mind, it will be helpful to consider factors typically central to the selection of the individual shot.

- The initial justification for selecting a shot is the *significance* of its subject matter and its *function* in the telling of the film's story. Someone or something needs to be depicted, and/or some action or moment needs to be captured.
- A shot might be needed to communicate an important increment of information, a reaction or a decision, a gesture or an act, or a shift of emotion or tone that constitutes some essential beat in the story.
- A section of a scene needs to be captured as an integral part of a scene's *coverage*— the totality of shots necessary for it to be cut together effectively. Without this section, the continuity (or apparent continuity) of the action in a scene would be broken.
- A shot might connect with, echo, or contrast with other shots in the scene, act, or elsewhere in the film.
- It might be selected to sustain a scene's flow of energy, its momentum and rhythm.
- It might convey spatial relationships.
- It might convey a passage of time.
- It might pose a question or answer one.
- It might tell a story in and of itself.
- It might offer a moment of poetry or intensity such as a vista, the fall of light on an object, or some instant of wonder or horror—a vignette of the natural world in *Nomadland*, for example, or one of the shocking images in *Hereditary*.
- It might offer the filmmaker's comment—critical, ironic, mischievous, questioning—on some element of the story.

Note: The filmmaker may have an intuitive motivation for showing something they or we might find hard to justify. If the resulting shot makes the final cut, if it works in some way, if its power and resonance seem undeniable, that is justification alone for its inclusion. The *poetry* of cinema, when it deepens the experience of the viewer, is not merely decorative but integral. At its best, it may defy analysis—cinema, indeed, is an art of vision in a figurative as well as literal sense.

Establishing Shots and Masters

A long-accepted approach to the choice of shot sizes as this progresses through a scene—not that this is utilized by all filmmakers—is rooted in the concepts of an *establishing shot* that sets the context for the scene and a *master shot*, static or moving, that provides the foundation to which shots from other angles and/or of closer sizes can be added.

The establishing shot shows a scene's setting, maybe its location, maybe its environment, whatever its nature, before its story begins to unfold. It is wide and generously framed, perhaps an interior, a room maybe, or perhaps a broad exterior expanse, maybe a street, a neighborhood, a vista of landscape. (Such a shot can also provide a note of punctuation, a breath in the transition from one scene, or one act, to another.) In past decades, there might have been more than one establishing shot to introduce a scene, each tighter than its predecessor, before a further progression of tighter shots would follow as the drama of a scene intensifies. There was a perception among some that cuts from very wide shots to CUs, without intervening sizes, would disorient audiences. This was never true, we might observe, when handled purposefully, when eye trace has been designed to direct our attention to a particular point in the outgoing frame that is the focus of an incoming closer shot.

As the visual language of cinema has shifted over the decades, any obligation to start a scene with an establishing shot has faded. It might therefore be more useful to refer to this category as a *setting* or *context shot*, one that can equally be placed later in a scene rather than at the beginning, revealing the place and space of the action at some significant moment.

The master shot is more a matter of the approach to the shooting and assembling of a scene, of its coverage, rather than a facet of visual language. Many directors conceive of a master before subsequent setups, while others will design a scene with its visual storytelling in mind—the sequence of images that will communicate story and emotion rather than capturing an event as it occurs on set. (It is nevertheless general practice in either case to shoot wider shots before going closer and tighter, as this establishes the lighting, the staging, and the continuity of a scene.)

Filmmakers may choose one mode or the other according to the nature of an individual scene. A merit of a master shot is that it offers filmmaker and cast continuity and flow of performance invaluable to both in the realization of additional setups. It also offers a spatial and temporal framework and a degree of insurance for the cutting room—there is always the master to return to when an individual setup fails to work.

A scene may of course be shot in one continuous take—a form of master in itself that tends to be wide but may include in its visual flow and shifting camera and framing considerably tighter sizes. An individual section of a scene may be designed as a "oner" (see *Hereditary*'s family séance in the case studies) to be followed by a progression of preselected setups—in effect a master placed before montage.

Note: Some filmmakers may shoot scenes or parts thereof as *tableaux*—generous WSs of minimal camera movement that contain a scene's entire action or a part thereof. When a scene's only coverage, this amounts to a master without additional sizes or angles added. Jim Jarmusch's 1986 *Down by Law* is a case in point, as is Hou Hsiao-hsien's 1998 *Flowers of Shanghai*. This approach, utilizing a *witnessing* or *observing* camera (see Chapter 9) tends to offer a third-person objective (but sometimes omniscient) narrative POV.

Subject

Further to the consideration of the *significance* of what a shot depicts as a criterion for its selection is its *nature*.

- Is this animate or inanimate, moving or still?
- Is it large or small?
- Is it an object, a place or setting, a character, or a group of characters—interacting or not?
- What emotions does it evoke?
- What action does it involve? What staging?
- Do staging and camera work together to combine several elements in a single shot—a *oner*—that might otherwise require separate setups? Or are individual, closer shots on elements, or contrasting angles on them, required?
- Even when the action might be contained in a single take, is it?
- Does the filmmaker provide for the modulation of the passage of time in the editing or does the single shot sustain tension without a cut? In other words, how much does the *flow of energy* played out in front of the lens determine the uninterrupted development and duration of the shot, and how much should that flow be left to the cutting together of individual shots?
- How much does the nature of the subject matter inform aspects of the shot? Does it suggest the shot be simple and static, simple and fluid, or does its complexity invite a complex, probably fluid approach to its shooting?

Simple, static shot: MCU of Bob Wells, addressing the RTR camp members in *Nomadland*.

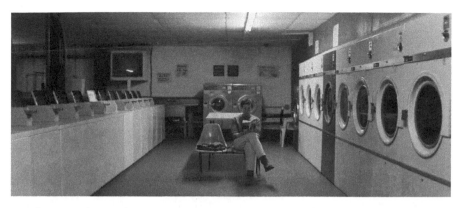

Simple, static shot: Wide on Fern sitting reading in a laundromat.

Simple, fluid shot: Fern interacts with her instructor as she learns to make a hole in a tire, the camera dollying left and panning right to contain the action.

An example of complex subject matter that invites a complex fluid shot can be found in the case study of *Hereditary*'s family séance scene, in which an apparently long opening shot brings Steve and Peter into position for Annie's attempt to raise the spirit of Charlie. Here, the convolutions of the family's emotional interactions are manifested in a staging with which the camera engages. The shot maintains

Complex, static shot: In Anthony Minghella's *The English Patient*, troops from opposing armies cross frame in contrasting lateral directions along layered planes (close foreground to background) as a figure emerges through a doorway in deep background. (A short pan introduces the shot.)

anticipation and tension throughout by a symbiosis of story and its representation, step by step, on screen.

A shot of this kind, now perhaps composited in postproduction rather than achieved in a single take, might constitute an entire film. This approach tends to emphasize the passage of "real time" but may disguise ellipses along the way. How the camera captures its subject matter and the impact of its nature on this involves the intricate interfunctionality of staging and camera placement and movement. This will inform shot size, framing, and angle and entail the "editing in camera" that will determine the ongoing placements of the fluid camera. Without cuts, the flow of energy must be captured in camera, except in those moments when sound design and music create rhythm and momentum to vitalize the image.

A fluid take of such duration will tend to entail the use of wider-angle lenses, which yield a greater depth of field and have the effect of making us feel we are *in* the space depicted, as *parallax*—the changing positions of what we see as the camera moves—is more evident. With sequence shots composited in postproduction, as opposed to being achieved within a single take, the lenses chosen for each section might vary, but the choice will be limited compared to that available for each when the sequence is cut together from shots of differing angles and sizes. Oners, in other words, offer flexibility in some senses but limitations in others.

Size

Shot size and the framing of a shot are obviously interlinked, but shots can be framed, angled, and composed in multiple ways whatever their size. Elements can be excluded or shown either in part or in totality, revealed to one extent or another by the chosen camera angle—characters standing behind a seated subject in a mid-shot, perhaps, their faces shown or not shown according to camera height and angle, whether level or raking. (See Chapter 9.) While keeping this interaction of the dynamics of the *form* of a shot in mind and the inevitable crossover of one with another, it will be helpful to consider each category individually over this and the following chapter.

A shot may depict a detail so microscopic as to be invisible to the human eye or a vista so vast as to include entire galaxies spread across the universe. It may also expand or contract from one to the other; the tighter the size, the greater the dramatic emphasis. A notable example of this aspect can be found in Alfred Hitchcock's *Notorious* (1946).

In *Notorious*, the WS of the party (see Alicia center frame in open-backed dress) tightens to the close shot of a key in Alicia's hand.

The filmmaker is by no means obliged to adopt a visual discourse so flexible and may limit their range of shot sizes according to their film's nature and requirements, to the aesthetics they choose, and to their sensibility and voice. *Nomadland* incorporates the small objects of everyday life and wide vistas of landscape, for example, while *Moonlight*'s social canvas and physical world determine an entirely appropriate spectrum less expansive (although including on the one hand "the block" on which Juan oversees his dealing and on the other the ECU of the gold "fronts" Black wears over his teeth). A range that is too restricted—limited largely to MCUs, for example— might become monotonous to the viewer, while inconsistent shot selection might weaken the connective tissue of a movie's visual language. (A filmmaker, however, might deliberately choose to restrict their approach in order to frustrate their audience or create in it a sense of claustrophobia, either perhaps to be countered at some significant step in the story.)

Another factor to be considered in the choice of shot size is the significance at any given moment of body language. Gestures, animation, shifts, and movements, whether slight or pronounced, may convey emotion, thought, intention, and subtext on the part of a character. Closer shots may fail to capture such a telling form of expression, which requires accommodation within the frame. Such a moment may prompt a cut to a wider shot (perhaps from a different angle or beginning a camera move) that changes the flow of emotion and energy, perhaps boosting both and freeing a scene from a repetition of intercut close reverses that we may find visually tedious.

To what degree might the size of a shot have its own inherent messaging, and what might this be? To what degree, on the contrary, might meaning depend on the visual discourse the filmmaker has designed—one in which intercut singles or 2-shots proliferate, one that makes use of a fluid camera that captures the action in an agile flow of image, or one in which CUs are sparse, so that when they occur they provide added emphasis (or on the contrary, when a vista might be all the more notable because vistas are rare in the film)?

A close shot on Chiron, in *Moonlight*'s classroom scene analyzed later, has the effect of keeping us close to his emotions, his thoughts as we perceive them, and his reactions. The filmmaker uses these shots as an integral resource in his following of the character's journey, in the articulation of Chiron's narrative POV, and in the modulation of our empathy for him. A close shot on antagonist Terrell, in the same scene, has a very different impact. He is a character we are far from comfortable being with. Here, his CUs present not an image of vulnerability, as in the case of Chiron, but of power and threat. Our sense of proximity does not invite empathy so much as the perception of danger. Close-ups on Terrell are not a component of Barry Jenkins's articulation of the character's narrative POV, since he does not invite us to follow that journey. Instead, they convey to us the disturbing power of the bully's hostility. Both in his case and Chiron's, the CUs accord their subjects an emphasis.

Wider shots will similarly have their effect on us in ways related to the nature of their subject matter and to the context in which they are presented. A character small in the frame might in general seem vulnerable, a larger one less so. Context is all, though. In the examples mentioned previously, of Cleo in *Roma* outside the movie theater and Fern in *Nomadland*, the former, although larger in the frame, comes across as more vulnerable because of the placement of the shot after her previous painful episode with Fermin. Fern, by contrast, is about to begin the odyssey the film follows. She may appear a lonely figure in the frame but seems far from helpless.

After Charlie's abrupt death in *Hereditary*, Ari Aster shows a devastated Peter in CUs, conveying his predicament also through wide vistas of his car in the expanse of the night, in which we cannot see him. The emptiness of the space in the latter size allows his distress, directly conveyed in his CU, to resonate in a way Alex Wolf's performance alone, despite its harrowing power, cannot.

(1) Peter, in a CU in *Hereditary*, registers the sudden death, moments before, of his sister.

(2) The lights of Peter's car, pinpricks against the night's dark expanse, intensify his devastation. (Note how the lights in Peter's eyes in [1] connect with the two lights of his car.)

The wider the shot, the less we feel ourselves a participant, the more an observer. That may leave us with a comprehensive, God-like view in which we see what individual characters cannot, especially if we find ourselves looking down on the scenario or place. It may leave us feeling helpless, particularly when we find ourselves witnessing an unpleasant event. With tighter sizes, in contrast, we cannot help but feel more involved in the action and emotion of the moment—as the CU on Peter demonstrates—even trapped in them.

The sense of proximity or distance from characters or objects that a shot size affords us can also offer information regarding spatial relationships—a factor of particular significance in the articulation of narrative POV. Hitchcock's *Rear Window* (1954) offers the quintessential lesson in how this works, since protagonist L. B. Jefferies is confined to his apartment with a broken leg throughout the film. He can look out on the back of the homes opposite but cannot get any nearer physically (even if later in the film he uses the telephoto lens of his camera to peer more closely at the lives of his neighbors). The dynamic is clearly articulated in the opening sequence: shots on L. B. Jefferies are closer, those in his POV wide so that we are placed with him in his environment, finding ourselves "with" him in his narrative POV. Related to that simple articulation of proximity and distance through respective shot sizes are cuts to closer sizes, both on Jefferies and the subject of his male gaze as his interest grows—a factor in the intensification of his narrative POV.

Later, when Lisa Freemont arrives in Jefferies's apartment, Hitchcock continues to employ shot sizes determined by the sense of our degree of proximity to and distance

(1) L. B. Jefferies gazes at a neighbor.

(2) The neighbor, a dancer, is shown in a WS—Jefferies's POV.

(3) Jefferies is shown in a closer shot as his interest is peeked.

from each character, placing us with Jefferies while keeping Freemont away from us. Shots on Jefferies are closer than those on Freemont; the two are never matched, even when she moves closer to him.

Here, the filmmaker's choice of shot size is precisely tailored to the spatial relationships of the characters and to our relationship with each.

(4) The next shot on the dancer is also tighter, reflecting Jefferies's interest.

(1) When Lisa arrives, Jefferies is shown in an MS.

(2) Lisa crosses the room into an LS.

(3) Lisa crosses forward into a loose MCU.

(4) From Lisa's MCU Hitchcock cuts to a tighter shot of Jefferies.

The articulation of narrative POV also impacts shot sizes (as it can camera placement and angle) when a character in whose POV we find ourselves motivates a cut to a *wider* size. An example of this occurs in Akira Kurasawa's *Throne of Blood*, when after his outburst upon seeing a ghost invisible to everyone else, Washizu barks out an order for his courtiers to settle.

Cuts and shot sizes are motivated by Washizu's action and emotions throughout the scene, this being a clear instance of his centrality. (Such a cut, from his single to a WS, also reveals his power over the court.)

(1) and (2) Washizu, in MS, issues a command that motivates a cut to a WS from the back of the room.

While this cut (and choice of lens) communicates the spatial nature of Washizu's environment, shot sizes may equally be chosen to deliberately *mislead* us, the spatial relationships conveyed at first glance proving false (in contrast to the articulation of space in *Rear Window*). Such a shift in our understanding occurs in the scene from Krzysztof Kieślowski's *Three Colors Blue* (discussed in Chapter 3), when the hitchhiking Antoine witnesses the results of a car crash.

(1) Antoine, in CU, turns. Cut to:

(2) WS of the crashed car, apparently his POV. Cut to:

(3) Antoine running to the car. Cut to:

(4) WS: he has farther to travel than (2) suggested.

The simple progression of closer and closer shots would not allow for this trick of storytelling, although there are, of course, circumstances in which such a series will be effective in raising tension. This can be seen in *Hereditary* in the episode in Charlie's classroom, which starts with a wide, establishing shot straddling four lines of desks. Our eye takes in the breadth of the room while being directed to the teacher, who crosses in the background from left to right. As she walks down Charlie's line, there's a cut to an OTS on Charlie, followed by Charlie's CU.

(1) WS on the classroom: the teacher crosses left to right before coming downstage toward Charlie (midground to right of center frame). (Note the horizontals and verticals.)

(2) The teacher approaches Charlie in a tightly framed OTS. (Note the diagonals.)

(3) Charlie in CU, the teacher behind her. Shortly afterward we find her in a BCU, shut off in the frame from the world around (4):

(4) Here, Aster shows context before detail, setting before drama. (1) might be described as an establishing shot (and should the take have been continued throughout the scene, as a master shot). As Charlie feels the pressure on her building, the shots tighten (and the angle shifts), leading to a BCU in which the constricted frame itself applies a visual pressure that conveys her discomfort.

In contrast, a scene may begin with a close shot, or several, in which setting, and context are *not* revealed, before cutting to a wider shot to show these. Perhaps we have been with the characters in a previous scene and assume we are in the same setting, only to discover that time has moved on and the characters are now in a different place. Perhaps the filmmaker wants to emphasize the drama before showing the setting. Perhaps we already know the setting and have no need of context. Perhaps there is a designed variation in how individual scenes begin—detail before context oscillating with context before detail. The former tells a story increment by increment, revealing the scene, while the latter directs the focus of the viewer to specific details in the scene.

Elsewhere, in *Hereditary*, for example, Aster begins a scene with a close shot on a model of a figure in bed, pulls back to reveal a second miniature figure being painted, then pulls still further back to show the painter: Annie. Only later in the scene does a wider mid 2-shot reveal the setting: her workroom.

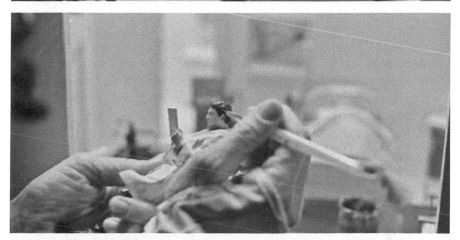

Detail before context in *Hereditary.* As the opening shot reveals one detail after another, Aster presents a visual narrative.

The scene reveals its setting by means of the wider shot and new angle that follows.

A further criterion for the choice of shot size might be the contrast between that of one scene and that of its following episode. In *Hereditary*, again, the meeting of Annie and Joan in the parking lot outside the art supply store that precedes the séance in the latter's apartment is shot in a single take that contrasts with the closer sizes of its successor. The impact of this second episode is consequently greater than it might have proved had the parking lot scene been shot on closer singles.

Finally, the aspect ratio of a film—a topic discussed in the section on composition—has a profound effect on the impact of shot size. A CU in Academy ratio, 1.33:1, will take up much of the frame. In a film in 2.40:1 it will occupy only a portion of the frame, leaving space for other elements; mise en scène here becomes critical: Is the subject to be placed to the left, right, or center of the frame, and what other elements are included elsewhere?

Framing

Cinema is a matter of what's in the frame and what's out.

—Martin Scorsese

There are, in general, two kinds of filmmakers: those who walk in the street with their head up, and those who walk with their head down. The former, in order to see what's happening around them, have to raise their head often and suddenly and to turn it left and right, embracing the field of vision with a series of glances. They see. The latter see nothing, they look, fixing their attention on the precise point that interests them. When they shoot a film, the framings of the former will be airy and fluid (Rossellini); those of the latter, tight to the millimeter (Hitchcock). . . . Bergman is rather in the first group, that of free cinema; Visconti, in the second, that of rigorous cinema.

—Jean-Luc Godard

These notes set out the considerations of the filmmaker as they decide on the framing of a shot.

- Framing finds and adjusts composition.
- What's *out* of a shot can be as potent as what's *in*.
- Space is an element as important as characters and objects; framing emptiness and negative space *into* a shot can be as significant a consideration as that of how much of a character, object, or setting might be framed *out*.
- Framing can be related to information the filmmaker wishes to communicate and information they wish to conceal.
- Whatever its formal or abstract nature, dramatic context affects the message a frame conveys.
- Framing is determined not only by the demands of the shot itself but by its connections to the shots around it.
- The purpose of a shot determines its framing as much as, and often more than, its subject matter.
- Framing can be a means of generating both suspense and surprise.
- Framing can offer punctuation and breath as well as tension.
- Framing works interfunctionally with aspect ratio, shot size, angle, depth of field, story, and storytelling.

The proficient filmmaker considers the criteria for framing in terms of both the shot itself and its relationship to others. How much "air" should there be around the subject? How little? How much might the degree of one or the other convey tension or release? The answers might reflect the sensibility of the filmmaker, perhaps of their culture. Filmmakers from predominantly individualistic cultures might perhaps opt for tighter framings, while those from predominantly collective cultures or ones that place the agency of the universe above that of the individual may opt for wider framings.

Shot size and framing might accommodate all of the action or a part only. When the filmmaker edits in camera (see the section on camera movement in Chapter 9), their framings of individual images might be determined by options available given the placement of elements on the set and to what degree the camera and its movement become active in modulating them.

If framing the components of the drama *in* is one consideration, then the framing *out* of unnecessary or distracting elements—be they characters or objects, or parts of those—is another. This can be seen in (3) above, in which the face of Charlie's teacher is not shown, then in (4), in which everything but Charlie is excluded. In *Moonlight*, in the scene in which Paula confronts Juan, Jenkins frames her companion out—he's initially seen in soft focus in the background—as the argument heats up.

Even when in soft focus in the background, the presence of Paula's unconcerned companion might distract from the intensity of her confrontation with Juan. Jenkins therefore frames him out as the scene develops.

Characters can also be removed from a shot by staging so that the space in a frame might remain more or less constant. In *Hereditary* this occurs when Steve receives a call from the cemetery about the desecration of Ellen's grave. Annie and Peter, present earlier in the scene, are not needed, indeed *must* be absent, so Aster has them walk out of shot while he *widens* the frame, trapping the lone Steve in the shot's geometry.

In *Hereditary*, Annie exits this scene, followed by Peter, as Steve listens to the call concerning the desecration of Ellen's grave. At the critical moment of receiving the news, Steve is shown alone, the empty depth of the hallway behind him. (Note the diagonals and the single-point perspective they offer—*ikones* suggestive of an inevitability of which Steve, facing away from them, remains unaware.)

The *frame within a frame* is an important means by which the filmmaker draws our attention to their subject and a potent resource the practical aesthetics that inform their decision-making. Here, parts of the set, foreground objects, or people (faces framed out, maybe) are employed to block out sections of the screen, emphasizing a particular portion of it so that a new aspect ratio is formed within the movie's. There is also a deepening of our sense of a character or characters, their actions, and their emotions. Jenkins does this effectively in *Moonlight* after Little has heated water for a bath.

The action of Little as he lifts a pan of heated water is heightened by the vertical frame within a frame, which offers new dynamics of composition. The contrast between foreground flat space and background depth imbues a static shot with visual energy and draws the eye to Little's struggle.

Later in the film, when Kevin calls Black, the filmmaker gives the former his own frame while breaking up the rest of the screen into several discrete frames.

When Jenkins shows Kevin in a restricted frame surrounded by other frames, he traps him visually through mise en scène and composition. Kevin's animate energy is contrasted with the static elements seen to frame left (deep space), frame right (flat space), and the horizontal strip in low foreground (flat space). The soft focus illustration to frame right of what appears to be a loving couple deftly complements Kevin's affectionate overtures to his former schoolmate.

In *Hereditary*, when the family return from Ellen's funeral and we see them at home for the first time, set design serves to create the frame within the frame. The nature of production designer Grace Yun's set for the Grahams' home in *Hereditary* affords Aster the opportunity to place the film's family in several frames within the frame—a visual symbol for their situational entrapment. (The symmetrical, receding diagonals of the lobby further suggest the sense of inescapable fate.)

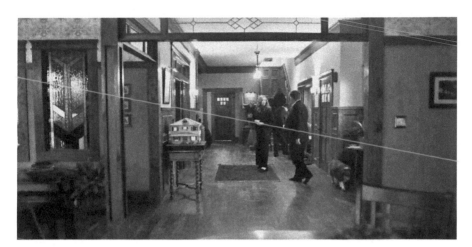

An example of frames within the frame in *Hereditary*.

The agility of variation and contrast that frames within frames offer stimulates our visual engagement. An important aspect of shot design, it presents the film-maker with compositional and framing opportunities above and beyond their film's fixed aspect ratio. These options will tend to be greater with 1.85:1 and 2.40:1 formats, where the lateral space affords more possibilities, than with 1.33:1 and 1.66:1, in which horizontals are less prominent. (2:1 offers both advantages, as can be seen in the *Hereditary* shot.)

Another mode of framing that wider screen formats present the filmmaker is the option known as *short siding*. Conventionally, when one character looks to another who is out of shot, they are placed to the opposite side of the frame: say character A looks to camera right to character B who is out of shot, then A would usually be placed to the left of the frame, their look to the right directing a lateral energy across the negative space in the frame suggestive of the distance between A and out-of-shot B. With short siding, however, character A is by contrast placed to the *right* of the frame, seemingly closer to character B, toward whom they are looking. (This can work equally in reverse, of course, with a character looking at or speaking to someone out of frame left.) The technique adds a visual inflection that a filmmaker can make use of in different ways, in different contexts. Jenkins demonstrates this in *Moonlight*, in the aforementioned phone conversation between Kevin and Black. The characters are in Florida and Georgia, respectively, but Jenkins conveys the attraction each feels for the other by placing Kevin to the right side of his frame, while Black edges toward the left side of his.

The suggested proximity of each, created through framing and mise en scène, through lighting, and through editing, conveys their emotional and sexual attraction. Although they are in separate shots, and in the world of the story are miles apart, they appear subject to a mutual bond. These framings demonstrate a clear instance of the filmmakers decision-making and their utilization of practical aesthetics in conveying subtext and emotion to the audience. (This is also a strong example of the interfunctionality of the crafts of cinema, with the performances of Kevin's Andre Holland and Black's Trevante Rhodes being integral to the scene's effectiveness.)

When Kevin calls Black in *Moonlight*, his placement, close to the right of frame, suggests an emotional proximity to Black, who is many miles away. Black, meanwhile, is placed closer to the left than to the right side of his frame.

Short siding offers variation in the lateral weighting of the frame, shifting attention and tension from one side to the other. In the process, it can render negative space less portentous. (It prompts an almost subconscious frame within a frame when we lose conscious awareness of the space to the negative side of a character.)

Consideration should be given also to the amount of headspace the filmmaker allows. The less the space between the top of a character's head and the top edge of the frame, the greater the emphasis on the image and the emotions it conveys. The earlier CUs of Kevin and Black during their phone conversation, for example, in which the tops of the heads are framed out, serves to stress the significance of the exchange. The shots from *Hereditary* of Steve receiving news from the cemetery, and of Charlie in the classroom, emphasize very different, less comfortable, emotions, but similarly allow for no headroom. The shot from *Nomadland* of Fern and the instructor, as she learns to punch a hole in a tire, although it allows for negligible space at the top of the frame, depicts by contrast a relaxed and playful event. Yet if the lack of headroom here is simply a consequence of shot size, the principle that less headroom brings tension to a shot, while more space deflates it, holds—the *Nomadland* episode engages us, and we want Fern to succeed in her task, even if the stakes are modest.

Where this dynamic of headroom's relation to tension breaks down, however, is in the approach to framing adopted by filmmaker Paweł Pawlikowski. In his 2013 *Ida*, he utilizes deliberately generous space in the top section of the frame.

Headroom dominates the frame in these shots from Paweł Pawlikowski's *Ida*.

In the 1.33:1 aspect ratio the film adopts, the vertical axis has a prominence lacking in wide formats. The filmmaker's choice is informed by his voice and by the creative vision of a film in which the agency of the individual is severely curtailed by their circumstances. In such a context, an approach to framing that might otherwise defuse dramatic tension fosters it. This is an illustration of how use and context can outweigh what might be considered an inherent aspect of cinematic language—a case of Wittgenstein over Block perhaps, and a singular mode of practical aesthetics. (Pawlikowski can be seen to have influenced other filmmakers such as Rebecca Hall, who adopts a similar dynamic in her 2021 *Passing*.)

The reader might reflect on how, when in a wider format there is empty space in a frame to left or right and the shot is framed for the entry of a new character, such anticipatory framing can prove either suspenseful or weak, depending on dramatic context. When there is no suspense in the story and we simply wait for a character to step in, the shot will lack energy, and tension will sag because when the character appears there is no surprise, as the space has long been demanding its occupant. When, on the other hand, we anticipate the appearance of a presence that might be antagonistic, and the character already in the shot is perhaps turned away, the empty space may yield tension, as we imagine a character coming to occupy it. When our eyes are directed away from that negative space—perhaps to the opposite side of the frame—and an element or character then enters it, the surprise can be palpable, as can be seen in *Hereditary* when Peter faces away from the darkness behind, looking to frame left.

In *Hereditary*, Peter looks to frame left, directing our eye path. In the following closer shot, Annie flies through the right portion of the frame, unseen by him but surprising us as our eyes shift to catch the fleeting image.

In another scene, Aster uses the empty space on one side of the frame to create tension there, then introduces a new element from the opposite side, thus creating a frisson or *jump scare*.

(1) In this scene from *Hereditary*, the family dog barks.

(2) Peter reacts in the reverse shot.

(3a) Tension to frame right (toward the dog, out of shot).

(3b) The hand suddenly reaching in from frame left shocks us.

Shots (1) and (2) set up the axis of tension between Peter and the dog. In (3a) the frame has tension to the right. When the hand reaches in, (3b), our eyes shift rapidly to the left of frame, precipitating our shock. (Here is an example of suspense and surprise working together—we anticipate a force of antagonism, but not in the section of the frame in which it appears.)

Aster can here be seen as exemplifying the precise filmmaker of Godard's description, one whose exact framings reflect his creative vision while functioning as deliberate practical aesthetics that determine our reactions. This scene illustrates also how important it is to distinguish between the categories of shot size and shot framing.

9
Camera

What do we mean by *camera*?

We might think of camera as *concept*. We should also consider it *practice*. Let us explore the notion of concept first, followed by the specifics of practice.

The relationship of the camera to the material it depicts and its function as visual storyteller can be complex, multifaceted, and shifting. Alexander Mackendrick's description of the camera in *On Film-Making: An Introduction to the Craft of the Director* as an *invisible, ubiquitous, winged, witness* helps us understand this—although might there be more to consider than these four categories? A highly accomplished, masterly filmmaker himself, was Mackendrick perhaps listing the tenets of his own sensibility rather than considering the multiplicity of approaches to be found in the language and aesthetics of the moving image?

While we cannot see the camera itself, we are not always entirely unaware of it. Indeed, we may at times sense its *invisible* presence, particularly when it moves, and when that motion is not disguised by the energy of what the camera shows—when it moves in a direction *counter* to the action, for example, or when it rises above the action or dives below, taking us on its own journey, or when it moves in complex fashion throughout a lengthy take, even throughout an entire movie—or when, very simply, it moves around a static subject. Dramatic and emotional context may serve to disguise a camera move, or a camera move may serve to give context to drama and emotion.

Many filmmakers will keep their camera studiously "invisible," while others will energize it, flaunting its presence as an integral component of their language. There is no "correct" approach. Intention on the part of the filmmaker to prompt our awareness or nonawareness of camera depends on their approach to style—very much an aspect of *voice*. One filmmaker will see the camera as a means of *capturing* their story, adhering to the notion of cinema as an art that conceals art, while another may conceive of it as an instrument of storytelling that cannot avoid *participating in* the emotion and energy of their film. To the latter, hiding the presence of the camera seems disingenuous; to the former, it is an imperative. Some may adopt either philosophy as they deem appropriate. Others, either unaware or indifferent, may prove inattentive to this aspect, so that perhaps our engagement with their work might be consequently lessened.

Nor is Mackendrick's second category necessarily true in every respect. Surely the camera is not exclusively *ubiquitous*? When a filmmaker cleaves to a particular character's narrative POV, for example, they may restrict camera placement and movement. They may opt not to show something a character cannot see even though it

The Art of the Filmmaker. Peter Markham, Oxford University Press. © Oxford University Press 2023.
DOI: 10.1093/oso/9780197631522.003.0010

might be useful for the audience to see it. They may wish to adhere to the constraints of a style they have adopted—no top shots, for example, or no raking camera angles. They may choose to avoid putting the camera anywhere that a person could not go—inside a fridge as someone opens its door, or inside a room *before* a character enters. On the other hand, a filmmaker may adopt an agility of camera placement, a flamboyance even, that the minimalist would eschew, in which case the camera becomes truly ubiquitous.

The third category also bears examination—some moving cameras might indeed be *winged*, while others, even if not static, might be more earthbound. What Mackendrick is describing here is the range of possibilities. Significant in his term is the notion of height. (See the later section in this chapter on top shots and the use of drones.) The term is eminently helpful, however, in suggesting the possibilities of the camera's mobility.

The concept of camera as *witness* does not appear to represent the full range of functions the camera offers. It can indeed be a witness to events, rendering us onlookers of the action. But what *kind* of a witness does it make us? Are we close or distant? Can we see everything, or are certain elements obscured? Can we see anything at all, or do we gather what is going on from what we hear? Is the camera always content to be a witness? When does it *witness* and when *observe*? Might it at times even be a spy, a *voyeur* along with a character, as in *Rear Window*, or without one, as in the same movie's opening? Could we say that the act of witnessing is innocent, that of observing knowing, that of spying willful? (Where the camera gives us the view of a voyeur *not* the POV of any character, this renders it—and of course us—a "peeping Tom." In this mode it becomes a *transgressive* camera.)

Does the camera sometimes *participate* in the action, even making itself *complicit*? Might it offer a comment on what it shows—by its angle (high, low, oblique, dutched), by the resulting mise en scène—thus rendering itself a *critical* camera? (Examples of the critical camera can be seen in Alfred Hitchcock's raking angle down on the Nazi Alex Sebastian upon his discovery that Alicia, his wife, is an American spy, and at the end of *Notorious*, when the doomed Alex, walking back to his murderous co-conspirators, is trapped in the rigid geometry of the shot's composition.)

We might refer to a static camera, simply observing the action, place, space, and object in an uninflected manner, perhaps in their entirety in the frame, with the lens at eye height, as a *passive* or *minimal camera*. It does little but look. It passes no comment, does not interact with what it shows, and does not reflect the energy or emotion of what it sees. This camera remains neutral, dispassionate; it does not impose. (The lighting of what it shoots is a separate consideration and may not be passive.) This is not to suggest that the filmmaker is necessarily passive also—theirs may be a deliberate choice, perhaps to avoid passing judgment, perhaps to offer a neutral, objective view or to allow for *cumulative* engagement with story and characters on the part of the audience: we watch, we wait, but before long we find ourselves drawn in, to be held for the rest of the movie.

When the framing is more deliberate, perhaps not showing an entire character, group, or object; maybe seeing it from a particular angle; raking steeply perhaps, or from above; maybe even looking away from an event; or concealing it behind some foreground obstruction, obscuring it so that the audience must do the work of imagining it—then the camera is something more than observing. It is more than a witness. This camera is *active*, a *dynamic camera*—not merely capturing the event so that it can be communicated by way of the screen to the audience but putting itself between the moment and the audience by presenting what's happening selectively.

An active camera entering the world of the film and its characters, when motivated by or reflecting its energy in some way, and when connecting with the emotion or visceral sensation of an event, we might call a *complicit camera*. This camera might be participating in the storytelling by angle, lensing, movement, framing, or mise en scène. In some instances, it might be adopting what could be described as *hyper POV*– placed in the most dynamic position, the most kinetic, the location of the most intense action, the greatest energy. It might thrust itself forward to reflect the vector of a projectile, for example, or be situated directly in the path of one oncoming. Less sensationally, it might relate to the narrative POV of a particular character, its progression of placement and/or movement the foundation for the editing that will connect us to that character above others.

The camera is of course rarely restricted to one specific function. Indeed, even within a single developing shot, it may be well be a *shapeshifting* camera, working in one mode one moment and another the next, as is the case in the scene from *Three Colors Red* described in Chapter 7. The final moments of Max Ophuls' 1952 *Le Plaisir* offer a particularly striking example of a shapeshifting camera.

Important in understanding the filmmaker's art is an awareness of the camera and how it can be used. The filmmaker's sensibility, their style, and the design of their film's language, as well as its constraints, agility, and nature form the determining factors in its functions.

Camera Placement and Angle

The inseparable topics of camera placement and angle encompass so many considerations and have so many applications in such a variety of contexts and situations as to render any comprehensive categorization deserving of its own book. The dramatic nature of the moment and its emotion, of its place in the scene, its function alongside others, its relation to the filmmaker's chosen visual discourse throughout their film, to the nature of a character, and to that of our connection as viewers all constitute possible foundations for the choice of placement and angle—quite apart from a filmmaker's intuition and individual vision.

Akira Kurosawa, for example, often used two or three cameras on an action, but commented that they should be placed only where a person *might* be positioned in that setting—atop a castle tower or hill, for instance, should such a feature be present in the episode, but be restricted to lower levels should there be no such elements. Another Japanese master, Yazujiro Ozu, invariably placed his camera at the eye level of the kneeling or sitting characters common to the social life he depicted. We might consider the camera of both directors to be a *human*, perhaps *humanist* camera. Placement that adheres to narrative POV, such as Hitchcock's *Rear Window* (where it does so predominantly if not strictly), offers another form of humanist camera.

More practically speaking—as the filmmaking reader will be aware—placement in relation to any particular shot size, as it pertains to the distance between camera and subject, will depend on the choice of lens. With wider lenses the camera will be placed closer to the subject; with longer lenses it will need to be farther away. (The dimensions of a set or the layout and nature of a location will determine the range of options available.)

Further considerations of placement will be related to the choice of angle, although with a fluid camera this topic becomes less amenable to categorization. Angles in this context that work within the flow and momentum of a longer "sequence" shot may not necessarily be those that might have been selected had coverage been broken up into separate takes. Here, the momentum, staging, performances, movement, and interaction of the characters mesh with camera placement, angle, and movement to give an organic whole that comes to life while telling the story. Such a shot may not stand alone, requiring further angles to complete the coverage required for editing (a feature of the "master shot").

Consideration of the choice of angle as this relates to a shot of a single character or object, or two of such, however, can provide a starting point for the reader's understanding of basic criteria the filmmaker might bring to bear on their selection. Even in these instances, the staging of a scene, the looks between characters, and the dimensions and configuration of a set or location will have an impact on the filmmaker's approach.

Background and its elements—what needs to be shown and what requires concealment—may be a factor in the filmmaker's choice of angle. Contextual or dramatic space—deep, mid, flat—might warrant the inclusion an angle grants, as might light, or darkness, or color, or a prop or object of significance not granted its own "insert" shot.

The articulation of narrative POV might come into play—a topic discussed later in this chapter.

Consideration might also be given to how the filmmaker can best facilitate performance. Experienced film actors will generally be less inhibited by the camera than nonactors. In the case of the latter, the filmmaker may place the camera further off the subject's eyeline, a less obtrusive angle benefiting the nonactor, even if it limits the director's options. (This approach is used to great effect by Andrea Arnold in her *American Honey* [2016], in which Sasha Lane's Star, the protagonist, is frequently seen in half-profile.)

These factors acknowledged, the criteria for the selection of angle for a static single can offer helpful insights.

Frontal Angles

When we see a character's two eyes, we generally feel more connected to them (depending on the nature of the character and the dramatic context of the shot) than when we observe them in profile and see one eye only. The human face with its nuances of expression forms our earliest, preverbal interlocutor, so a front-on MS, MCU, or CU can provide a stronger connection to a character. The face brings a direct communication of emotion, while we project our own familiar emotions back onto the fictional being we are watching. We also gain insights into the *micro-story* of a character's thoughts and feelings. (Shot size, framing, camera movement, and context of course serve to modulate this effect.)

The connection between us and a character is at its strongest when their eyeline is closest to the axis of the lens. The farther from the axis of the lens a character's eyeline is, the weaker our connection to them may become, again depending on context—on how closely we have been following a character's journey, how well we have come to know them, how much we share in their emotions, and the prior and subsequent angles on what they are seeing.

Examples of eyelines close to the axis of the lens are shown in Chapter 6 with the bruised Chiron seeing himself in a mirror in *Moonlight*, and in Chapter 8 with Peter reeling from the sudden death of Charlie in *Hereditary*.

When a character turns to us and looks *directly* into the axis of the lens to address us, they are said to be "breaking the fourth wall." This disturbs the illusion of a film's fictional world, destroying our suspension of belief. (See comments later in this chapter on *Funny Games*.) When, however, character A, in directing their look into the axis of the lens, is understood to be looking directly at character B, this can put us in the immediate perception and emotion of the character to whom that look is directed. Far from destroying the illusion of the fiction, this has the effect of putting us in the midst of the drama.

When two actors in a scene are experienced and can hold their eyelines close to the lens axis, even directly into it, we are taken directly into the drama of their exchange and feel ourselves spatially and emotionally between the two. With such eyelines, neither actor can look at the other on the set, as the camera stands between them. An instance of this occurs in *Moonlight*, between Paula and Chiron. (See p. 102.)

Later in the film, Chiron, as Black, dreams of Kevin, whom Barry Jenkins shows looking directly into the lens (even though Chiron has never seen the adult Kevin!). The shot immerses us in the homoeroticism of Chiron's psyche. (See also p. 102.)

When, by contrast, a character turns to address *us, the audience*, perhaps to comment on the action, the effect is like a stage play's aside. As in the theater, so in film this tends to involve a tone of irony, often comedic, perhaps darkly so, that serves to distance us from the events we are witnessing. In Michael Haneke's *Funny Games*, Arno Frisch's Paul winks at us as he goes about his business of murdering a family for thrills, appalling us but at the same time rendering us—as an audience viewing

When both Paula and Ashton Sander's Chiron look directly into the lens, the cuts from one to the other have the effect of placing us between them and heightening our emotional experience.

Kevin turns to camera in Black's (Chiron's) dream.

Paul, played by Arno Frisch, turns to us and winks, prompting us to acknowledge our entertainment in witnessing his lethal antics.

a thriller—complicit in the appeal of the genre's sadistic violence. Here, the choice of camera angle has a moral dimension, reinforcing the critique posed by a movie that denies us the emotional catharsis (although not its realizational counterpart) that might excuse our enjoyment of its brutality.

Profiles and Half-Profiles

Angles and shot sizes are frequently matched when there is cross-cutting between characters, whether each single is close to or off the eyeline or in half- or full profile. This may be the result of a merely grammatical rather than narrative approach, but on the other hand it may serve to raise the tension in a scene. In *Hereditary*, in the first section of Annie's nightmare-within-a-nightmare, Ari Aster employs a frontal single of Annie and a frontal angle on the ant-covered Peter asleep in bed. As the following section begins, he cuts to a wide profile 2-shot, then opts for profile singles before employing frontal singles, and in bringing the eyelines closer to the axis of the lens he escalates the horror.

(1).

(2).

(3). Aster cuts from a wide profile 2-shot of Annie and Peter (1), to matching profiles (2) and (3), putting us in a third-person narrative POV (although this occurs in Annie's nightmare—so in context is subjective). When the nightmare intensifies, he shifts to more front-on singles (4) and (5), drawing us further into the episode's horror.

(4).

(5). The profile singles direct lateral energy across the frame. The shift to the frontal angles, with eyelines *not entirely* close to the axis of the lens, maintains that lateral tension while directing the energy more toward the camera and us.

While profile shots often convey antagonism—as in this example from *Hereditary*—they may however communicate the very opposite, offering connection rather than conflict. Since there may be no distance between two characters in a romantic scenario, there can simply be nowhere else to put the camera to access a front-on angle. Context, character, performance, and tone will here lend a profile 2-shot the appropriate emotion.

In Hitchcock's *Rear Window*, the profile kiss between Lisa Freemont and L. B. Jefferies suggests romantic intimacy rather than conflict.

Two characters innocently greeting each other, or sitting, talking on either side of a table, might be shown in a profile 2-shot, equally without any hint of conflict—as is the case in *Moonlight*, when Black (Chiron) and Kevin reconnect in the diner.

The placing in the story of Black's reunion with Kevin and the performances of the actors convey a mood of harmony and affection in this profile 2-shot. As the scene develops, and Kevin attempts to break down Black's emotional defenses, Jenkins adopts matching OTS reverses to articulate Kevin's purposeful playfulness.

The half profile, in which we see both of a character's eyes but their look is as close to the lateral axis as to that of the lens, perhaps more so, offers something of both vectors. Half profiles may be matched cut (in which case we are likely to look at the characters as witnesses of their scene rather than being brought *into* its emotion)—or they may not, as is the case in *Nomadland*, when Fern registers for employment. Here she is shown in half profile, while the clerk to whom she's speaking is seen in an OTS shot. The result is that we both observe Fern in her single and share in her perception of the clerk—but we do not share in the clerk's perception of Fern, as indeed we should not, given that she's a minor character and we are not entering her narrative POV.

(1) Fern is shown in half profile. We see both her eyes, but her look is away from the axis of the lens.

(2) The clerk to whom Fern is speaking is shown over Fern's shoulder, whose perception we share while she remains present in the frame. Note: OTS shots bring eyelines closer to the axis of the lens to bring us closer to a foreground character's POV while keeping them present in the frame. (A similar approach can be seen in Andrea Arnold's previously mentioned *American Honey*.)

When close eyelines are avoided throughout a scene, perhaps throughout an entire film, however, we may perhaps be in danger of being rendered distanced observers. While such a style might be a deliberately removed positioning of the audience to the material, the reader might reflect on whether it may indicate that the filmmaker is avoiding the emotional pain of their characters or inviting little empathy with them.

As with matching shot sizes when cross-cutting, matching angles are far from mandatory. In Hitchcock's *The Wrong Man* (1956), for example, in an exchange between Manny and Rose Balestrero, Hitchcock chooses to depict the protagonist at a 90 degree angle from the axis of their exchange. This keeps us in the narrative POV of Manny that Hitchcock has established from the start of the film.

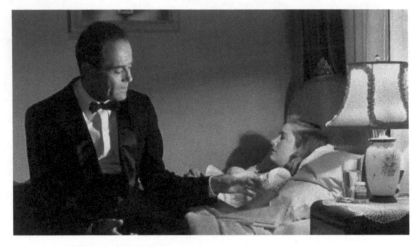

(1) A wide profile 2-shot of Manny and Rose Ballestrero from *The Wrong Man*.

(2) The single on Rose.

(3) The reverse single on Manny is *not* from Rose's matching angle but shows him in profile.

(4) As Manny turns away from Rose in his reverse, he turns toward camera, and so to us.

(5) After the conversation, Manny is shown in a single, his look close to the axis of the lens, as he reflects on the couple's financial problems. The angle has shifted further to camera right, and the lamp is excluded. The effect of these nonmatching angles puts us in Manny's narrative POV, rendering us alone with the character as he ponders a solution to his problem. (It perhaps also creates the suspicion of emotional distance between him and Rose.)

The Back Shot

Alexander Mackendrick commented that while profiles tend to offer us a more objective sense of a character than a frontal view, the angle that shows the back of their head brings us, paradoxically, closer to them. In *Moonlight*, when Little turns away from us to find Paula arriving, Barry Jenkins chooses to hold the shot for a moment, keeping the focus on the back of his head rather than racking to Paula, thus maintaining our connection with the boy even if there's no cut to his reaction.

Little turns away from the camera as Paula arrives. The resulting brief back shot, as Jenkins briefly holds him in focus rather than racking to Paula, paradoxically maintains our connection to him. (The focus on Little is accentuated by an anamorphic lens that softens the background.)

Later in the film, as Chiron returns home after school, the camera follows him. Throughout the flow of the shot, we have the sense of the events of his day we have just witnessed resonating in his mind. As so often with this angle, the shot from behind also serves to convey a sense of the character's vulnerability.

As Chiron, seen from the back, returns home after dramatic events at school, we remain connected to his emotion, even though we are denied a view of his face.

Such an angle can also be a means of creating suspense—we might be kept in ignorance as to how a character is reacting, the filmmaker making us wait either for the character to turn to the camera, or for a 180 degree cut that reveals their expression. Indeed, if we anticipate one reaction but discover the opposite, we experience not only suspense but also surprise. A similar phenomenon occurs when there's a revelation so momentous that any reaction might seem either inadequate or redundant. Rather than relying on an actor's performance to capture adequate emotion, the back angle poses questions to us: *How is the character responding?* and *How do I, myself feel?* Again, if the character's reaction is subsequently revealed to be calm, or perhaps one of amusement, while we've expected alarm, we experience surprise.

Another reason the filmmaker might show a character from the back is when, rather than our not knowing their emotion, we are fully aware of it—in particular, when it is painful. To show pain on a character's face in such an instance might prove redundant. Here, we are left to imagine their expression on the screen of the mind—often the more powerful "screen"; the filmmaker denies us the voyeurism that might be afforded by front-on views of difficult emotions, which rather than connecting us to a character either renders their agony unwatchable or, on the contrary, reduces them to a spectacle of pain presented for our entertainment.

A filmmaker might choose a back shot to precede more direct angles as they ramp up the intensity of emotion. When Annie first visits Joan in *Hereditary*, Aster sets the scene with an establishing shot in which we see her from the back, with Joan seated to her side. We hear her tearful outpouring and feel her anguish before Aster cuts to her frontal single. In this way, he avoids prompting us to look away from this display of pain, instead drawing in our empathy for his character.

(1) When Annie visits Joan in *Hereditary*, Aster shows her hesitant as her host invites her to join her for tea.

(2) The back shot of Annie already seated provides a crisp transition from the previous shot (1) while denying us the sight of her anguish.

(3) Having drawn us into the scene, Aster cuts to the front-on single, which further elicits our empathy for Annie.

The back shot might also be used when the filmmaker wishes to conceal a character's emotion as they go about an action, or to hide their identity altogether.

The angle also has the merit of showing both a character and their destination within the frame. As demonstrated in the end sequence of *Nomadland*, as Fern walks away from the camera in a symmetrical composition, the reader might consider how this can have the effect of suggesting a character is on a path to their destiny. Such an angle can also be seen in Michael Mann's *The Insider* (1999), when Russell Crowe's Jeffrey Wigand, having met with Al Pacino's Lowell Bergman for the first time, walks down a hotel corridor.

The symmetrical composition, receding diagonals, frames within the frame, and single-point perspective combine to render this angle suggestive of a character en route to their fate.

Finally, such an angle might be employed in the course of a filmmaker's *introduction* of a character—as an increment in the all-important task of "announcing" them. Filmmakers may make us wait before we see the face of a protagonist, for example, selecting angles and frames to tease us before fully revealing the face of the character. (Little, in *Moonlight*, is seen initially from behind, the camera barely able to hold him in the frame as he runs—see the case study in Part III.) When a star is playing the role, and the audience come to a movie to see them, this can create suspense as they wait to catch sight of a familiar lead.

The Raking Angle

Raking or extreme angles may be used simply to accommodate characters in the frame—for example, when one is seated and another, whose face also needs to be shown, stands behind them or to their side, or simply when one character is taller than another. In such instances, the camera needs to be angled up or down.

Although a steep angle may merely be the means of containing the heads of the two characters within the frame, it gives the shot a charge. This may relate to a power dynamic, with character A, higher in the frame, having authority over B below. When cross-cutting, the filmmaker might select matching diagonals—singles or OTSs up one way, down the other—or on the other hand may use one angle up to higher character A but as a reverse choose a camera height closer to the level of the lower character B's eyes. In this latter angle, B will be seen looking up, over the camera toward A. In such an instance, we share B's impression of the powerful A but do not share B's reverse eyeline, looking down, on the powerless A. This approach can be seen in the *Moonlight* case study of the scene in the condemned apartment scene between Little and Juan. The angle on Juan is from Little's eye level, looking up to him, while that on Little is not from Juan's but from the boy's eye level, so not looking down on him. This has the effect of placing us in the perception and emotion of Little.

A raking or low angle that empowers one character and disempowers another can be seen in this frame from Orson Welles's *Citizen Kane* (1941). Such angles are prominent in the film, used also to elevate the stature and significance of the characters, who at times seem like giants or gods.

The low angle emphasizes the power of the foreground figure.

The *low* angle here makes the characters seem gigantic.

The *high* raking angle here serves to accentuate the diagonals.

A raking angle may also be used in order to accommodate multiple elements within the frame:

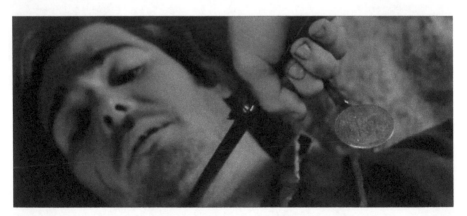

In Martin Scorsese's *Gangs of New York* (2002), this raking angle shows Henry Thomas's Jonny, with Amsterdam's knife at his throat, Amsterdam's hand, and the medallion Jonny recognizes. (Scorsese's eclectic practical aesthetics inform his ever-agile visual discourse.)

Extreme angles (and perhaps extreme lensing) may constitute an aspect of the language of a genre. Thrillers, action movies, and horror movies—in which the drama itself is extreme—often employ exaggerated angles appropriate to their heightened realism. On a social realist canvas or in a drama of nuanced, less exaggerated action and emotion, by contrast, such perspectives might seem out of place. That said, Charlotte Wells's *Aftersun* (2022), a compassionately observed daughter-father drama, reveals a breathtaking flexibility of camera angle.

Decisive angles might be a facet of the aesthetics a filmmaker chooses for their movie. They might wish to subvert a genre's conventions or may want to echo those of another. Hitchcock's high, raking angles reflect his creative vision, his camera bearing down on characters as if to impose the judgment of the universe upon them. In such instances, these angles, not necessarily chosen to contain elements in the frame, bring us into the filmmaker's vision of the world and our place in it.

A flexibility of angles on the part of the filmmaker will afford them the option to select optimum composition and mise en scène. In Steven Spielberg's *West Side Story* (2021), for example, the variety of angles, chosen not merely for pictorial flamboyance—although many yield frames that are visually intoxicating—but for storytelling, composition, energy flow, and editorial effectiveness, render the spectacle exhilarating but at the same time functional in terms of narrative and emotion. The story is about a romance across communities manifested on screen through staging and dance, and Spielberg's inventive choices of angle allow him to depict Justin Peck's choreography to maximum effect. This is particularly evident in his choice of top or overhead shots.

Top Shots

More extreme than the raking angle is the top shot, the *bird's-eye view*. When the filmmaker adopts a top shot, not the POV of any character, it privileges us with a godlike perspective. The top shot might be utilized for a multitude of purposes. It might present the optimum angle on a moment, event, or setting; render an incident visible that from a lower angle would remain hidden; connect elements in the frame; yield a contrasting geometry to earthbound views; simply offer context; convey a critical comment; or reflect the filmmaker's attitude to their material.

A bird's-eye view chosen simply for cosmetic embellishment might offer pictorial merits but have negligible narrative or dramatic purpose. One selected for its emotional power, however, and placed in a sequence of shots to which it contributes meaning, may provide a beat of telling impact.

In *Hereditary*, when for the first time we see Steve in his office, events around him are beginning to spiral out of control. The high angle here works as an establishing shot while suggesting the presence of a determinist power. The impression of control and order the frame gives makes for an ironic contrast to the character's impotence against the gathering forces of evil and the crescendo of trauma besetting his family. Aster's shot conveys this tension between stability and instability by its ordered composition on the one hand—afforded by the high angle—and on the other a mise en scène in which Steve is placed to the less stable right of frame while the more stable left contains little but empty chairs pointed diagonally (accusingly?) toward him and so exerting visual tension. The shot that follows maintains the predominant geometry of line (horizontal and vertical) but shows us an email Steve is writing concerning Annie's mental deterioration—over which he has no control. This is followed in turn by a BCU of him (lacking headroom) that conveys his anxiety, then a shot of an email concerning the desecration of Ellen's grave.

Aster's godlike perspective articulates his film's vision of his characters' impotence in the face of fate. Like the heroes of Sophocles's Greek tragedy *The Women of Trachis*, on which Peter's teacher gives a class, they have no choice in the matter of their destinies. Steve comes across as alone and vulnerable in the face of a ruthlessly ordered universe.

(1) *Hereditary*'s top shot of Steve in his office. The ordered composition, which renders the space flat; the placement of the character to the less stable frame right; and the diagonals created by the chairs frame left that point to him—together with the moment's dramatic context—create visual tension. The following shots derive charge from this:

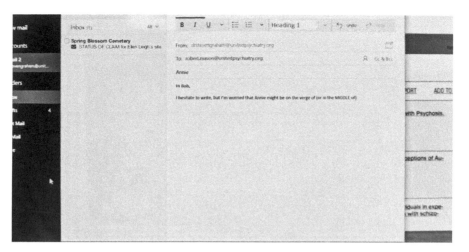

(2) Insert of Steve's email about Annie's disturbing behavior. Note the affinity of flat space and horizontal/vertical geometry.

(3) BCU of Steve as he receives notification of an email from the cemetery, a contrast to the dehumanized shots before and after.

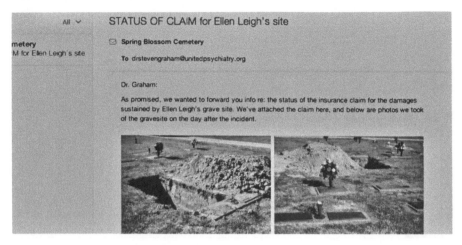

(4) Insert of email showing desecration of Ellen's grave. Back to flat space and ordered geometry.

When characters lie horizontally, a high angle may yield the optimum perspective. This is the case elsewhere in *Hereditary*, in Peter's nightmare. (See earlier frames from this episode in the section on framing.)

Peter writhes on his bed as hands grab his head in *Hereditary*.

A top shot might also be effective when the axis of movement is vertical. When, in *Gangs of New York*, Daniel Day Lewis's Bill the Butcher, having survived Amsterdam's assassination attempt, hurls a meat cleaver into the air, Martin Scorsese selects a high angle to bring the spinning implement toward the lens.

As the cleaver falls back, its energy is transferred to the camera, which descends at breathtaking speed toward the splayed, hapless Amsterdam. We do not see the cleaver as the camera descends, but its presence is articulated by the plunging camera and by the swishing sound the object—supposedly—makes.

(1) The spinning cleaver, thrown by Bill the Butcher, hurtles toward the camera in a high angle in *Gangs of New York*. This has the effect of bringing the energy of the shot directly toward us.

(2) The cleaver is also shown laterally, to capture its spinning motion and prolong its journey.

The introduction of drones has resulted in greater use of extreme wide bird's-eye views showing vistas of whole neighborhoods and landscapes, a godlike perspective indeed! The availability of this technology may at times be the sole reason behind its use, although the opportunities it offers for showing a film's world, as well as the freedom of angle and camera movement a drone offers, cannot be denied. The sensation of flight, even vertigo, that we the audience derive from such shots can constitute a potent aspect of a film's address.

The Dutched Angle

A staple of thrillers and horror films and derived from German Expressionist cinema—*dutched* is perhaps a corruption of Deutsch—the slanted angle renders horizontals and verticals as diagonals, lending energy and drama to a frame while disorienting us. Carol

Reed's *The Third Man* (1949) makes famous use of the dutched angle, while among the case studies, Peter's vision of the revenant Charlie in *Hereditary* provides a startling example.

Elsewhere in his movie, Aster goes further, depicting the world upside down as Annie approaches Joan's apartment. He also adopts this technique in *Midsommar*.

The apparition of Charlie, seen from Peter's POV as he lies in bed, is shown in a dutched angle.

Angles on the Axis of the Drama

An angle might be chosen to *depict* a moment, action, or look, in a *lateral* axis—horizontally (as in *Moonlight*'s profile 2-shot in the diner) or vertically. This angle renders us a witness to what we see, but an angle may on the contrary be selected to bring us *into* the vector of its energy by placing the lens along or close to the "axis of the drama" (as in the aforementioned shot from *Gangs of New York*). Here, the viewer's experience is more direct. When a character looks at someone or something, for instance, the filmmaker may cut to a *POV shot* of what the character sees. In this case, the lens is placed in the position of the character's eyes so that we the audience share in their perception. The camera may also move as the character moves, showing what they are seeing, which will intensify our connection to the character perceptually, if not always cognitively or emotionally. On the other hand, the angle chosen might *not* be that of the character's subjective POV but its direct opposite, *from the other side of what they are looking at*, so that what the character sees is in the foreground and the character is in midground or background to the far side of it.

An example of this can be found in *Hereditary*'s party scene, when Peter tempts Charlie with chocolate cake in order to rid himself of her. The cut from his look to the cake is not to the cake from his or his sister's POV, but to a WS with it in foreground (in soft focus) and the siblings behind in midground. Although we are looking *at* them, this keeps us with their perception and feelings.

(1a) The camera depicts the axis of the Charlie-Peter altercation laterally in a profile 2-shot. (Note: there is also the deep axis afforded by Bridget's observation of the siblings; she is shown in soft focus in the background.)

(1b) Peter turns right to look at the cake, motivating the cut from the lateral axis to:

(2a) the camera bringing us *into* the axis of the drama—which runs between the siblings and the cake—seen not in a POV shot from their position but foreground in soft focus. When Peter exits, focus is racked to the cake:

(2b) The racked focus communicates Charlie's interest in the cake (while the knife cutting it suggests she will eat a slice).

Camera Height and Character Eye Level

When the lens is below—even slightly below—the eye level of a character, the shot may afford them the suggestion of power. It may also have the effect of imparting dignity, particularly if a character is of modest status or holds negligible power in the story. When the lens is placed above eye level, there may be a suggestion of weakness—the higher the lens, the stronger the impression, or the angle might subliminally convey pressure on the character. With the lens on the same level as a character's eyes, we will tend to feel more of a connection, although this will depend on context—use, as so often, is the determinant of meaning.

Camera Movement

Note: In considering camera movement, it will be useful to consider the three axes of direction: the lateral (*x-axis*), the vertical (*y-axis*), and the deep (*z-axis*).

When the camera moves—and it can move in many ways—that movement can be motivated or unmotivated by the action it shoots. It can take from the energy and direction of an event, running with or against and counter to what it shows. It might *partake in* that energy or on the other hand be witness to it, altogether independent, moving stealthily, slowly, even imperceptibly while the action it depicts is rapid (or it may move quickly over a subject that moves slowly or is static). The reader might consider whether a camera move has a purpose, and if so what it might be. To what does it lead, what does it reveal as it travels, and what final image does it deliver? How does it affect our engagement with the moment, with

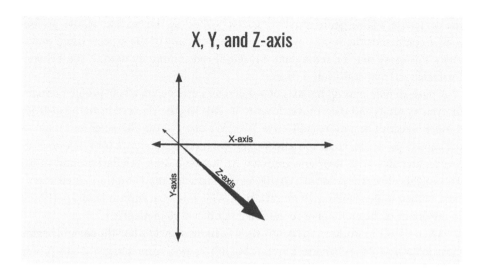

X, Y, and Z-axis

the characters? Does it bring us into the action or take us away, distancing us for a more objective, even critical perspective? Does it match the style and overall visual discourse of the film?

The push-in and pull-out are perhaps the simplest modes of camera movement. The first, when moving from a frontal MCU, say, to a CU, generally marks a moment of significance, giving emphasis to the shot's subject. The character perhaps perceives something of importance, a realization dawns on them, or, in contrast, they are struggling to understand something. Perhaps they are suddenly under emotional pressure, or they experience tension, or maybe shame. They must make a decision or *have* made a decision. Perhaps the attention of everyone else in the scene focuses on them, or they are telling a story that's becoming ever more compelling. They are revealing a truth, maybe offering a confession. They are anticipating a development, certain or uncertain. In many instances, the push-in brings us into greater intimacy with a character. On the other hand, it may seem as if the filmmaker is antagonizing them. (Camera as punisher of an errant character, perhaps?) Use, in other words, is all.

Most push-ins will be achieved by a dolly, a Steadicam, or perhaps a handheld camera—which will tend to be less smooth and more noticeable. We might be intensely aware of the camera when the filmmaker adopts a zoom, although a zoom judiciously combined with a dolly move might be disguised. Zooms draw attention to themselves because they are not mimetic of human perception. Use of them tends to go in and out of fashion.

The speed of such a movement will have an impact on what is conveyed and on whether we notice it. Too fast and it might seem melodramatic. Too slow and we the audience might get ahead of it—should we be aware of it. If a push-in does not mesh with the filmmaker's style, it may draw attention to itself. If it seems incongruous in the context of a film's genre, it may "take us out" of the movie. If an actor's performance commands the frame, alone communicating any of the aspects listed previously, this move may be redundant. Indeed, if too commonly used, it can become formulaic and may constitute a cliché.

A push-in may start *off* the axis of a character's eyeline, on a half-profile perhaps, or even a profile, and then move closer to it. This has the effect of bringing us from a more objective to a more subjective POV. We observe the character and then, as the camera pushes in, come to share in their emotional experience (or find ourselves faced—literally—with their antagonism). At the same time, the background shifts. This might convey the sense of a change in the character, their emotions, their cognition, or their understanding. (It might also provide a new background more pertinent to the drama of the moment or reveal some significant element of it.)

When a push-in works in the contrasting fashion, namely when the camera begins close to the axis of the character's eyeline but moves away from it to give a half-profile or profile, our experience will shift from that of the character to a more objective one and perhaps to what is happening around them—the looks or action of other characters beside them, perhaps. In both moves, the character provides a *pivot* for the camera movement, relating it to the action and rendering it less obvious.

A push-in, or a zoom, might be more substantial, starting with a view of a setting, then coming into a closer shot to emphasize the action: context before detail. Such is the case in *Moonlight*, when we find Juan and Little in a diner after the film's opening sequences. (See the case study in Part III; Jenkins begins with a WS showing diner and customers with Juan and Little center frame. The camera very slowly, almost imperceptibly, zooms in to give a closer 2-shot in which Juan turns to engage Little before a cut to reverse OTS shots.)

The push-in to Peter's bedroom (a z-axis move)—from model to actual room at the end of *Hereditary*'s opening shot, energized and afforded tension by the score— leads to the surprise discovery of a "real" room. (See the case study in Part III.) Not only does this emphasize its subject, but the move also brings about its transformation. (The filmmaker can achieve the opposite effect by having their camera pull back to reveal context or action of which we have previously been unaware—the detail-before-context approach. This can of course be achieved by cutting to a WS, but a less immediate transition may offer a more measured, compelling shift. A cut, by contrast, is over before we know it.)

While pushing forward along the z-axis, the camera might pan in the opposite direction with an approaching character as they come toward and past the lens, holding on them so we then see them recede. This can work also for a lateral cross—for example, as a character moves right to left, the camera performs a parallel move left to right while panning right to left to hold the character in shot. Such a shot becomes more dynamic than a simple parallel track because the background behind the character shifts more quickly. This is an example of a *countermove*, in which the direction the camera travels is opposite to that of the shot's subject.

Movement along the lateral x-axis might be either a pan or a dolly or a combination of both. In such a move, when the shot shifts from composition to composition, the filmmaker *edits in camera*—presenting a sequence of distinct images that might otherwise require separate setups. Movement between each will be decisive, the camera traveling more slowly as it passes the relevant image, perhaps pausing to allow us to take in the relevant information. Such is the case early in Hitchcock's *Rear Window* when, by means of a complex lateral move, we are taken from a view of his neighbors across the way to a CU of Jefferies as he sleeps, down to the plaster over his broken leg on which we read his name, out to an LS of the character reclining in his chair, left to a broken stills camera, then in and up to pause on a photograph of race cars crashing, further up to another showing an explosion and firefighters, quickly left to reveal more journalistic photos of dramatic events, down and across camera equipment to the negative print of a woman on a magazine cover, then further left to a pile of fashion magazines. This complex move—involving not only an overall left-to-right x-axis progression but vertical y-axis and deep z-axis dynamics, serves to tell Jefferies's backstory without a word of dialogue, thus "announcing" his character. A move working in this manner might be said to constitute the visual equivalent of a run-on sentence.

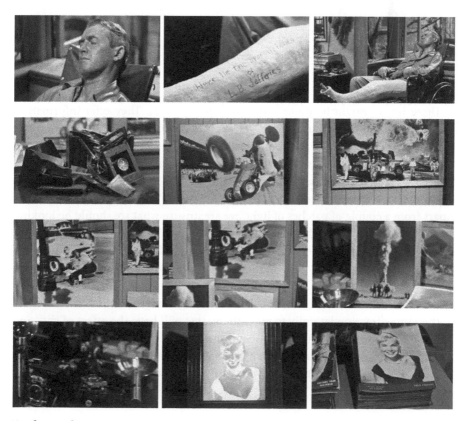

Key frames from *Rear Window* as Hitchcock's complex camera moves along x-, y-, and z-axes, capturing images that reveal L.B. Jefferies's current situation and backstory, "announcing" the movie's protagonist.

A lateral movement might by contrast proceed at a constant pace that allows us just enough time to shift our attention from one element to the next. In *Moonlight*, Jenkins shows us young participants about to start a game of soccer. His camera pans right at a brisk speed calculated to allow us sufficient time to register the face of each boy.

Frames from the pan right and push-in past a row of boys in *Moonlight*. The pan is brisk but allows us to register the face of each boy.

These moves might be described as *narrative* moves. They offer information sequentially by guiding our eyes to points in the frame. A lateral camera move that by contrast allows our attention to wander over the shot, without guiding our eye trace and so leaving us to search for elements of significance, might be considered a *descriptive* move. This approach is used to great effect in *Hereditary*'s opening shot. Here, the pan is conceived as a means of prompting our anxiety. Apart from a couple of patches of light, we are unsure what we should be looking at. As the camera pans right, we anticipate the appearance of some unknown element, whether character or object. (See the case study in Part III.) The pan also gives emphasis to the final push-in on the model house and Peter's bedroom that follows in the same shot.

When a character is seen to move forward diagonally, and the camera dollies in the same direction laterally to meet them, this will have the effect of showing the character more in profile at the beginning of the shot and more frontally at its end as they come closer to the lens, perhaps into a CU, their eyeline nearing the axis of the lens. Here, the camera is active rather than passive, progressively boosting the energy of the shot rather than simply witnessing or observing the action.

As previously stated, camera moves may be supplemented by the placing of a foreground "pivot," whether character or object. This can be between the camera and the character crossing. The dynamics set out earlier are given added complexity by the pivot, which remains static in foreground in the frame as the camera dollies around it, shooting a character crossing behind. In terms of staging, a pivot may be static or moving, but as the camera moves around it, the pivot remains more or less in situ in the frame.

Pivoting moves may be brief. During the family séance scene in *Hereditary*, as Peter turns his head to look behind him, the camera dollies left to right with his head turning right to left. (See the case study in Part III.) Given the dramatic context, the move startles us while the direction of Peter's look suggests a possible new location— the back of the room—for any spirit that might manifest itself. Once again, the camera not only functions as a witness to that look but is complicit in the rendering of it, the bold, abrupt move prompting our reaction.

In the opening scene to *Moonlight*, Jenkins pivots the camera around Terrence and Azu as he reveals the streets of their neighborhood in the shot's swirling background. (See the case study in Part III.) In the process, he shows Juan at key moments, adjacent and listening as the circular movement progresses. Staging and camera here work symbiotically to tell the story and generate energy on the screen. The shot, meanwhile, is complex, utilizing not only pivots but pans, Steadicam tracking, and static placement.

Vertical camera moves—along the y-axis—may be simple, in the form of tilts (vertical pans) and booms (vertical dollies). More pronounced moves, facilitated by cranes and more recently by drones, can have a profound effect. In *Hereditary* there is a simple boom down as Annie peeks under Joan's table during their séance, and another as Steve repeats the movement during the family séance. (See the case study in Part III.) These actions link us to the characters as we share in their experience. A more pronounced y-axis move occurs as Charlie's casket is lowered into the earth, motivating the camera to execute a corresponding descent.

Here the camera performs a *katabasis*, a descent, that leaves us feeling distinctly uneasy. We lose sight of the coffin but find its movement continued by the camera, which takes us into a darkness that ends the film's first movement/act. Indeed, this sinking camera brings us, quite literally, down to earth. A rising camera, by contrast, frequently "uplifts" us with its weightless ascent, or *anabasis*. (See p. 130.)

A notable example of a rising camera can be found at the end of the prelude to Martin Scorsese's *Gangs of New York*, when after the death of priest Vallon, the camera ascends to the heavens (along with his spirit?) to reveal the island of Manhattan in 1846. The bravura movement, serving to reveal the setting, place, and time of this epic movie, is an example of Mackendrick's "winged" camera. (See p. 131.)

As Charlie's casket is lowered in *Hereditary*, the camera correspondingly booms down into the bowels of the earth.

After Priest Vallon's death in *Gangs of New York*, Martin Scorsese's bravura rising camera takes us up to the heavens as it punctuates the end of the film's prelude.

A camera move forward, along the z-axis, takes us *into* the action. Whether motivated or unmotivated, it suggests a *dynamic* camera, one that is no mere witness but an integral component of the energy of the scene or the moment. This is evident, for example, in the *Moonlight* episode described earlier, when Chiron returns home after an emotional day. The camera shares in the energy of the character, moving at his speed and along his path toward his home. It *involves* us, rather than permitting us to stand back and simply observe. In the same film, Juan's opening walk from his car to Terrence and Azu (see the case study in Part III) motivates a z-axis camera move that takes us into his world of drug deals on the block.

Camera movement may be steady or unsteady. For much of the history of cinema, cameras were too heavy for much handheld work. There were, however, exceptions, such as some of the approach of cinematographer Jules Kruger in Abel Gance's innovative epic *Napoleon* (1927) and in less well-known films such as Delmer Dave's *Dark Passage* (1947)—in the opening of which an unsteady, apparently handheld camera is used to show the POV of the protagonist. (Unsteady POV shots are a common form of the handheld mode.) With the influence of French New Wave, of documentary, as cameras have become increasingly portable, as approaches to lighting have become more flexible, and as digital filmmaking has flourished, handheld, unsteady camera work has become more pervasive. On its own terms it is neither correct nor incorrect—what matters is how an unsteady camera relates both to its material and to the visual discourse the filmmaker has chosen throughout their movie:

- The filmmaker may adopt it for specific scenes or moments, or use it throughout an entire movie.
- It might reflect the energy of the moment.
- It may be appropriate to the cultural and social canvas of the film.
- It might render us uneasy.
- It might simply reflect the flow of everyday life, avoiding any hint of undue formality or decorum. Or the filmmaker might use it subversively as an aspect of style that challenges the nature and energy of the world it captures.
- It might work in none of these ways, be used solely for convenience—the speed at which a shot can be achieved—or it might be used to avoid decisive shot size, framing, or angle.
- On the other hand, handheld work can make the camera-actor symbiosis more organic, affording a more free and flexible interaction.

Lensing

Depth of field is an important concept for the reader to understand. Depth in a shot can be segmented into focal planes. With a wide-angle lens and ample light, and depending on the cinematographer's chosen stop, an image might be in focus from the foreground, through the midground, to the background and even beyond With a long lens, in contrast, there may be only a narrow focal plane that is sharp. Neutral lenses, closer to the human eye, will achieve an effect somewhere in between, depending on available light and chosen stop (and the precise quality and characteristics of the lens). The exacting complexities of the technical details that comprise this aspect of the cinematographer's complex art—a craft that combines the skill of visual storytelling with an informed knowledge of the physics of lensing and light—need not greatly concern the reader so long as they understand the broad principles set out earlier.

What, however, might be the effect of different depths of fields on our response, emotionally and cognitively?

With deep focus, every element in the frame will be sharp. Once thought appropriate for comedies, along with broad and bright lighting, this approach has largely fallen out of fashion in this respect. Deep focus will of course show setting and world as well as the action of a shot, so when this is appropriate—when the environment is of particular significance—this can be particularly effective. The physical universe becomes, in effect, a character in the scene. Deep focus is particularly effective when applied to raking angles that reveal ceilings or floors. Complex receding backgrounds, perhaps seen through doorways or other portals, give a sense of depth to the image that a narrower focal plane will obscure. Scope and scale behind the action will also be emphasized. Action itself, meanwhile, can be placed in the foreground, midground, or background while maintaining sharpness on elements in all other planes. Movement along the z-axis will seem more pronounced than it would be to the human eye. (Masterly use of wide-angle lenses can be seen in Greg Toland's cinematography in *Citizen Kane*, achieved through the precise nature of his lenses and the *f-stops* he employed: the amount of light the lens allows to pass through it and the light the camera lets into it.)

When, in contrast, the focus is restricted to a particular plane, and when other areas are softer, our attention will be drawn to what is sharp. In a deep 2-shot, the filmmaker may shift focus from a character in the foreground who speaks (perhaps in profile or facing the camera) to a character deeper in the shot, who responds, or more broadly put, they may rack focus from one significant element to another. The decision of when to rack focus, to whom or what to rack, or whether to rack focus at all is a specific aspect of the filmmaker's storytelling craft. Such varying of the emphasis within a shot may not necessarily be evident on first viewing but on subsequent engagement can reveal much about the thought processes of the filmmaker. (See how, as shown earlier, Jenkins, in *Moonlight*, chooses to keep focus on the back of Little's head as he turns to his mother's approach, rather than racking focus to Paula.) This visual resource is, in effect, another form of editing in camera—an effect apparent in *Hereditary* when Charlie, in class, is shown in profile and the focus is racked rapidly to a bird hitting a window off to her side, then slowly back to her as we register her lack of reaction and its contrast with that of her classmates.

A long lens giving a narrow depth of field has the effect of compressing depth and perspective (as opposed to the exaggeration of these elements afforded by a wide-angle lens) and lessening our sense of movement by the camera or character along the z-axis. This may convey a sense of visual pressure, even of claustrophobia, and emphasize the drama of the action as the setting of the scene in effect disappears and our attention is directed to significant characters or objects alone.

When the filmmaker shoots different shot sizes from the same angle, using different lenses, and the camera remains in the same position, the background becomes softer and less evident the longer the lens that is used. Since this very often relates to the pitch of the drama and tension as a scene progresses, the softening of background and the heightening of emphasis on a character's expressions and gestures will invariably prove appropriate.

A similar effect can be seen when the camera pushes in for a tighter shot size. As the subject comes closer to the lens, the ratio of the distances between character and camera and background and camera is increased, with the background consequently becoming less sharp. Such an effect is evident in the family séance scene from *Hereditary*. (See the case study in Part III.)

It's worth noting that longer *anamorphic* lenses are required to achieve shot sizes identical to those rendered by *spherical* lenses. This results in a narrowed depth of field so that, other considerations discounted, the background given by an anamorphic lens CU will be softer than that of the equivalent spherical lens CU.

There are other differences in quality between spherical and the squeezed anamorphic lenses. Soft background points of light in the former will be circular, while in the latter, in what is known as the *bokeh*, they will be oval in shape. Older anamorphics give more lens distortion, although this has been corrected in newer lenses. Racking focus with an anamorphic lens will cause a "breathing" effect as the vertical axis is expanded or contracted, and background and foreground shift position slightly in the frame. These lenses also yield a wider field of view than their spherical counterparts while creating greater lens flare, generally blue in color. Filmmakers wanting the world and environment to be prominent might opt for spherical lenses; those whose characters might be less aware of or alienated from their backgrounds might opt for anamorphic lenses. Others might employ both for different sections of their movies.

The bokeh of the anamorphic lens is evident in the limited depth of field and oval-shaped street lights in this frame from *Moonlight*.

Anamorphic blue lens flare in *Moonlight*.

The modulation and indeed manipulation of space as we perceive it in a movie—something that is achieved by decisive lensing—is an important resource in cinema's visual language. A filmmaker may choose to make use of it, or they may not. Some will prefer to use neutral lenses consistently. This approach offers more of an approximation to human perception and may coincide with the filmmaker's philosophy and voice. Others will embrace a flexibility of lens selection, choosing to match our perception to each beat of a scene. More flamboyant, inflected lensing will tend to give rise to more heightened realism, while more adherence to neutral, uninflected lensing might tend to create a more naturalistic canvas. Choices to go in either direction, or a path in between the two, may be rooted in the genre within which the filmmaker is working. There is no single correct approach. The filmmaker chooses to work with the nature of their movie, whether conforming to its conventions or subverting them, and with their instinct and vision as a visual storyteller.

10

Editing

The Nature of Cuts and Transitions

It is the very eloquence of the cinema that is constructed in the editing room.
—Orson Welles

The Art of the Editor

Editorial art is comprised of much more than the simple act of joining shots together. The skills of the editor are at the very epicenter of visual and auditory storytelling. Together with the director, and under their auspices, the editor—in the best of all worlds—is the final arbiter of the story to be told and of how to tell it. When to make a cut, when not to make one, which available size and angle to select, which take to use, what material (shots, scenes, entire sequences) should be included in the final cut and what left out, what order suits the narrative and which scenes might need to be reordered—these constitute some of the questions director and editor encounter. Like the director, the editor is concerned both with the detail of the scene, with the granular development of an episode, and also with the architecture of the entire film. The flow of emotion, energy, and tension; the audience's shifting relationships to characters; the dissemination or concealment of information; and how such aspects relate to the movie's passage and structure—these are primary concerns of the editor.

The editing of a film determines the meaning of individual moments and scenes. The timing of a cut bears upon the meaning of the incoming shot while modulating the effect of the one outgoing. The order of shots and indeed of entire scenes and sequences affects the meaning of any individual narrative unit. (See the later section on how reading the screenplay after viewings of the film provides insight into how any reordering of scenes informs their meaning and drama. The omission of scenes can further have a profound impact on the narrative.)

Walter Murch's six criteria for making the cut—and just as importantly, for not making the cut (an equally active decision)—listed in his book *In The Blink of an Eye*, offer invaluable insight into the editorial process. Murch lays them out in order of priority as he sees it:

The Art of the Filmmaker. Peter Markham, Oxford University Press. © Oxford University Press 2023. DOI: 10.1093/oso/9780197631522.003.0011

1. Emotion. (Presumably, this might refer both to the emotions within the film and those we feel as viewers.)
2. Story. (Storytelling as the all-important duty of the filmmaker.)
3. Rhythm. (*Rhythm* connects to the flow of energy and is a preferable term to *pace*, which tends to imply that speed is an imperative. It is not.)
4. Eye trace or path. (See Chapter 7.)
5. Planarity. (The two dimensions of the screen and how this relates to what is known as the 180 degree line: the invisible vector between two characters as they look at each other: A looks left to right, B right to left. When an incoming shot crosses this line, however, A looks left to right, but so does B. We might therefore understand them to be looking not at each other but in the same direction. Ozu ignores this dictum, yet most of us accept, indeed revere, his language.)
6. Space. (The three dimensions of the film's world. Murch is known for rarely having visited a location or set since he wishes to create our sense of space and its modulation through editing and without preconceptions derived from actuality. The fictional space the screen depicts, he shows us, is not necessarily the same as the physical space in which the action was staged. It is presented in two dimensions. It changes its nature, deepening, shortening, widening, narrowing, and at times approximating to our daily sense of it, at others pursuing its own dimensionality.)

Narrative POV

To Murch's criteria could be added narrative POV—which character or characters we are "with"; who is our conduit into the story, the drama, and the emotion; and how this determines who we should be seeing, when we should be seeing them, and from what angle and in what shot size. It might be argued that this is related to the first category of emotion, but it's important to recognize it as a specific consideration since it also affects how the audience relates to the perception and cognition of particular characters. Narrative POV is a complex aspect of visual storytelling, one with few hard and fast rules, but the reader might consider which characters they feel most strongly connected to in a film and how much of that connection is prompted not only by dramatic circumstance and by the nature and actions of a particular character—whether one empathizes with them or not—but by the visual language the filmmaker employs in telling the story and, specifically, how this relates to a film's editing.

Cutting from a character's look to a shot of what they see while not cutting from another's to their perception might suggest we are in that first character's narrative POV. When the filmmaker spends time on a character's reactions as another character speaks, that again can place us "with" them. A character's movement might motivate a cut, perhaps to a wider shot so that they remain in the frame—another means by which the filmmaker articulates their narrative POV. One character's move might prompt camera movement while another's does not—again an indication we might be "with" the former. An angle chosen can also place us with a character—see the example in Chapter 9 from Hitchcock's *The Wrong Man*, in which the protagonist Manny turns away from Rose and toward camera, and us, as he reflects on his predicament.

The concept of narrative POV, particularly as it relates to editing, is much broader than the stratagem known as the *POV shot*. The filmmaker shows a character's face and their look, cuts to what they see, cuts to their reaction, and holds for their moment of understanding and perhaps for longer to show them appearing to take a decision then perhaps beginning to speak or take an action as a consequence. (Such a sequence of behavior might be thought of as a *micro-story*.) Thus, we see, understand, and share in the character's perception and comprehension. The world of the character is *our* world too. The character is our conduit into the story, drama, and emotion, even if the shots used are not always the subjective perception of the character. (This approach bears parallels with the literary term *third person intimate* or *limited*, by which we enter the thoughts and feelings of a character although the writer does not describe them in the first person.)

When the filmmaker cuts from a character to something they do *not* see or are unaware of, this takes us *outside* their experience. The narrative POV becomes *third person objective* or *omniscient*: *objective* if we see but do not understand the characters' thoughts or feelings, *omniscient* if we see and understand the perceptions and emotions of all or most.

The Cut

Neophyte filmmakers often cut on dialogue. Cuts should come with the flow of subtext, emotion, action, and movement—this latter being fundamental to rendering a cut smooth, particularly to a new angle. Who speaks is of less importance than who communicates, through looks, or blinks, or gestures, or who perceives, realizes, feels, reacts, then acts.

A cut might also relate to changes in the axis of the drama—see the shots illustrated earlier, in the *Hereditary* party scene when Peter indicates the chocolate cake to Charlie.

Further categories that inform the cut, or the lack of one, or the combination of successive cuts, might be the fostering of suspense, of surprise, of shock. A cut made later than we wish for in some contexts might hold us in suspense, in others bore us. An unexpected cut might surprise or shock us, although when wrongly judged it might startle us to no good purpose. These criteria, though, can be included in Murch's category of rhythm.

Repetition of shots can be used to convey a sense of entrapment, perhaps to render us impatient with the situation—as is the case in *Hereditary* when, outside the group therapy venue, the voluble Joan prevents Annie from driving away. Repeated angles may also serve to avoid showing us other elements in a scene, ones we might be ignorant of or perhaps suspect might be present and about to become apparent. Repetition might also provide focus on a continuing exchange between characters, when constantly changing shot size and/or angle would diffuse the drama and distract us. The family dinner scene in *Hereditary* is a notable example of this. (See the case study in Part III.) In other circumstances, however, repeated sizes and angles may feel monotonous. Context is all.

Modulation of Space and Time

As opposed to its reality on the set or the location, the nature of space on the screen, which may already have been modulated by lens choices, can in the cutting room be created, refined, rendered malleable, ambiguous and made to serve the drama. Through selection of available coverage and angles the editor may offer a faithful recreation of physical reality or its fictional counterpart.

As with space, the modulation, and indeed the manipulation of *the passage of time*, is of prime importance in the editing process. Time can be compressed or expanded across the cut. A conversation shot on reverse singles might consist of individual shots shortened or held in the editing process, which changes its onscreen duration from the original length of an exchange on set. Gaps between the dialogue can be altered, more or less time can be given to a reaction before the next line of dialogue or the next look, or one line might be laid over another as if one character is interrupting their interlocutor.

Time may also be compressed (or expanded) as a character crosses from one place to another. In the first angle they come toward camera, while in the reverse that might come with a cut, we see them walk away. The point at which the cut is made might render them closer to (or further from) their destination so that they appear to arrive in less or more time than it would have taken them, physically, to cross the space in question. There might also be a cut to the place of their arrival, either sooner or later than we have anticipated, given our understanding of the space and distance involved.

Simultaneous actions may also demonstrate manipulated, indeed cheated, time. When an antagonist chases a character, they may be made to appear closer to them than they actually are, so that at the last moment the pursued can be seen to escape the pursuer in the nick of time. Such a contrivance is regularly employed in thrillers and action movies, in which we readily accept the misdirection. To be credible and suspenseful, it must be expertly assembled.

Transitions

Transitions between scenes warrant special consideration in the editorial art. Often conveying an ellipsis in the passage of time while offering punctuation of varying accent, this cut (it may be a dissolve) serves both to separate and conjoin narrative units. A film transition, in terms of its visual characteristics, may be one of affinity, of contrast, or of both.

Transition of contrast in *Nomadland*:

(1) Interior: populated, artificial light, expanding diagonals; Fern in profile.

(2) Exterior: Fern alone, natural light, contracting diagonals, shown from the back.

Transition of affinity in *Nomadland*:

(1) Wide, lateral axis, left to right eye trace, low horizon, three-quarter sky.

(2) Wide, lateral axis, right to left eye trace (to front of moving train, traveling left to right), low horizon, three-quarter sky.

Transition of both affinity and contrast in *Nomadland*:

(1) Affinity: wide, landscape, lateral axis, three-quarter sky. Contrast: day, vehicle, deep axis of road, blue-grey sky, vector to frame right.

(2) Affinity: wide, landscape, lateral axis, three-quarter sky. Contrast: evening, person, right to left axis of Fern's walk, red-streaked sky, vector to frame left.

A transition in *Gangs of New York*, from Amsterdam's Bible thrown in the river to celebrations in Manhattan, exemplifies the combination of affinity and contrast in a transition.

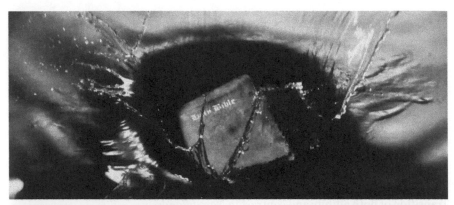

Affinity in this transition: composition, center-punched subject (Bible, Abraham Lincoln outline), framing, circular geometry, contrast between dark and light, energy and direction of explosions (water/fireworks), rhythm, words on screen (Holy Bible, SLAVERY ABOLISHED). Contrast: Shot size (CU/WS), day/night, water/fire, monochrome/color, sinking/rising, suggested amorality/suggested moral progress.

Transitions are central to the flow of the narrative. Many will have been planned by the screenwriter and/or the director. Others will have been discovered during the editing process—when a scene ends earlier than previously planned, for example, or when scenes have been reordered or omitted and new connections have had to be articulated. (Connections are narrative and dramatic as well as visual of course—the flow of emotion and cognition integral.)

The reader might bear in mind how their own cultural approach can have an impact on their response to transitions, and indeed to cuts in general. The imperative in mainstream American cinema is to *cut to the chase*. Once a character or characters have left the frame, there must be a cut to the next shot or scene and further action. Energy must be relentless, the screen constantly dynamic. It may be, however, that empty space such as a room devoid of characters will allow the dramatic import of a scene to resonate, or that an incoming shot might depict emptiness and stasis. The pillow shots (as described by Roger Ebert) of Yasujiro Ozu's films are a famous case in point and a clear example of filmmaking from a very different cultural perspective than the imperatives of a breathless, individualistic cinema. Here, emptiness suggests meaning, while patient rhythm proves as compelling as the acceleration of pace that marks so many American commercial movies, gripping as this so often proves. That said, the work of filmmakers across the world, and indeed within the United States, rarely fit such broad, convenient categorization. It is for the reader to note multiple examples of these differing approaches, all that comes between them, and of the oscillation between the two in the films of any individual filmmaker or in any movie.

Emptiness and stasis in pillow shots from Yasujiro's *An Autumn Afternoon* (1962).

The function of transitions as a means of punctuation between narrative units—scenes and sequences, acts, or movements—also helps us to understand the richness of this facet of cinematic language. The transition may be not only from one episode to another, one place to another, one time to another, one group of characters to another, but also from one tone to another, one flow of energy and level of tension to another—a restarting of tension maybe, for scenes that follow climactic action and/or drama. They may move us from one stage of understanding to another—through a revelation perhaps or new information that enables us to answer a question the story has posed. They may serve to give charge to a new scene that without the impact of the drama of its predecessor might prove less suspenseful. They may also articulate the stanchions of a film's structure—transitions between acts or movements often proving more pronounced than those between scenes or sequences.

11
Sound and Music in Relation to the Screen

Sound

There never was a "silent cinema"—even if silence itself may prove potent against a film's soundscape. Musical accompaniment, mimetic of action on the screen, was an essential part of the audience's engagement before the advent of the "talkies." Providing score and soundscape, musicians brought movies to life, mimicking life's sounds on their instruments, translating its visual energy into sonic momentum and rhythm, setting the tone and emotion of a scene, playing to cultural references—films without this art would have been bereft of life.

To consider the practical aesthetics of the screen without insight into the interaction of sound design, not merely as a supplementary resource but as a coequal, codependent language, would be to diminish the richness of the cinematic address. Robert Bresson's comment quoted in Chapter 3 about the ear going toward the within, the eye to the outer, pinpoints how sound works within us, conveying emotions, prompting images on the screen of the mind, and deepening our engagement.

Sound has several functions. As a means of understanding the multitasking of sound design, the categories of sonic purpose might be delineated as discussed in the following sections.

Verisimilitude

The most obvious aspect of sound design is its function in creating the illusion of reality. The sounds of the environment, without any particular emphasis, without dramatic significance or narrative purpose, and not always consciously heard by us the audience, impart a sense of the life of a setting. The fabric of a world, its nature, activities, breadth, and depth, is readily conjured by its soundscape. What need not be shown would take up too much time, too many resources, and too much of the budget to shoot and can be evoked by effective sound design. Indeed, a film without this sonic dimension might appear curiously dead.

When specific scenes and moments are shown without background accompaniment, however, their tension and drama may in some circumstances be intensified.

The Art of the Filmmaker. Peter Markham, Oxford University Press. © Oxford University Press 2023.
DOI: 10.1093/oso/9780197631522.003.0012

The contrast between broad and deep sonic scope in some scenes and its restriction in others, or in specific beats within a scene, will have a potent impact on our engagement. Without necessarily being aware of the modulation, we find our connection to events on the screen heightened. Such is the case throughout *Hereditary*, in which the ticking of the clock, heard through much of the interior scenes in the Graham home, is absent at key moments—the family séance is one episode in which this occurs. In the same way that changing to a longer lens narrows the focal plane and softens foreground and background, one might consider the concept of the *sonic* plane and its effect. Does the soundscape stretch outward into the world beyond the scene, or is it constrained to the immediate events we are watching? In other words, not only does a soundscape serve to create the illusion of a world, but it may also serve to define the boundaries of its drama.

The Screen of the Mind

While we might be barely conscious of some background sonic elements, others emanating from out of shot might be designed to heighten our awareness. These will evoke images on the screen of the mind—often more powerful than what is depicted. (Images lacking sound, by contrast, do not evoke sounds in our internal ear.) We may have seen the source of a sound before and so recall the image or activity associated with it. Perhaps we have seen a similar event earlier in a movie, so that when we hear it repeated, although we do not see it again, we remember it, projecting its images onto our internal screen. We might also *not* have seen the source of a familiar sound but recognize its source or—rightly or wrongly— guess at it.

Eye Trace

The filmmaker can determine the point upon which our eyes settle in a shot by linking a sound to its source on the screen. This sound may be rendered louder in the mix to draw the eye to a specific visual element. As the shot continues, the dynamics of volume and register may further direct our eyes across the screen.

Narrative POV

When the narrative POV of a scene rests with a certain character, sound can be utilized to convey that character's subjective sense. Sounds that we know are of particular significance to that character but less so for others may be emphasized in the mix.

Subliminal Messaging

Distant sounds we perceive barely consciously can convey hidden messages. In Alfred Hitchcock's *Notorious*, for example, a distant train whistle can be heard in an early scene as Devlin attempts to recruit Alicia as a spy. The faint sound, which we hardly notice, suggests at a deep level the notion of travel. The ticking of the clock in *Hereditary*, which we soon fail to register consciously, communicates a sense of time passing relentlessly. The distant barking of the family's dog in the film, meanwhile, is a means by which Ari Aster heightens our anxiety.

Tonal Dissonance and Irony

The filmmaker may make use of incongruous background sounds to highlight the tone of an episode. The innocent sound of children playing, or of celebratory diegetic music, for example, might be contrasted with some ominous event shown on the screen. Such an effect may be subliminal or pronounced. When it is the latter, this may represent critical comment on the part of the filmmaker on the nature of an episode. Incongruity of tone creates divided reactions in us, prompting more intense engagement on our part. When sound matches fury on screen, our response can be strong indeed and deeply visceral, but too much unvarying sonic reinforcement can yield decreasing returns as it becomes increasingly redundant.

Register

Lower registers can be used to prompt anticipation, tension, and foreboding. Emphasizing them in the equalization of the mix can have impact, especially in a movie theater's auditorium ,where we experience bass notes more intensely. The higher pitch of sounds such as bird song and a gentle breeze in trees may by contrast prompt a sense of lightness—although prolonged, grating high frequencies such has those heard in *Hereditary's* score may on the contrary induce anxiety.

Immersive Experience

Sound from speakers situated around the auditorium of a movie theater serves to envelop us in the emotional and visceral experience of a movie. While our eyes are focused on the screen, the world of the film, its energy, and the power of its drama surround us. We cannot be distanced from what we see, cannot be mere witnesses, but are brought, experientially, into a movie's heightened reality. Such sonic envelopment might contrast with a somewhat distanced engagement offered by a witnessing/ observing camera.

Silence

The decision to subtract sound and deliberately implement silence is as important a step for the sound designer as the addition of effects. Robbed of sound, we feel uneasy and long for its return, thus experiencing suspense. When a scene is quiet, absence of sound is entirely appropriate, but when an episode is noisy, the muting, even eradication, of sound can prove viscerally chilling.

Music

A film might have *non-diegetic music* (score or source music not derived from an immediate setting, added to the soundscape) or *diegetic music* (drawn from the world of the film). Either way, as part of a film's soundscape, music can prove more than a veneer or simple reinforcement to its drama.

The functions of music in film might be compared with those of sound.

Verisimilitude

Diegetic music from radios, TVs, musicians, and other sources serves to convey a sense of period, place, and social milieu. When distant, such music expands the sonic plane while evoking the feeling of daily life.

Narrative POV and Subliminal Messaging

Musical themes and stings (short musical phrases employed to heighten the drama of a moment) that the filmmaker uses in association with a particular character may draw our attention to them at appropriate moments. We may even come to associate a character with a specific instrument: in Hitchcock's *The Wrong Man*, protagonist Manny Balestrero plays double bass. The film's score includes passages from this instrument at key moments, subliminally connecting us to Manny.

Tonal Dissonance and Irony

Source or diegetic music may be particularly effective when used ironically. When the emotions of an event and the tone of the music conflict, the dissonance can prove especially compelling. When, on the other hand, a song or piece of music accompanying an episode projects the same emotions, it may prove redundant. Other dissonance may be created by music that is anachronistic or culturally incongruous. In *Moonlight*, Barry Jenkins accompanies a raucous game of soccer played by Little's peers with Mozart's *Laudate Dominum* from his *Vesperae Solennes de Confessore*, projecting a dignity onto the boys (and revealing it *within* them) that contrasts with their chaotic, rumbustious antics. Sofia Coppola's *Marie Antoinette* (2006) juxtaposes tracks from English post-punk bands with the French eighteenth-century milieu of Louis XIV, offering in the process fresh perspective on her regal characters as youthful rebels.

Register

As with sound, a score's lower register can create a sense of foreboding. The pulsating bass throb that *Hereditary*'s composer Colin Stetson introduces at key points is one example. The film's insistent high strings also prompt feelings of anxiety.

Immersive Experience

A film's score, when effectively judged and when appropriate to a film's genre and identity, can heighten our emotional and visceral engagement intensely. This is the intention of many filmmakers, while others will make more complex use of score and source music. Restrained approaches may prove telling—Chloe Zhao's use of Ludovico Einaudi's plaintive score in *Nomadland* lends poignancy to simple montages of travel. Her judiciously spare addition of his simple themes adds to the power of the episodes they accompany.

Music may have been employed to convey emotion absent in the film. It may have been added without thought in a bid to fill any possible gap in tension and drama. It may have the same function as the narrative and emotion on the screen, a redundant element added for insurance. In some instances, the reader might consider whether, just as a filmmaker may have packed the screen with visual overkill, so their composer might have filled every register of pitch—high, middle, low—and whether this might have created a redundant orchestral wash that overwhelms all else.

A filmmaker, on the contrary, may have chosen to add *no* music to their film, relying solely on the aesthetics of the moving image and its interfunctional soundscape to convey emotion and tone. Bresson, for example, was studious in his eschewal of score. Music in his cinema had to be strictly diegetic. Most of his work avoids music altogether, his soundscape as austere as his visual aesthetic.

12
Reading the Screenplay

When the reader has access to a film's screenplay (not a transcription of the completed movie but a draft that existed before the shoot), a comparison between script and screen can help reveal the substrata and development of the narrative and its representation on the screen. What are the omissions, additions, and revisions? What reordering of scenes and sequences has there been? How has this affected narrative and emotional flow, and how has the story been changed? What information, what explanations have been added or subtracted? Has any repetition been eliminated? What needed to be clear in the screenplay but does not need clarification on the screen? What worked in the screenplay but needs additional elements on the screen so that we may understand it?

Above all, what do images do that words cannot, and vice versa? Have lines of screenplay dialogue been omitted in the cut because nuances of performance and looks render verbal articulation unnecessary? What do these changes tell us about the practical aesthetics of the screen? How do they inform our understanding of the evolutionary process that occurs as one form of discourse is transformed into another?

A screenplay may be thought of as a template or blueprint for the film. While the filmmaker does not simply parrot the screenplay (the screen is not the page), they ignore the writer's connective tissue—its architecture, intricacies, and depth—at their peril, and indeed, at the peril of the movie. (The screenwriter is of course a filmmaker too.) The screen may multitask in a way that words on the page cannot, but this multitasking is best when it grows organically from the script. A screenwriter can give a sense of rhythm and tone in their sentences, their punctuation, and the idiom they choose. How that sense has informed the visual discourse of a movie can be revealed to the reader by a close comparison of page and screen.

It is important to understand that the "writing" of a film does not finish with the work of the screenwriter. It continues through preproduction, the shoot, and postproduction—in the cutting room, the color-timing, the Foley work (postproduction sound effects), and the sound mix. The precise identity of a film becomes evident, even asserts itself at some point during this process—or filmmakers hope it does. Filmmaking is a voyage of discovery, although preferably mapped. Something of the nature of that voyage may become clear to us by understanding how a screenplay has been brought to life on the screen and how the film has found its autonomy through that transformation.

The Art of the Filmmaker. Peter Markham, Oxford University Press. © Oxford University Press 2023.
DOI: 10.1093/oso/9780197631522.003.0013

The screenwriter does not have the benefit of hindsight granted the director and editor, so changes from the screenplay apparent in the film should not be seen as indicative of shortcomings on their part but as revealing of the evolutionary nature of the filmmaking process. Changes, however, may leave residues of previous intentions, rendering a film, in a sense, as palimpsest replete with evidence below its surface of its evolution. What may have worked in one manner has been made to work in another way in the film itself, or perhaps at times something remains in place from the screenplay but lacks its former purpose. What counts is function. Superfluous, distracting, disconnected elements weaken a film's flow and authority. When the latter qualities are present in the screenplay and also on the screen, even if modulated, perhaps even transformed, but each faithful to the other, the filmmakers' work has been realized.

PART III

THE CASE STUDIES

The Three Filmmakers

Ari Aster *Hereditary* (2018)
Barry Jenkins, *Moonlight* (2016)
Chloe Zhao, *Nomadland* (2020)

These three films have been chosen for the diversity of their filmmakers, for the variety of their genre and subject matter, and for the outstanding cinematic art they demonstrate. The fresh vision, energy, and approach of each of these movies, together with the breadth of sensibility exemplified by the three filmmakers, render them paradigms of the art of the filmmaker. Each film excelled both critically and commercially, especially *Hereditary*, crossing often impermeable boundaries between "arthouse" and commercial cinema.

Screenplays are available for *Hereditary* and *Moonlight*—not transcripts of the movies themselves, but preshooting scripts that reveal significant differences from the completed works. This is an aspect of filmmaking vital for the reader to understand. What works on the page may not be so efficacious on the screen and vice versa. The first language serves the second, while the second brings the film to life.

The screenplay available online for *Nomadland* offers an intriguing mix of shooting script and transcript of the completed film, a document that in combination with the movie reveals insights into the filmmaking art of writer-director-editor Chloe Zhao.

Three sequences each from *Hereditary* and *Moonlight* are analyzed in detail. The art of *Nomadland* is analyzed in three sections that observe specific aspects of the filmmaker's approach.

The Art of the Filmmaker. Peter Markham, Oxford University Press. © Oxford University Press 2023.
DOI: 10.1093/oso/9780197631522.003.0014

Ari Aster

Hereditary

Aster's feature debut was a success both at the box office and with critics, and as such it offers inspiration to students of the filmmaker's art and informed readers generally. The precocious accomplishment of this director perhaps renders the virtues of his craft more accessible to those who might otherwise feel daunted by the stature of cinema history's giants—even if Aster has been rated by Bong Joon-ho as one of the world's leading new filmmakers. Unique in straddling the domains of arthouse and genre, Aster's film works on multiple levels: as an anatomy of grief, as a family drama, and as a model of the horror genre, replete with its tropes and conventions, subverted, reinvented, and rejuvenated. A perfect case study in how to make a substantial film that works for both the informed viewer and mass audiences, *Hereditary*'s rigor renders it invaluable for the insights into the art of the filmmaker that it offers.

Hereditary is a genre movie. But what is its genre? Horror, of course, but what genre of horror? Horror of possession, surely. A horror of myth made immediate, too, of the past overtaking the present. Ghost story horror also. Physical, visceral horror, under-the-skin horror. But if it is, as Aster himself says, also a tragedy, a family tragedy, the story of a latter-day doomed house of Atreus, it's a conspiracy thriller too. Such cross-fertilization of genre invites the depth of this filmmaker's discourse and the practical aesthetics through which this is articulated—all of which can be seen from the three sequences chosen for analysis. It also points to the filmmaker's self-awareness: of the tropes of the horror movie; of cinematic language, tone, camera, and editing; and of artifice itself and its contrast to but interplay with "reality" through its mischievous levels of fictionality. Such sure-footed navigation of narrative and its heightened representation on the screen offers the reader an exemplary class in the filmic art.

Hereditary is not adapted from another source but is the original creation of the filmmaker. Its world, while it has everyday elements—classrooms, teenagers' parties, grief counseling groups—is far from everyday. The film's tenebrous house and rooms, its plethora of nightmarish incident, and its alternating *katabases* and *anabases* place it in a realm of its own. Yet the lessons that can be drawn from its forensic viewing reveal universal principles that might be applied to the art of the filmmaker across the board.

Essential in such an exploration of Aster's art is his articulation of his film's prelude. In these scenes he acculturates his audience to his film, as a shot-by-shot analysis demonstrates. The dinner scene utilizes the interaction of performance and editing

The Art of the Filmmaker. Peter Markham, Oxford University Press. © Oxford University Press 2023.
DOI: 10.1093/oso/9780197631522.003.0015

as it builds to its explosive climax. Strongly manifesting the family drama aspect of *Hereditary*, the episode reveals uncomfortable psychological truths. Yet the loss of control of its characters contrasts with a stealthy handling on the part of its filmmaker, meticulous yet vibrant, precise yet emotionally telling. The *grand guignol* of the family séance scene, meanwhile, shows an interfunctionality of staging, camera placement and movement, editing, and sound that together serve its practical aesthetics.

Aspect ratio: 2:1

Lenses: spherical

Hereditary

The Prelude

The prelude is comprised of the following sections:

One: Opening Caption—the Family

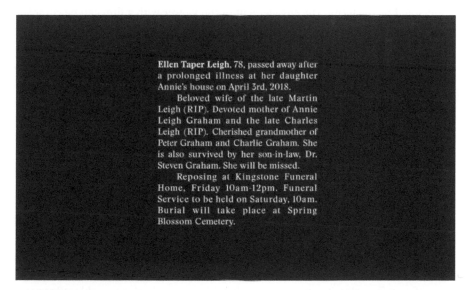

A death, a family, a funeral.

The Art of the Filmmaker. Peter Markham, Oxford University Press. © Oxford University Press 2023.
DOI: 10.1093/oso/9780197631522.003.0016

Summary

We see what appears to be the formal announcement in a local paper of the death and forthcoming funeral of a woman, a grandmother, whose family's names are listed.

Questions

Audience: Will I have time to read this? Who are these people? Am I absorbing this information?

Reader: Why begin a film with text and not an image? What does this caption do? What does it suggest about the characters, their attitudes, their world, and their place in it? What tone does it set? How much time is the audience given to read the caption?

Commentary

In waiting for a film to begin, we anticipate an initial image. When instead we encounter a caption, our expectation of visual engagement is confounded: here the screen presents no image but fifteen lines of text, white on black, a welter of information conveyed not in pictures but in words.

A filmmaker might consider the opening of their film as a means by which they activate the audience. Why should a filmmaker *activate* their audience, and what can we understand by the term? The engagement of the viewer with a film can be complex, multifunctional in nature, and shifting throughout. A filmmaker might therefore choose to initiate the audience in a manner appropriate to the demands and expectations of their ensuing film. *Hereditary* is dense in terms of both content and address to the extent that our engagement as an audience needs necessarily to be active, alert, and focused. By presenting us with so much information, Ari Aster acculturates us in the demands his film is to make. Even at its opening, he expects nothing less than complete attention. This is to be a film made not merely for the purpose of diversion but as the vehicle for rich and challenging cinematic involvement. The density of information concerning events, characters, and their relationships in this caption and the compression of the passage of time (past, present, and future)—the degree of exposition giving a sense of both backstory and story to come, in particular the expectation of a forthcoming funeral and its concomitant period of mourning—make for the necessity of immediate absorption, on our part, of a considerable amount of data.

We get the impression, from the number of names given in a few sentences, of a tightly knit family unit, perhaps formal in its attitudes or at least bound by expectations of such formality. The suggestion is that this is a family of reasonable affluence, if not ostentatious wealth, one in a fixed configuration, somewhat claustrophobic, perhaps inescapable. A succession of generations, central to the story and themes of the film, is presented in immediately comprehensible fashion.

There is barely enough time for us to read the caption before it begins to fade. A low chord is introduced while we are busy reading, so that we become aware of it only after its build has begun. Aster thus startles us with an element of tension we apprehend only after it has been introduced. Note too, how the last word of the text is *cemetery*—even if we have not absorbed all the information offered, we may well have registered the ominous note thus provided as Aster cuts to the movie's first shot.

Conclusion

Information: The death of Ellen Graham, a grandmother. The Graham family. Ellen's upcoming funeral.
Emotion: Unease.
Visceral sensation: Mild claustrophobia, anxiety.
Vision: Death and continuing life—the flow of the generations.

The economy and effectiveness of this caption present an object lesson in multifunctional storytelling. Information, tension, and the visceral sensation prompted by the crescendoing chord come together in no more than twenty-six seconds (within the fade-in and fade-out).

Two: The Setting and the Family—Steve and Peter

(1a) WS through a window. Pull back, pan left: (1b) Slow pan/dolly left, settling finally on:

(1c) A model house. Push in to the bedroom to its left. As it fills the frame a character walks in: (1d).

Summary

The treehouse and Annie's workroom are introduced. Steve and Peter are introduced, along with the family dog. A question is raised as to the whereabouts of Peter's sister.

Questions

Audience: What is the importance of the treehouse? When will we get to find out? Why is Peter so slothful on the morning of the funeral? What was his relationship to his grandmother?
Reader: Why spend so much time panning around this room? Why not begin the film with a character? Why wait to start telling the story? Why the affinity of color and light, rather than the contrasts expected from the horror genre? Why the transition from model room to real room? Why the lateral, "flat space" depiction of Peter's bedroom?

Commentary

The first image of the treehouse appears abruptly as the crescendoing chord heard over the opening caption, having reached its climax, yields to silence. Silence can be very unsettling in a movie, and Aster, having put us on edge with a combination of the caption and the accompanying roar of the chord, creates further unease by presenting an image that—were it not for that echoing silence—might otherwise appear innocuous. Already there is a strong indication of an acute awareness of film language on the part of the filmmaker—we see the frame of the window within the frame of the screen and observe a house beyond a house. The camera looks out, moreover, while placing us *inside* the room, a room about which, at this point, we know nothing. Immediately, as the opening titles appear, the camera begins to pull back slightly, a new score quietly introduced along with the ticking of a clock, the latter perhaps suggesting the countdown to an event. Thus, the building of tension continues. When a camera moves back, especially in a confined space—and here with a chord again building—and we cannot see what is behind, this can prompt a subliminal sense of disquiet.

The window appears to be tightly shut, suggesting no possibility of escape. The slow, descriptive pan that follows establishes the room and its contents, as we can do little but try to absorb the mass of detail. The camera thus teases us with the anticipation of some revelation. Meanwhile new elements are introduced in the music, maintaining the flow of energy and tension even as the camera continues its deliberately slothful journey. Apart from the sheen of a mirror and a lighted lamp, Aster gives us no specific object among the general disorganization and clutter of the room upon which to focus our eyes. Indeed, without a clear direction as to eye path, we tend to feel disoriented, yearning for single points in the frame upon which to fix our gaze. *Where is this leading?* we ask. *What are we supposed to be looking at? When am I going to see something as frightening as this music portends?* The affinity of color and tone in the room offers little of the expressionist language, contrast, and key lighting typical of the horror movie genre. Why? Is it to save that visual vocabulary for later, not employing the currency of the genre at the outset, so that when it is utilized it will be to greater effect? If so, this would reveal a confident avoidance of redundancy and overstatement on the filmmaker's part.

The camera passes a closed door, a hint of the house interior beyond, while the lighted lamp against the far wall suggests a human presence. *Are we going to see someone?* we wonder. *Who though? And when?*

Note how the camera move is not articulated for the purposes of editing in camera but to yield a deliberately slow-paced exploration. It does not move from composition to composition but wanders across the room—a descriptive camera rather than a narrative one, apparently passive rather than dynamic. Yet we find ourselves at its mercy. Although it appears to be an *observing* camera, it is *complicit* in the intentions of the filmmaker, who uses it to create the sense of what Alexander McKendrick described as *anticipation mingled with uncertainty.*

Finally, with low notes of woodwind, the camera settles on a large model of a house set upon a table, its rooms open to our gaze. No sooner has it settled than it begins to push in. Thus, a shot that began by looking *out* of the room now becomes one looking *into* one. Contrasts, opposites, are fundamental to dramatic narrative and its representation on the screen, and here Aster shows a visual symmetry that affords his filmmaking stylistic authority. There's the hint of another contrast too—between life and fiction.

The camera continues to push in, to a bedroom on the second floor of the model, the score supplemented by a footstep-like percussive sound that helps build the flow of energy and the increasing tension created by the camera's forward motion. A modest pool of light, falling upon the chest against the far wall of this bedroom, at last provides a focus for our eyes. The camera dollies in until the room fills the frame, the score increasingly busy with new sounds and rhythms. As this happens, a figure lying in bed is revealed behind a foreground object—a camera on a tripod? (It is a telescope for astronomy, in fact.) At this point there's a knock on the door to frame right and . . .

A character walks in!

This startles us. What was a model room has become "real," make-believe transformed into reality—within the make-believe of the movie, at least. This playfulness—the oscillation of fiction and reality—is further orchestrated by the flat-on frontal view of the room, as if we were looking at a theater stage under a proscenium arch. This also gives a sense, in terms of narrative POV, of third person *objective*—distanced from the characters, we simply watch rather than empathize with them. (Were we to know more of their thoughts and feelings, this approach might become third-person *omniscient*—all-knowing.)

Come on Peter. Wake up Peter! Wake up! There's your suit! the character says, crossing right to left to the bed, followed by a dog. Peter, in the bed, fails to stir until the man, evidently his father (Steve), asks him if he knows where his sister slept last night. Steve then exits with one final command, *Come on Peter, get up!*, which brings the shot to an end. He has mentioned the name *Peter* three times. We surely know it by now and will remember it. The astute viewer, meanwhile, might connect this Peter to the one named in the opening caption.

Three characters have been introduced, perhaps four:

1. The father, who seems to be a parent who holds the household together.
2. Peter, a slothful youth who needs a reprimand to get him out of bed.
3. A sister we have not yet seen, given to behaving unusually.
4. (Maybe) the person responsible for the models and the mess in the room over which the camera has just traveled, the clutter perhaps indicating an aspect of their character.

There's another element of connective tissue here too: the black suits are surely to be worn at the funeral mentioned in the opening caption.

Conclusion

Information: The introduction of two main characters, a father (Steve) and a son, Peter. Peter's slothfulness. Steve as the family organizer. Peter has a troublesome sister, a third character. There is an event about to take place. The family have a dog, an indication of regular domesticity, so do not seem to be a chronically dysfunctional unit, yet.
Emotion: Irritability (Peter). Impatience (Steve).
Visceral sensation: Unease (audience).
Vision: The osmosis of fiction and life. The doubling of elements: treehouse and model house.

The attention Aster pays to the obligations of dramatic narrative—its drive and connective tissue —and its nexus with the visual language of the screen, is rigorous indeed. As an opening shot, his preface is replete with multifunctional elements:

1. The introduction of a world, a specific environment.

2. A tone of foreboding conveyed by the accompanying score, by an *unmotivated camera*— suggesting the presence of a force outside of and invisible to the characters—and by the interplay of reality and fiction.
3. A self-awareness, on the part of the filmmaker, of his filmmaking.
4. The "announcing" of three of the film's main characters and their relationships, and a hint of a fourth.
5. The setting up of the grandmother's funeral.

Three: The Setting and the Family—Steve and Annie

(1a) Starting on Steve's walk, camera booms down to reveal Annie (1b).

Summary

Steve leaves the house to look for Peter's sister while Annie waits in the car.

Questions

Audience: Does Steve think he'll find Peter's sister in the treehouse? Will he? When will we see her? Why does the woman in the car (surely his wife) not help Steve to hurry their children? Will the family arrive at the funeral in time?

Reader: How does the filmmaker maintain our engagement visually? How does he handle his introduction of the new character?

Commentary

In a WS, Steve crosses from right to left—in contrast to the left to right direction of his exit from the bedroom—and heads for the treehouse. (The director is ringing the changes in terms of *screen direction*, scene to scene, shot to shot, and in this manner keeping us engaged.) Steve's determined walk is perhaps an indication of his methodical nature.

The camera booms down to reveal in the foreground a woman sitting in a car. We assume she is Steve's wife. Note how, for a split second, she is introduced in profile, looking right to left, but quickly turns away to look toward Steve—robbing us of our initial view of her—then turns back so that we have a second moment sufficient to register her features.

Conclusion

Information: Steve assumes his daughter may have slept in the treehouse—indeed, her sleeping there might be a regular occurrence. Annie is introduced. Her impatience, perhaps with her husband, perhaps also with their tardy children, suggests the family are running behind with the morning's schedule. She is sitting in the passenger seat, so Steve will be the driver, functioning—as it seems he invariably does—as the parent who attends to the practicalities of daily life.

Emotion: Irritation, exasperation (Annie).

Visceral sensation: Continuing unease (audience).
Vision: The doubling of elements: Two houses, two cars.

Again, there is a multiplicity of function within a single shot. The story moves on while important elements are introduced. The currency of fraught emotion is conveyed with the introduction of the irritable Annie, while insight into the workings of the family unit is broadened and deepened. The audience is left wanting to reconnect with Steve, to be taken into the treehouse to meet his daughter.

Four: The Setting and the Family—Steve and Charlie

(1) Steve rises through a trap door, turns. Cut to: (2) Charlie rising in the reverse shot.

(1) MS of Charlie.

Summary

Steve finds Charlie in the tree house.

Questions

Audience: Why does Charlie choose to sleep away from the family? Why here? What is the meaning of her line, *It's OK?*
Reader: How does the *announcing* (introduction) of Charlie differ from those of Peter and Annie? What is the geometry of line the filmmaker adopts here?

Commentary

Charlie is introduced, and in contrast to the announcing of the previous characters, is present in the first frame. Steve appears through the open trap door, face toward camera, yielding the first (partly obscured) MS of him, and must turn to discover Charlie. This is in itself a story (a "micro-story"): Steve appears, does not see Charlie, turns, and then sees her. That motivates a cut to the reverse angle, past Charlie to him, in which Charlie stands. The subsequent MS gives us a clear view of Charlie and her disheveled demeanor—a sign, we might assume, of her discombobulated character. Her orange top is introduced. This garment and its color will become *memes* in the film—elements repeated with differing significance and meaning.

Charlie's reply to Steve's concern that she might contract pneumonia from the freezing night, *It's OK*, seems odd and not something, at this point, that we understand. The shot, as she stands, suggests a geometry mirrored in many of the film's compositions—the sloping roof behind her and the hint of a church it implies—barely if at all noticeable at this point but a seed for further development. The diagonals of this scene contrast with the horizontals and verticals of the earlier bedroom scene. Staging is significant too, Charlie becoming higher than Steve and looking down on him, only his head and shoulders visible—this raking angle a hint, perhaps, at some power over him she might possess. His exhortation *Come on! Let's go! We're late!* adds to the sense of the clock imposed on the characters' actions—time is moving on, and they need to catch up with their schedule. The tardiness of the children in the face of the parents' need to arrive at the funeral punctually creates a friction that compels us to follow the story to see whether their simple objective will be achieved.

Conclusion

Information: This is Charlie, Peter's sister. She is problematic and behaves oddly. She wears an orange top. The treehouse offers her a retreat from the family house. The family are late for the funeral.
Emotion: Pique, exasperation (Steve).
Visceral sensation: Physical chill (Steve). Chill (audience).
Vision: The crypto-religious hint of the arched roof behind Charlie.

With this third scene, and the third shot of the film, all four of the main characters have been introduced, even if Peter is yet to be seen clearly. We have a sense of the characteristics of each and of their relationship to the others. Key locations have been established: Annie's workroom, Peter's bedroom, the house (although not its several other rooms), the treehouse, exterior and interior, and (to a degree) the geography of the Grahams' property. The two cars, Annie's and Steve's, have also made an appearance. The filmmaker has been marshaling the components of his story, suggesting its emotional foundations, conveying a strong sense of urgency and frustration among the family, and presenting an opening sequence that drives his story toward to the next event.

Five: Transition to the Funeral—Ellen Graham Insert

Summary

A portrait, presumably of deceased grandmother Ellen, is shown in a formally composed static insert that lacks context.

Questions

Audience: *Who* is this? (We know from the first line of the film's opening caption.) *Where* is this? *When* is this? How do we feel about this woman?
Reader: What are the visual elements of affinity and contrast evident in the transition from the previous shot?

Ellen Graham's portrait.

Commentary

Aster ends the previous scene on the MS of Charlie and cuts directly to the uncontextualized portrait photograph of her grandmother, suggesting a bond between the two characters. Our eye trace on Charlie is close to that on the grandmother, our gaze barely shifting from shot to shot. There is on the one hand an *affinity* of mise en scène (subject center placed), and color between the two shots—orange/red, ocher/brown (suggesting a connection between the two characters)—and on the other hand a *contrast* between the geometry of line in Charlie's shot and that of the portrait insert (diagonals to horizontals and verticals) and between a "live" character and one in a portrait. The transition is crisp, marking a passage in time and place from the treehouse. The unremarkable woman the picture reveals, and the white carnations and lilies in the foreground to either side, would seem to imply innocence and ordinariness—a deliberate misdirection on the filmmaker's part. The low woodwind that we hear, however, adds a strong hint of tonal dissonance.

Conclusion

Information: This is Ellen the grandmother.
Emotion: Neutral (audience).
Visceral sensation: A chill from the low woodwind note (audience).
Vision: A precarious, misleading harmony counterpointed by an unsettling score—order about to be undone.

Charlie's connection with Ellen, her grandmother—introduced albeit only in her portrait—is strongly hinted at by the transition from one scene to the next. This is important: Charlie is closer to Ellen than anyone else in the family, the precise nature of their bond one we are to discover. Seeing the portrait alone in the shot without context renders Ellen, even though she is dead, a significant character: she possesses the frame—and in somewhat regal fashion.

Six: The Funeral—Annie's Eulogy

Summary

At the funeral, Annie steps up to give her eulogy, a halting speech that reveals not only something of the character traits of both her mother and herself but also their troubled relationship. The speech soon falters.

(1a) Annie steps into the shot, frame left:

(1b) Boom up and dolly left around Annie as she speaks to:

(1c) Annie in half-profile, looking left to right.

Questions

Audience: What was Annie's exact relationship to her mother? What was Ellen doing in secret, and why did she hide this? If Ellen was so private, why are there so many mourners?

Reader: How does the camera move add tension? Why has the door to the back been left open?

Commentary

A symmetry of composition in the portrait is continued in the shot that follows as Annie sets down her notepad and steps into frame, back to camera. The door at the far end is open, unusual perhaps in such circumstances but admitting a backlight to render Annie's figure more dominant. There's much exposition, given through Annie's lines, about Ellen, and Annie's distanced relationship with her, so it's instructive to understand how Aster bolsters this with a tension created first by Toni Colette's masterly performance—all wary hesitation and halting unease—and second by a camera that booms up and dollies around Annie to reveal her profile (left to right in contrast to her earlier, first profile, right to left—we are already getting a more complete sense of her). The dollying continues before settling once Annie's eyes have both been revealed (and Aster's "announcement" of her as a main character is *almost* complete). The score has ceased so that when Annie pauses there is an uncomfortable silence—uncomfortable to *her* audience no doubt, but above all to us, the audience of the film.

Conclusion

Information: Ellen was *a secretive and private woman* with *private rituals, private friends, private anxieties.* Annie does not seem to have known her mother or her activities well.
Emotion: Loneliness, reticence (Annie). Quiet foreboding (audience).
Visceral sensation: Nervousness (Annie, audience).
Vision: A daughter confronted by her mother's world, of which she has been unaware.

Seven: The Funeral—Charlie and Ellen

Summary

As we hear Annie pick up her speech, we see Charlie in the line passing Ellen's casket. She stops to look at her grandmother before catching the eye of a blond stranger at the back of the room.

(1a) Reveal MS of Charlie. Push in as she comes forward to (1b) her MCU. Cut to:

(2) Charlie's POV of Ellen. Cut to: (3) closer on Ellen's sigil. Cut back to:

(1c) Charlie turning to see a mysterious stranger deep in the shot.

Questions

Audience: What is the significance of Ellen's sigil? Who is the blond man who locks eyes with Charlie?

Reader: What information is Aster communicating, both visually and through Annie's continuing eulogy? How does he organize the passage of time?

Commentary

Aster breaks visually with the flow of linear time as, in the disquieting lacuna of Annie's hesitation, he cuts to a line of mourners paying their respects to Ellen, lying in an open casket. As Annie returns to her eulogy we are put in two present tenses— one conveyed visually, the other through dialogue. In the former narrative, Steve and Peter face out of frame, clearing the shot to reveal Charlie, who stops by the casket— bedecked with white lilies, which remind us of the insert shot. (Because Aster frames out the faces of Steve and Peter, the reveal of Charlie—whose face he does show—is emphasized.) In this new shot, the background is deep, a contrast to the previous shot of Annie with its lateral, midspace background.

Since Charlie's look at her grandmother is shown—motivated by Annie's lines *She was a very difficult woman to read. If you ever thought you knew what was going on with her . . . and God forbid you tried to confront that*—while the glances of Steve and Peter are not, there is the suggestion of a singular connection between the girl and the dead woman. From the shot of Ellen, its angle implying Charlie's POV (and its diagonal composition ramping up the sense of drama), Aster cuts to a (not too close) insert of Ellen's sigil medallion—one that is to become a *key image* throughout the movie. There is a moment of triangulation—the intrusion of a third force—when Charlie turns to lock eyes with a smiling stranger at the back of the room, an uncomfortable event for which no explanation is offered. This unsettles us by way of its tonal contrast to Annie's line *She could be the sweetest, warmest, most loving person in the world,* and with the introduction of a ghostly score.

Conclusion

Information: There is a pronounced connection between Charlie and Ellen. Ellen wore a sigil medallion the significance of which we do not yet understand. A mysterious stranger has a knowing sense of Charlie.
Emotion: Response to Ellen undecipherable (Charlie), puzzlement at the stranger, may be (Charlie).
Visceral sensation: A continuing subcutaneous chill (audience).
Vision: The juxtaposition of neatness (Ellen) and untidiness (Charlie), and more importantly of death and childhood.

Eight: The Funeral—Annie's Eulogy Continued

Summary

Annie reveals more about Ellen and herself, both tending to stubbornness. Peter and Steve listen while Charlie, evidently given to making a habitual clicking sound, draws her mother's face on a sketch pad, which an irritated Steve closes. Annie registers this.

Questions

Audience: What is the significance of Charlie's clicking sound? Why does she draw an ugly caricature of her mother? If this behavior is typical, what does it portend?
Reader: What is the effect of showing Peter in MCU for the first time? How is Charlie's click introduced and explained?

(1) MS of Annie. Cut to: (2) MCU of Peter. Cut to:

(3a) CU of Steve. Cut to: (3b) Steve looking down. Cut to:

(4) His POV, Charlie's sketch pad. Cut to: (5) CU of Charlie (she makes a clicking sound).

(6) 3-shot of Steve, Charlie, and Peter. Cut to: (7) wide on Annie and Ellen's portrait.

Commentary

We return to Annie, now seen frontally in an MS, a clear view of her for which we the audience have been made to wait and which completes Aster's introduction of her as we learn she is as stubborn as her mother. The dual time of the previous scene reverts to the single present of her eulogy. We hear a strange clicking sound, Annie shooting a look that prompts a cut to a MCU of Peter—the first close shot of him, which completes the announcement of his character that began in the film's opening scene. (The cut to Peter on Annie's comment about stubbornness suggests that her son might also be prone to this.) The source of the click or *tock* sound remains unexplained.

A closer shot on Steve follows, in which, as we hear a second *tock*, he turns into a profile that motivates a cut to his POV of a grotesque drawing—Charlie's sketch of her mother—then a CU on Charlie, who gives a third *tock* (now we know she is the one making the sound). There's a cut to a WS showing all three seated family members, other mourners present behind, in which Steve closes Charlie's sketchbook. The configuration in the 3-shot is lateral, as opposed to the earlier deep-space composition of Charlie and the stranger—a hint here perhaps of enforced family harmony.

Aster, in this sequence of shots, presents a MCU of Peter, a CU of Steve, Charlie's sketchbook with its drawing—the face of Annie—a CU of Charlie, and then Steve, Charlie, and Peter together in a single frame, as Steve, managing a problematic situation as always, closes the sketchbook. His subsequent look at Annie motivates a cut to her, a shot in which the portrait of her mother is placed to one side, camera right, a bunch of the white lilies to her other side, camera left—a visual connection to the initial insert showing Ellen's portrait between bunches of lilies. Annie has meanwhile said about Ellen—furthering the depth of our understanding—*that if she ever was mistaken, that was your opinion, and you were wrong.*

Conclusion

Information: Peter appears to be somewhat in a world of his own. Charlie is troubled and seemingly resentful of her mother. Judging from Steve's mildly irritated reaction to her drawing, she is given to sketching such grotesque portraits. Ellen was a woman of contradictions, warm but stubborn, the latter quality shared by Annie, and perhaps Peter.

Emotion: Fear, resentment (Annie). Irritation (Steve). Anger (Charlie—seen in the drawing of her mother).

Visceral sensation: A continuing subcutaneous chill (audience).

Vision: A precarious, misleading harmony. The family unit as an arena of friction and conflict.

A Note on the Funeral Thus Far

The welter of information the filmmaker provides in three brief scenes is communicated by his use of all the resources of the filmmaker. Annie's dialogue, Toni Collette's performance, Aster's staging, shot selection, camera placement, editing, and the score are combined and juxtaposed to allow for the dense, simultaneous expression of multiple elements conveying both information and emotion. Yet there is always clarity, Aster avoiding confusion through the precision of his storytelling, which might be seen as an example of Walter Murch's rule of "two and a half": the concept that with fewer than two and a half elements, an audience might become bored, with more it finds itself confused, and with two and a half it remains engaged. We *listen* to Annie's words, *watch* the actions of the characters, and *hear* the score (hearing perhaps an example of Murch's "half").

Nine: The Funeral—Final Scene

Summary

Charlie, watching as a funeral director moistens Ellen's lips with oil, bites a chunk from a chocolate bar. Steve leans into the frame, asking his daughter whether it contains nuts. Annie repeats the inquiry as Steve leads daughter and mother out of the room. Peter follows.

(1a) A mourner passes Ellen's casket.

(1b) A funeral director appears. Cut to:

(2) CU of hand moistening the corpse's lips. Cut to: (3) wide MS of Charlie watching. Cut to:

(4a) MCU of Charlie as she bites a chocolate bar. (4b) Steve steps into the frame.

(4c) Steve leads Charlie out as Annie enters the frame. (4d) Peter is the last to leave.

Questions

Audience: What was special about the relationship between Charlie and her grand-mother? How serious is Charlie's nut allergy?

Reader: How does the filmmaker connect Charlie to Ellen here? Why does Aster have Steve's question of the possibility of nuts in Charlie's chocolate be repeated by Annie, thus ensuring we register the information? What does the manner of Peter's exit—apart from and behind the others—suggest?

Commentary

The incoming shot looks toward a window, whereas the outgoing shot of the previous scene looked toward a wall. In that sense this is a transition of contrast, although in the way both shots share an aspect of lateral, midspace, it is also a transition of affinity. Both aspects are clearly realized in a decisive cut that links the new scene to the old while also making a clean break from it.

This first shot, over Charlie's shoulder, begins as a mourner crosses out of frame from the center to the left, revealing Ellen in her casket. Annie's turn to the right in the previous shot has drawn our eye directly to the man crossing in this new scene, his movement affording the incoming shot an energy, while concealing, albeit briefly, a central element: Ellen in her open casket.

Continuing our view over Charlie's shoulder, the funeral director steps in from the right of frame, following the direction of the extra's movement, to moisten Ellen's lips. It isn't immediately obvious that Charlie is the character in soft focus to the right of frame over whose shoulder we view the action; this is revealed with a generous MS of the quizzical Charlie, who reaches into her pocket. One mourner stands to the left of frame, another in shadow through the doorway to the right. The eye therefore rests immediately on the black-clad Charlie. The uncluttered background—the painting, three vases of white lilies (reminders of the shot of grandmother's portrait), set against a blank wall—facilitates this. The movement of Charlie's right hand then renders seamless the cut to the movement of the funeral director's hand as she adds the final touches to the corpse's lips. This tighter shot signifies a considerable degree of fascination on the part of Charlie. (With the oil on the lips, Aster perhaps provides a subliminal message, one of resurrection.) The funeral director exits to the left, wiping the frame, the shot ending on Ellen's profile.

There follows a cut to a MCU of Charlie, alone in the frame, as she bites from a chocolate bar. This tighter shot, matching the previous tighter shot on Ellen, emphasizes her preoccupation with what she has just witnessed. Steve steps in, seemingly unaware of the focus of his daughter's attention, to ask whether her chocolate contains nuts. The shot continues as he leads Charlie back to the doorway, Annie stepping into frame to repeat his question. Peter enters the shot and briefly looks back—Aster ensuring we register him—as the family exit, together in one shot for the first time in the movie, their introduction complete as its prelude is coming to an end. An ominous chord fades up as we mix through to the driveway leading up to the family house for the next sequence.

Conclusion

Information: Charlie has a profound connection to her grandmother. She likes chocolate and is allergic to nuts. Charlie and Peter seem somewhat disconnected from their parents, although in different ways.
Emotion: Unsettled (Charlie). Disquiet (audience). Note—we worry for Charlie yet are worried *by* her. She seems vulnerable yet is not entirely sympathetic.
Visceral sensation: The application of a cream applied to the lips of the dead woman maintains the chill of these early scenes. The contrast with the chocolate on Charlie's living lips prompts in us a tactile sense.
Vision: The juxtaposition of life and death.

Screenplay versus Film

In the screenplay, the first shot of the film is described as beginning not on a treehouse seen through a window, but within Annie's workroom. The effectiveness of the opening frame in the movie and the continuing shot would be lost—the immediate introduction of the treehouse, along with the questions this poses, the frame-within-a-frame composition, the loss of eye path as the camera moves away from the window to pan around the room, and the contrast between the treehouse and Annie's model house—would each be lacking were the film to have followed the screenplay. The second scene—Steve walking out of the house to the treehouse and Annie revealed, impatient, in the car—would introduce two completely new elements (the treehouse and Annie), not just one (Annie), which would render it less effective; the parceling out of increments of information generally needs to be paced, and the introduction of Annie in particular deserves its own unimpeded moment.

In the screenplay, Annie is described as *wearing a delicate NECKLACE bearing an ORNATE SIGIL, which she compulsively fingers*. Were the sigil thus introduced it would have connected this key motif to Annie rather than Ellen. Annie wears a sigil in the film, but by making us wait to see it clearly until we see Ellen, when we see it from Charlie's POV furthermore, Aster links it closely to Ellen and Charlie.

The screenplay has Charlie's drawing pad present in the treehouse scene. In the film it is absent, awaiting its revelation during Annie's eulogy. The introduction of Charlie, asleep in the treehouse, is thus not weakened by extraneous information and renders our registering of her immediate. The shoebox described on the page is present, although not immediately noticeable.

In the screenplay, the funeral service begins with a description of those in attendance, the introduction of Ellen's open casket, and her photo. A *large woman* is speaking, Charlie makes a clicking noise with her tongue, and a bird flies in. All this before Annie begins her speech. Again, Aster introduces important elements more decisively in his film. Rather than setting the scene—as he does in the screenplay—he chooses to begin the service in medias res as Annie steps up to speak. Economy wins out over description. The element of the bird, perhaps a foreshadowing of the pigeon that flies into the window of Charlie's classroom later in the movie, is also excised. Too much strangeness might militate against the film's tone of insidious chill. In the movie, Aster does not explain the nature of Charlie's click immediately but makes us wait to discover its source—in the process emphasizing its importance.

As written, the scene in which Charlie pauses by the open casket occurs after the completion of Annie's eulogy. This makes sense in terms of the address the screenplay makes to the reader. In his film Aster places this episode midway through the eulogy, making use of the juxtaposition of the visual presentation of one scene with the dialogue from another for more economical, interconnected storytelling.

The screenplay has Charlie bite into her chocolate bar in the family car on the way home. In the film this happens as she gazes at Ellen in her casket, reinforcing the connection first established when the mourners file past the grandmother. Also, it would seem unlikely that Charlie would take out chocolate in the car in front of her parents. The practical restrictions of shooting inside a car would in addition have yielded limited camera placement and shot choice, making it difficult to isolate Charlie within the frame. What's more, storytelling does not always benefit from following the journey of characters from one place to the next. Showing us the family leaving the funeral, then arriving home—but not having us witness the journey in between—helps the story move on and boosts its narrative energy.

In the screenplay, the car scene includes a conversation about the bird earlier described flying into the funeral service. Without that element in the film, reference to it is of course unnecessary. More than that, Annie's line as written, *That was too weird. The* timing? *It felt it was like my Mom* not only would have made the significance of the incident explicit but also would have accorded the characters an awareness of the supernatural that might have diluted the suspense that we feel—more attuned as we are to the eeriness Aster builds. Charlie's line in the script *I don't like going back without Grandma* similarly overstates what the filmmaker establishes through visual language and the subtext it conveys.

Aster the screenwriter did not have the hindsight possessed by Aster the director. What the screenplay needs to make clear, the movie can suggest. The delicate but vital balance of information and suggestion, descriptive clarity, and communication through events and actions can be realized to best effect through the evolutionary process of writing, previsualization, rehearsal, shooting, and editing. Few filmmakers start from an all-knowing position, and there are few who don't benefit from the enrichment afforded by the processes that follow.

Transition to the Following Sequence

The film cuts to the family car driving up to the house, then to the house interior *before* the family enter. Were that second cut to occur as the door opens, we would not experience a moment to ourselves in the empty lobby. The switch here to a purely third-person *objective* narrative POV echoes the initial pan around Annie's workroom in that it suggests, at a subliminal level, a force outside the family's human presence. The storyteller crosses a boundary before his characters do. Were he to have adhered strictly to their journey—and in another film this might prove effective in connecting us more closely to their emotions and experiences—he would not be setting up a narrative POV in which we not only know and feel what the individual characters do but also know (or at least suspect) *more* than they do. The *hierarchy of knowledge* that Aster establishes here proves increasingly effective as the movie progresses.

(1) Wide on the return home. Cut to (2) the empty lobby, prior to the family's entrance.

As it is, seeing the hall interior, the foreground sitting room, and background stairs before the family enter offers a beat in which we absorb this environment and its configuration. If our attention were purely on the characters and not their home, that information would be less clearly communicated. This is an example of an effective dissemination of increments of information. Also, the unpopulated moment can be seen as punctuation before the beginning of the new act or movement that follows the film's prelude.

Hereditary

The Dinner

This scene is comprised of four sections:

One: The Simmer
Two: The Explosion
Three: Peter's Riposte
Four: Annie's Exit

One: The Simmer

Outgoing shot of previous scene.

The Art of the Filmmaker. Peter Markham, Oxford University Press. © Oxford University Press 2023.
DOI: 10.1093/oso/9780197631522.003.0017

(1) Opening group shot.

(2) MS/MCU of Annie.

(3) MS/MCU of Peter.

(4) MS/MCU of Steve.

(1) Sets up the scene. Without dialogue, there are then cuts from (2) to (3), then again from (2) to (3). Peter's line and look at Steve prompts the cut to him (4). Following this, and using these three setups, there are successive cuts to Annie/Peter/Annie/Peter/ Annie/Peter/Annie/Peter/Annie/Peter/Annie/Peter/Steve/Annie/Peter/Annie/ Peter/Annie. As Annie erupts with anger, the scene moves on to its next section.

Summary

The family pick at their dinners silently until Peter compliments Steve on his cooking. Resenting their implied alliance, Annie sneers, prompting Peter—who is convinced she holds him responsible for Charlie's death—to ask her to explain what's on her mind and riling her to the extent that she loses her temper.

Questions

Audience: How long can this tension last without emotional mayhem breaking out? Reader: Why start with a WS? Why repeat the same setups? Why not cut to different shot sizes and angles? Why never return to the opening WS?

Commentary

The transition from the previous scene works in both narrative and visual respects.

In the outgoing interaction, Steve, seeing Annie painting a model of the aftermath of Charlie's death, worries Peter might see it. Annie replies that it has nothing to do with Peter but is *a neutral view of the accident*. (Is she trying to distance herself from her own sense of guilt?) Angrily announcing that dinner is served, Steve walks out, leaving Annie to add the finishing touches to her tiny model of Charlie's severed head. The cutout of the scene comes an instant after Steve has turned the corner in the background—Ari Aster won't allow the bickering couple their freedom from each other for more than a frame or two! Note also that Steve does not shut the door behind him. Furious with Annie as he is, he leaves open a path to reconciliation. Doors left open or closed at the end of scenes often convey contrasting meanings, informing the ongoing narrative in contrasting ways.

Steve leaves Annie in the outgoing story beat of the prior scene, only to immediately rejoin her in the incoming beat of the next, Peter now present. The protracted silence of the new shot, accentuated by the remorseless ticking of the clock and the distant thrum of cicadas, and punctuated by the sporadic clatter of flatware on plates—indicating that the friction between husband and wife has not abated—is laced with tension and suspense. Will anyone talk? If so, who? Will what they say provoke fresh altercation? To see Steve leave Annie's workroom but then abruptly find the couple together again startles and unsettles us; it traps the characters in their conflict as it traps us as observers of it. The presence of Peter in the frame, meanwhile, adds to our apprehension: Will he soon come across Annie's model? Would the sight of it deepen his trauma? Does he know of his parents' bitter exchange that preceded the dinner? Probably not, in which case he's unprepared for its continuation now.

The hierarchy of knowledge and the dramatic irony it renders this opening shot, communicated by the transition and its elision of passing time, are clear. We know what Steve and Annie each know, and we and the couple know that Peter remains ignorant. Aster now has Peter become a third force brought to bear on his parents' fragile relationship, soon to precipitate its further deterioration and lead to Annie's exit at the end of the scene—a contrast to Steve's departure in the previous episode.

The visual components of the transition are as assured as their narrative counterparts. The physical space of the different rooms and its representation in the respective lensing and framing are similar. In the incoming shot, the depth of field is narrower than that of the outgoing, suggesting a neutral lens was used for Annie's room, and something a little longer for the dinner scene opener—the slightly narrower focal plane emphasizing the tension and entrapping the characters visually. Each composition offers a single-point perspective to the center of the frame—where Steve exits in the first, the corner of the room in the second. Annie is present, center frame in both shots. These are aspects of affinity that connect the shots. There are also components that furnish the cut with contrasts that suggest the story has moved on—Annie faces camera in the outgoing shot but is faced away from camera in the incoming. While she is alone with Steve leaving at the last instant of the prior mise en scène, Peter and Steve are placed to either side of her in the new episode; there is an open door to the back of the previous shot but only the dark corner in the new one. The new mise en scène also works as a visual riposte to Steve's concern for Peter expressed in his altercation with Annie, who now comes between father and son in the frame, the potential threat to Peter that she and her model pose rendered latent through staging and angle.

The filmmaker might have chosen to begin the scene with the single of Steve, his mute ire apparent, then cut to that of Annie, refusing to look at him, then to Peter, finally revealing his presence, then perhaps last of all to the group shot, revealing their spatial relationships. He might have chosen to begin with an insert of a knife and fork cutting food on a plate, then revealed the character performing the action, or maybe with this action in the foreground, tilting up to reveal the character opposite—the permutations are many. The result, however, would surely have proved less dramatic, less tense, and less compelling than the transition he selects. (Another consideration to bear in mind is the effect of varying the nature of the shots employed to start different scenes. Adopting a uniform approach throughout a film can become monotonous—better to adopt the method suited to the particular circumstances of the transition, while considering not only the new scene but previous and subsequent episodes also. Note: This can present the filmmaker with challenges when reordering scenes in the edit.)

Moving on from the transition to the scene itself, the first cut to Annie comes before a word has been spoken. Steve's looks at her, then his look down as he reflects on her mood, motivate this. Annie's eyes are down as she toys with her food. Peter's hand can be seen in the right foreground, soft in focus. Annie throws a look at Peter that motivates a new cut back to him—all the more effective for the subliminal sense of him in her shot. He looks at her, then attends to the food on his plate. Nobody, it seems, wants to eat—picking at their meal provides the characters with a *business* that reveals, under the surface, their concerns. The cut back to Annie here, although she offers no look at the others, is important in that it suggests opposition between mother and son and foreshadows the ensuing verbal conflict. It also comes before the angle returns to Peter, when in attempting to break the ice, or perhaps to goad Annie, he compliments his father on the dinner, a remark motivating the cut to Steve. Annie's isolation is thus contrasted with the bonding of father and son.

From Steve's *Thanks buddy!* the scene cuts again to Annie for her sneer, then to Peter, who fixes his look on her, to Annie again, then to Peter, holding his accusatory stare. After an unbearable silence, Peter asks his mother if she's okay. We see Annie look up, throw glances at Peter and Steve, then respond to the challenge of Peter's subtext: not his spoken *Are you okay Mom?* but his subtextual meaning: *You are not okay.* The scene now cuts from Annie to Peter for his *Is there something on your mind?*, his way of suggesting subtextually *You hold me responsible for Charlie's death!* (He hopes for her reassurance that she *does not* hold him responsible because *he holds himself* responsible.) In her reverse shot Annie counters by throwing Peter's question back at him and starting to deliver the very message he fears.

The two characters are embarked on a journey of confrontation—driven by the guilt both feel—that they are powerless to stop, their comments, loaded at first, growing increasingly direct. When Peter suggests there's something Annie wants to say, Steve, off camera, asks him to demur. Annie's retort to Peter, that he would sneer at anything she says, makes clear her husband's inability to control an exchange spiraling out of control. Peter seizes on her exact words and repeats them, claiming he would never sneer at her while doing precisely that. The pace of cutting speeds up as the sparring of mother and son grows ever more bitter. There's a cut off Peter to Steve, who by his admonition *Peter!* indicates he would prefer to cross swords with his son rather than Annie. Steve's look from Peter to Annie motivates a brief cut to her, after which there's a return to Peter. The characters now speak over each other, their voices rising as the filmmaker cuts back to Annie, then to Peter, who yells his response—a loss of control that provokes Annie, abruptly rising from her seat, to finally explode.

There's a stricture, occasionally heard, that filmmakers should avoid cutting back to the same shot, that such repetition yields tedium, and that changes of framing and/or angle should be sought to aid an imperative of "rising tension." In this scene's opening section, the same setup on Steve is repeated twice, on Peter ten times, and on Annie eleven times. The resulting montage captivates us as the tension rises unbearably. As with the transition into the scene, the characters find themselves trapped, as do we, in the initial unspoken enmity; in the developing rancor that follows; in the visual repetition (the repeated shot sizes and angles new filmmakers may find themselves warned against); in the cutting; and above all in the emotion, friction, and crescendo of conflict. Repetition here is the means of maintaining and building tension. Variation would diffuse it. What is simple, what remains the same, enables what is complex and exponential in its development, keeping it potent under the surface. As the scene progresses, there will come tighter framings, which prove all the more effective for the restraint shown throughout this prelude.

The limiting of angles and shot sizes in a scene of intense emotion such as this also serves to aid performance. The greater the coverage, the more the takes in which the actors must perform. Energy and spontaneity tend to wane over the course of the hours required to shoot a scene of this nature, so more extensive coverage may lead to diminishing returns, even from an accomplished cast such as this one.

Another mantra sometimes aimed at the aspiring director is that characters in a scene need to keep moving. (Perhaps this is derived from theater, where kinetic blocking might be considered preferable to stasis.) Here the characters remain static, rooted to the spot. As with changes of framing and angle, movement would offer release for characters and audience. Any escape from tension, however, is to be achieved only by an emotional eruption which, we will discover, is no release at all.

A further lesson to be taken from Aster's approach as the scene develops, is how his staging and shooting avoid any possibility of breaking the "180 degree rule": what is known as *crossing the line*. With the camera placed in the gap between each of the other two characters, with consistent adherence to the resulting angle, Annie looks camera right at Peter and left at Steve; Peter looks left at Annie, right at Steve; and Steve looks left at Peter and right at Annie. In such simplicity lies function and elegance. We are always clear about where the characters are and at whom they are looking.

Conclusion

Information: Annie and Peter are at loggerheads for reasons as yet unknown. Steve wants to defuse the situation.

Emotion: Simmering resentment, hatred, guilt (Annie, Peter). Fear (Steve).

Visceral sensation: Bile (Annie and Peter). Dread (audience).

Vision: Family strife at its most savage when silent. Emotional conflict exacerbated when characters cannot move.

Through silence, sound, and looks; through subtextual accusation building to its spoken counterpart; and through visual repetition, Aster sets the scene for what is to follow. The contrast with the section to come renders its fury all the more overwhelming.

Two: The Explosion

Annie rises in an MCU (5). Steve reacts in a tight MCU (6). Annie rants in an MS (7), the same setup as (2). Peter, in MCU (8), listens but says nothing. Back to Annie's MCU as she continues (5), with Steve's appalled reaction then shown, Peter soft in left foreground, frame left (6). The shots then alternate between Annie's MCU and Peter's

(5) MCU of Annie.

(6) MCU of Steve.

(7) MS of Annie.

(8) MCU of Peter.

After these shots, (5) MCU of Annie repeated, (6) MCU of Steve, (5) MCU of Annie, (8) MCU of Peter, (5) MCU of Annie.

(9) Wide 3-shot, cut to (8) MCU of Peter, (7) MS of Annie, (4) MS of Steve, (3) MS of Peter, (2) MS of Annie.

MCU before the cut to a wide 3-shot, Steve center frame, Annie's eyeline now right to left (9). Back to Peter's MCU, then to Annie's MS, continuing with the MSs of Steve, Peter, and Annie. As Annie sits, the scene moves on to its next section.

Summary

Annie reprimands Peter, bemoaning his lack of gratitude for her motherhood but going on to raise the topic of Charlie's death and accusing him of being responsible. Refusing to forgive him, she deplores the inability of anyone in the family to admit what they've done.

Questions

Audience: How much more of Annie's cruelty can Peter take? How much more can *we* take? Why doesn't Steve stop this?
Reader: Where can the scene go once emotion is ratcheted up so forcefully? What does the wide 3-shot add?

Commentary

Annie's furious explosion, marked by her rise, prompts Aster to use her tighter MCU, yet he returns to the MS after the cut to Steve. He surely covered her rise in both sizes but opted for the tighter for the power it affords the moment. Coming back to her MS shows her body language. That revealed, a return to the MCU works for the next part of the scene. The cut to Steve for his immediate reaction after Annie's first MCU is significant in that it both emphasizes the shock of her sudden outburst and lets us know that he's as startled as we are. Part of Peter's profile can be seen in soft focus in frame left foreground, and although the eye is obviously drawn to Steve, the inclusion is a subliminal reminder that it is the youth who is bearing the brunt of Annie's temper.

Aster cuts back to Annie in her MS before cutting to the open-mouthed Peter in his own MCU, his emotional pain all too evident through his stunned silence. There follows a series of matching MCUs as the filmmaker pummels us remorselessly with Annie's escalating rage, mindful to insert again the horrified Steve's MCU, his impotence deliberately marked. Looking at the shots on Peter, we catch glimpses of Annie's hand, waved in his face. When we see this, if only subliminally, we retain the image of her features, contorted with her wrath. Notable too is how Aster holds on Peter as his mother yells *Your sister is dead. She's gone forever.* This would be shocking enough were he to show Annie saying it, but holding on Peter as he takes in its lacerating message is harrowing to the point of being unbearable. We want to look away, but so compelling is the drama and so unflinching the performance by actor Alex Wolff that for most of us, such relief proves impossible.

The cut to the new 3-shot midway through this stretch of the scene comes with Annie's line *then maybe we could do something with this.* That *we* motivates the ironic cut to the family, a unit incapable of dealing with its tragedy. The shot works in other respects also. Its mise en scène puts visual pressure on Steve, center frame and sandwiched between the haranguing Annie and the chastised Peter. He's helpless to intervene even if his very placement shows him to be the intervening component of the mise en scène. Annie, meanwhile, now looks at Peter, not from left to right as in previous shots, but from right to left, so that when she again accuses him of not taking *responsibility for anything,* her attack's fresh vector affords its vehemence additional force; she is, visually, surrounding him. He cannot escape. She, meanwhile, is placed on what is generally regarded as the unstable right of frame. To find any measure of equilibrium she needs to make her way to the left—which she manages to do only at the end of the scene.

The filmmaker offers this new angle after two and a half minutes of repeated angles. This affords an energy boost to the storytelling, it allows the welter of emotion to reverberate throughout the room and into the deep background, and it brings each of the characters together on the screen for a moment in which their pain as a family is shared despite their gulf of opposition and individual personal dysfunction. The horizontals and verticals of the production design, meanwhile, as shown in the composition, serve to provide frames within the frame, a means of further visually ensnaring the characters in their environment and thus their predicament.

With the subsequent cut to Peter's MCU, the entire emotional power of that WS is projected onto him. His look at Annie has shifted from left to right, to right to left, accentuating the sense of her surrounding him. Annie is now seen in an MS, her body language and emotional exhaustion clear as she issues one final cry of anguish, claiming that *nobody admits anything they've done.* The MS invites another on Steve, mute still as all he can do is observe. He transfers his look to Peter, now seen also in MS. The damage done in the tighter shots is now given time to sink in with looser framings as the pace slows and energy saps. The breath is short-lived, however; Annie quietens and sits down, bringing this section of the scene to a close. It will be Peter who, unable to let the sleeping dogs of Annie's abuse lie, cannot prevent himself from rekindling the conflict.

It's worth noting, in respect of the two sizes used for the singles on each character, that this can also prove efficacious in the process of shooting. The change of lens but not of angle or lighting takes up less time than a shift of axis. It may be tempting for the director to move on to a new setup once they have their desired take, but they might be mindful of how invaluable a tighter size can prove and how simple a task its shooting can be. While this book does not aim to describe the processes of physical production, it should be noted, in a case like this, how considerations of practicality in the shoot may coincide with those of optimal visual language.

Conclusion

Information: Annie's outburst wounds Peter deeply and renders Steve incapable of protecting his son.
Emotion: Rage (Annie). Pain (Peter). Helplessness (Steve). Alarm (audience).
Visceral sensation: This section of the scene might be described as "stomach churning" (audience).
Vision: Jungian projection as a dynamic of family relationships: Annie attempts to transfer her feelings of guilt over Charlie's death to Peter, while Peter similarly projects his guilt onto Annie.

This section forms the climax of the scene. The visual language is assured, the screenwriting adept, but it is through their interfunctionality and organic connectivity with the performances of Gabriel Byrne, Alex Wolff, and Toni Colette that the full dramatic power of the episode is realized. If *Hereditary* is a horror movie (of demonic conspiracy, of demonic possession), it is also a family tragedy. Here, that latter aspect comes to the fore. Whereas the former presents a fantasy (in such compelling fashion it becomes immersive), the psychological realism of this ferocious minute of screen time resonates with the authority of universal human experience.

As Annie sits, we might be excused for breathing a sigh of relief. That would prove premature however, given the flow of the following section.

Three: Peter's Riposte

Annie sits in her original MS (7). Peter in MCU shoots an accusing stare (8). The tighter size motivates the cut to Annie in her own MCU (5) as she fails to react. Peter throws the issue of guilt back at her, prompting the return to his MCU (8). She reacts

(7) Continued MS of Annie.   (8) Continued MCU of Peter. Held.

(5) Continued MCU of Annie. Held. Cut to (8) Peter, to (7) Annie. Cut to:

(4) Continued MS of Steve. Cut to (5) Annie, to (4) Steve.

(5), at which point Steve, in his looser MS (4), attempts to stop the emotional combat. As he repeats his demand, Annie snarls at Peter (5), then turns to Steve. Steve's MS (4) is repeated.

Summary

Peter accuses Annie of responsibility for Charlie's death. Steve demands that the pair cease their fracas.

Questions

Audience: When will this agony end? Can Annie and Peter ever be reconciled?
Reader: What lessons can be drawn from not having Annie storm out at the end of the previous section? What's gained by continuing the scene after its climax?

Commentary

By holding on the MS of Annie as she sits and again toys with her meal—as though, maybe, she regrets what she has said—there seems to be a breath for characters and audience to recover from the scene's unremitting tension. With the following cut to the MCU of Peter as he stares accusingly at her, and with the return of the earlier protracted silence, however, the excruciating antagonism is re-established. Peter says nothing, and when Aster cuts back to Annie, it's in her MCU, the tauter framing marking a return to the scene's harrowing tension. The shot is held until Peter's line *What about you Mom?*, after which comes the cut back to him for his line *She didn't want to go to the party. So why was she there?* Showing Annie as we hear Peter's first words—his response to the emotional agony she has just inflicted on him— accentuates our sense of her vulnerability. Although we are looking *at* Annie, we are put *with* her as we empathize with her distress. It also provides a ramping up of the drama when we come to Peter for his subsequent comment, a rhetorical question that finally reveals his agenda and prompts the cut to Annie for her reaction of disbelief.

Note how, although Peter has thus far been the vulnerable character in the exchange, Annie now becomes the one to suffer the brickbats. The rewards, as such, of Aster's use of *omniscient narrative POV*—by which we share cognition and empathize and feel emotion with each of the characters—are demonstrated by this switch in the power play between mother and son. If we feel the anguish of Peter in the face of Annie's abuse and perhaps long for him to fight back, when he does just that we are offered little by way of gratification. With the shoe on the other foot, it is *his* behavior that appalls us, his mother's pain that we feel. In this transfer of empathy lies a source of considerable suspense: by never being allowed to settle with any one character for long, we find ourselves constantly uncertain with whom we will find ourselves or what their emotional state might be. This unpredictable path is articulated through Aster's shot selection and editing, writing, directing, and storytelling working together.

At this point, Steve attempts to prevent matters from proceeding even further, his looser framing a reflection of the releasing of tension he hopes in vain to prompt but perhaps also of his emotional distance from the others. Annie's glare at Peter and subsequent turn to him for her reply *Fine!* comes in her MCU by contrast, his reaction following once more in his disempowering MS before there comes the cut to the fresh angle of the WS that ends the scene.

Conclusion

Information: Peter responds to Annie by accusing her of causing Charlie's death.
Emotion: Bitter anger (Peter). Pain and guilt (Annie). Despair (Steve).
Visceral sensation: A further stomach-churning section (audience).
Vision: The feedback loop of projected guilt and accusation.

Four: Annie's Exit

Summary

Annie leaves.

(10) Wide. Annie rises, leaves.

(11) Steve attempts to comfort Peter, gives up, cannot eat his dinner.

Questions

Audience: When will we have relief from this emotional pain?
Reader: How does this lingering WS work so effectively?

Commentary

Such generous final framing might in other circumstances denote a relaxation of tension. In this instance however, the toxic emotion of the preceding minutes reverberates throughout the frame. The flat-space background of the room's wall with its verticals and horizontals, the diagonals to left and right of frame, the sloping beams of the ceiling, and the lamp hanging over the table to highlight the faces of Annie and Steve impose visual pressure on the characters. The sudden sense of loneliness that composition and mise en scène present—everyone diminished in a frame that offers only pools of light isolated within a canvas of shadow—also evokes the irony of the scenario: the family antagonism is intensely claustrophobic yet resonates throughout their surrounding space.

The extensive negative space to the left of the group renders Annie's retreat longer to make and more uncomfortable to watch. Aster holds the shot after she's gone, never cutting to singles of Steve and Peter. Perhaps he continued the singles but decided not to use them since lingering on the WS proves more discomforting. Alfred Hitchcock said the director should *make the audience suffer as much as possible*—and this is what Aster does. Indeed, with Annie gone, the shot loses none of its emotional impact. Steve may be small in the chasm of the frame, but his beats of emotion find poignant expression in the shot, his frustration, his attempt to comfort Peter, and his final despair each articulated through a performance that is a match for the visual language and gauged to function in the context of the frame. The size of the characters in the composition, dwarfed by the dimensions of the room and coming at the end of such a grueling episode, might suggest how puny their lives are in the face of fate (and, indeed, at the hands of their writer-director!). The framing thus serves to reveal a classical tragedy unfolding before our eyes in the guise of horror movie and family drama.

The shot, like the section before, allows time for the intense emotion of the family conflict to resonate. Another common dictum of the screenwriting teacher is to "cut to the chase." Just as at the beginning of the scene, when the filmmaker cuts not to the chase but to the suspense, here he lingers on the final moments of the scene before moving to the next episode. By modulating the pitch of the drama rather than attempting a constant rising frenzy, the filmmaker holds the engagement of his audience while contouring the emotional journeys of each main character. Tension not on the surface lies potent under it. When the hysteria dies down, reflection on the part of characters and audience delivers emotional reverberation.

Conclusion

Information: Annie leaves.
Emotion: Guilt (Annie). Despair (Steve, Peter).
Visceral sensation: Wrenching concussion (Steve, audience).

Vision: Human emotion as remorselessly intense yet puny in the face of the universe.

Finally, the reader will find it worth noting that there has been an intricate dialogue of looks throughout the scene as eloquent as its spoken exchange. They indicate the rich interconnectivity of an episode much of which takes place in silence.

Screenplay versus Film

At the end of the previous scene, Steve left the door behind Annie open as he stormed out. The screenplay by contrast describes how *he SLAMS the door behind him*. The open door, the conduit for Annie to follow him, seems the more effective option. Slamming the door shut would be appropriate to Steve's annoyance, but his not doing so offers both a revealing subtext (he wants her to follow him) and a connection to the dinner scene. It works in the moment but also in context. Slamming shut the door would have worked in the moment but not in context.

In the screenplay there's a scene preceding the Annie-Steve workroom episode between Steve and Peter that takes place in Peter's room. Steve suggests Peter might benefit from counseling but fails to persuade him. There's a note of disconnection between the two at the end, a wariness on Peter's part that would render the moment of mutual solidarity between the two early in the dinner scene an inconsistency in the film's otherwise meticulous tracing of their shifting relationship. Steve's conciliatory behavior is sufficiently conveyed throughout the film without any need for individual scenes such as this, and besides, a focus on his well-meaning attempts to diffuse the family drama might do just that—not for the family but for us, the audience.

In the screenplay there's the following direction: *Annie, Steve, and Peter sit at the dinner table. A fourth chair divides Annie and Peter.* That chair—Charlie's—is not shown in the film. It isn't there as it probably would not have been, given the period of time since the daughter's death—indeterminate but surely a matter of weeks. Nor need it be present for the sake of a scene that works powerfully without it. Annie's raising of the issue of responsibility for Charlie's demise seems motivated by her work on the model prior to the dinner, when she tells Steve it is *a neutral view*—her attempt to distance herself evidently not succeeding.

There follows this description: *Annie is fuming from her last interaction with Steve. Beside her glass: an unswallowed pill.* The pill is not shown in the film. We have seen Annie taking medication shortly before, during her first visit to Joan, but how would we know the pill here is *unswallowed*? We haven't seen her decline to swallow it. For all we know, she could be intending to swallow it later. Not only is it not needed, but it might prove confusing.

From there on, the scene in the film closely adheres to the scripted version. There's no mention of specific looks, so vital to the interactions. These are left to the instincts of the actors.

What follows this episode in the screenplay is, however, significantly different. The film cuts to a brightly colored miniature in Annie's workshop. We then see a haggard Annie, who sees a note to herself to keep working. There follows a cut to her leaving an art supply store where she meets Joan again. In the screenplay all of this occurs later. Immediately after the dinner comes a scene on the page in which Steve confronts Annie over her outburst. The exchange becomes a postmortem of the previous scene, both its text and subtext, that results in Annie blaming herself and Steve claiming *We have no control over anything*. Next comes a scene in Peter's room in which Steve attempts to console his son but succeeds only in provoking his self-deprecation. There follows a brief scene in which Annie apologizes to Steve. Only after this does the screenplay move back to Annie's workroom.

These intervening scenes, omitted in the movie, are unnecessary. Steve's repeated conciliatory sorties have the effect of lessening tension and re-examining the meaning of previous scenes in little need of explanation. His declaration of human powerlessness is the voice of the film speaking, not the character, a needlessly explicit message. The self-recrimination of Annie and Peter make clear what is potent in the subtext of the dinner scene. Annie's apology deflates our ongoing apprehension. Steve the peacemaking character is leading Aster the screenwriter in a placatory direction entirely the opposite to the one Aster the director correctly pursues in the film. The script is too caring of its characters. The film is merciless.

Transition to the Following Sequence

(1) Insert: Annie's miniature (Annie's POV).   (2) MCU of Annie.

The contrast between the darkly shadowed dining room and the brightly lit pastel colors of Annie's miniature startles us while suggesting time has moved on—information confirmed when we see the long-lensed MCU of a drawn, subdued Annie in a change of costume. The transition from a real room (real within the fiction of the film) to a model room (a fiction within the fiction of the film), also an element of contrast, echoes the filmmaker's play of life and fiction introduced in the opening shot of the movie and given further illustration by the model—witnessed two scenes before—of the moments after Charlie's death. The comparison between large and small spaces offers a further contrast. The cut, though, is from one room to another, one interior to another—an element of affinity to connect outgoing and incoming scenes. Sound-wise, the steady but barely noticeable ticking of the clock in the dining room stops as we come to the model. The effect, however, is to go from silence to silence—again an element of affinity in the transition—so that the reverberations of the previous scene linger. Tonally also, the somber outgoing and incoming moments match.

Hereditary

The Family Séance

This scene can be broken down into five sections:

    One: Scene Prelude
    Two: Annie Exhorts Steve and Peter
    Three: The Invocation of Charlie
    Four: The Possession of Annie
    Five: The Resolution

One: Scene Prelude

Starting on a miniature house (1a), its folksy style at odds with Annie's usual work, the camera dollies left and booms up to find Steve and Peter descending the stairs in the background, then pans right and pushes forward, motivated by the advance of father and son, pausing briefly (1b) before they walk through the lobby toward the living room, where Annie is revealed deep in shot (1c). Continuing its dolly forward, the camera tracks around Steve and Peter to give a profile 2-shot, looking right to left as they briefly settle (1d).

Summary

Following from previous scenes in which Annie wakes Peter and Steve, father and son venture downstairs.

Questions

Audience: Why is this model house so unlike Annie's other constructions? What is it that Annie wants Steve and Peter to try?

Reader: How does the filmmaker create energy and convey suspense? How does he motivate camera movement? How does he render a simple journey from one place to another a story in itself?

The Art of the Filmmaker. Peter Markham, Oxford University Press. © Oxford University Press 2023.
DOI: 10.1093/oso/9780197631522.003.0018

Outgoing shot of previous scene: Steve's POV of Peter. (Note the frame within a frame.)

(1a) Stacked miniature house. Dolly left, pan right. (1b) From feet on stairs (seen moving through the bannisters) pan right, track forward.

(1c) Track forward.

(1d) Dolly to the left of Steve and Peter. (Followed by dolly to 1e).

Commentary

As the filmmaker cuts from Steve's POV of Peter through the open bedroom door to the shot of the folksy stacked house below the stairs, our eyes remain fixed to center frame. In this sense, and given the similarity of color and subdued lighting, this is a smooth transition of *affinity*, while cutting from a character to an object is a transition of *contrast*—the duality both connects successive elements and creates a sense of the story moving forward. The miniature house itself, different from Annie's other creations and barely noticeable in any previous scene, begs the question as to its origin. Is it perhaps a treasured possession of Annie's, something from her childhood, somewhat grotesque, a gift from her demonic mother? In the back of shot in three previous scenes, it's evidently a considered object, one that unsettles us slightly, thus foreshadowing the horror of the upcoming episode.

The stacked house provides the pivot for the camera's dolly left as it pans right to find the feet of Peter, then Steve as together they descend the stairs, each pausing briefly (along with the camera) before stepping into the lobby. (We hear their footsteps from the top of the scene.) Why their hesitation? The stairs might be understood as domain 1, the lobby as domain 2, the dining room area as domain 3. With each new territory, their uncertainty grows. The hesitation is credible psychologically, then; neither character is clear about Annie's intentions, and both are consequently wary of what might be about to transpire. When Steve, in his usual role as the one to offer reassurance, whispers to Peter, *It's okay*, their journey continues into the lobby, motivating the camera to dolly forward as they approach the dining room, in which Annie is preparing for the séance, then catching up with them to give the profile 2-shot as they pause at the room's threshold. There's a second moment of stasis here, on the part of both the characters, who hesitate to move into the room, and the camera. Like the first moment, it is significant: Steve and Peter are about to move into domain 3—territory that Annie is marking out as being under her purview. How does Aster provide Steve with the motivation to proceed further? Steve has already reassured Peter at the foot of the stairs. It would be easy, but dull, to repeat this, and besides, now that he's on the verge of territory Annie is making her own, his trepidation has intensified. *It's freezing in here*, he explains. *I'm going to close the windows*. Simple, clear motivation for his action—and now he crosses into the room.

Aster has told the story of the journey from the stairs to the dining room, a walk of three stages, punctuated by two pauses.

Annie's breathlessness, meanwhile, heard throughout these opening moments and emphasized in the sound mix, creates a sense of urgency that vests the measured pace of the shot thus far with energy, tension, and suspense. She's eager to get started—but on what?

Conclusion

Information: Steve has evidently agreed to Annie's request. Annie is anxious to proceed.
Emotion: Impatience. Unease (Steve, Peter). Foreboding (audience).
Visceral sensation: Suspense, the steady rise of adrenalin (audience).
Vision: Meta gothic (stacked house miniature). Territorial/boundary instinct primal in us.
Using staging and camera, and by not cutting, Aster locks the audience into a journey with his characters toward a place of potential danger.

Two: Annie Exhorts Steve and Peter

Steve leaves Peter to cross left into the living room, motivating the camera to dolly left, giving a deep 2-shot, Annie in the foreground to camera left, back to camera,

(1e) Invisible edit as Annie's back comes to fill the frame. Pan to: (1f).

(1g) Lateral 3-shot. Push in to: (1h) Steve/Annie. Pan right to:

(1i) Annie/Peter. Pan left back to (1h) then pull out to: (1g). Then cut to (2a) for the next section.

Steve in the center/right of the frame in the background (1e). When Annie sits, the camera booms down to keep her in the frame, settling as she urges Steve to follow her instructions. Steve resists, so she rises to drag the table to the right, closer to Peter. (On her rise, her back fills the frame, at which point there is an invisible cut that gives the appearance of a continuing take.) The camera now pans and dollies right to contain the action and find Peter to the right of the frame in the resulting 3-shot (1f). Annie drags him toward the table before turning to pull Steve in also, the composition now a lateral 3-shot, the table in the foreground (1g). As Annie issues instructions and Steve protests, the camera pushes in and holds on a mid 2-shot of Steve and Annie (1h), panning right to a 2-shot of Annie and Peter when Steve bids him leave (1i). When Annie begs him, Peter says he'll stay, his look at his father prompting a pan left to a repeat of the Steve-Annie 2-shot, the camera then slowly pulling back to a repeat of the lateral 3-shot (1g), holding this until Annie summons the spirit of Charlie, at which point the long sequence shot that began with the opening of the scene ends and Aster cuts to a profile single of Steve for his reaction. (See the next section.)

Summary

Annie cajoles Steve and Peter into position for the séance. She then invokes Charlie's spirit.

Questions

Audience: How can Annie persuade Steve to agree to take part in the séance? How will he react when he learns of her intentions? Will she be able to raise the spirit of Charlie?

Reader: Why has Aster chosen to shoot the scene thus far in an apparent single take? Why no visible cuts?

Commentary

The filmmaker gives Steve motivation for entering the dining room—to shut the windows because he feels cold. When Annie instructs him not to, he stops in his tracks. Annie, by winning this initial skirmish, takes command. When she sits and orders the others to follow suit, Steve refuses to budge, though. His stubborn silence forces her to act, and she rises to push the table toward Peter; if she can't get the others to the table, she will take the table to the others. (This spares the scene a circular exchange of dialogue between her and Steve, difficult for a writer to resolve.) Notice how Aster has shifted the energy from Steve to Annie, placed in the foreground, larger in the frame, while her action motivates camera movement—she has become the active character, barking instructions and dragging the others into position to either side of her. She now mentions Charlie. This provokes annoyance from Steve, prompting the camera to push in to a 2-shot of the couple, the tension between them energizing the frame. Annie announces that she's a medium; the nature of her intentions is beginning to become clear to Steve. (The audience is of course aware of the earlier séance with Joan, of which Steve and Peter were, and remain, ignorant. When Annie mentions her new acquaintance, we therefore realize, much earlier than the other two characters, what is about to transpire.)

Steve orders Peter to bed, motivating the pan right to an Annie-Peter 2-shot. Annie argues that he must stay, as the family need to be together for the purposes of what is about to take place, and when he agrees, the look he shoots at Steve prompts the camera to pan left, returning to the previous Steve-Annie composition. Notice that Annie is present in both shots, the visual link between father and son but one over which the obsessively managerial Steve has no control. As Annie pleads with the silent Steve to participate, the camera eases back to bring Peter into the frame, thus consolidating her victory—it is she who is dictating camera movement and framing. Her control of the scenario is reflected in this prompting of camera angle and movement and visual language, and thus in what we see.

Steve wearily shakes his head and eventually accepts the hand she offers, the camera continuing to pull back to return to the earlier lateral 3-shot (although tighter), Annie in center frame and the table with glass and candle in the foreground. This visual symmetry presents a precarious harmony to be violently disrupted as the scene continues.

At each point, the camera captures and conveys the drama—the friction, the tension, the configuration of characters from each moment—by movement, framing, and depth of field, the background softer with the push-ins from the 3-shots to the 2-shots. In the Steve-Annie 2-shots, Steve, the character representing family stability, is to the stable left of frame, with Annie, opting for the unpredictable, to the unstable right. In the Annie-Peter 2-shot, Annie, the mother, is to the stronger left, and Peter, the vulnerable son, is to the weaker right.

Conclusion

Information: Annie assumes agency and directs the others. She's about to stage a séance. Steve is impatiently resistant, Peter acquiescent.
Emotion: Exasperation (characters). Uneasy anticipation (audience).
Visceral sensation: Anxiety (Steve, Peter, audience).
Vision: Family conflict the conduit to horror.

The apparent single take the filmmaker employs from the opening shot of the stacked house through the end of this section has the subliminal effect of making us feel as powerless as Steve and Peter in the face of Annie's demands. "Real time" can directly place us in the world and actions of a scene, as it does here, bringing us closer to the narrative POV, emotionally and viscerally, of the characters with whom we enter the scene. Cuts within these two sections of steadily building tension might have disturbed that spatial, temporal, visual, and narrative continuum, offering us a measure of release that the filmmaker must avoid. In the following sections, the pace of the drama accelerates as the scene proceeds, by contrast, through cuts. With each cut, the audience has to catch up with the story and characters as the scene moves forward to the breathless panic of its climax. Without this contrast to the simmering suspense of this opening sequence shot (if achieved in two takes with an invisible join)—which lasts over two and a half minutes—the scene's contrasting second section might have proved less effective.

The sequence shot, moreover, contrasts strongly both with the editorial style of the previous séance with Joan and with that of the family dinner scene before it. In those scenarios, the characters are seated and static, while in this one they cross from the stairs to the lobby to the dining room, the staging of which provides an energy that motivates camera movement and selection of angle, composition, and framing. Only when Annie summons Charlie does the filmmaker cut to a profile CU of Steve. The grip of the opening shot is now broken, a new spell conjured.

Three: The Invocation of Charlie

When Annie summons Charlie, the sequence shot is interrupted by a cut to a profile CU of Steve looking left to right at her (2a). The camera pans to a CU of Annie (2b) as

(2a) MCU of Steve. Pan to: (2b) MCU of Annie. Cut to

(3a) 2-shot of Annie/Peter. Dolly to:

(3b) Peter/Annie. Cut to Annie (2b). Tilt down to:

(2c) Pull out, tilt/boom up to:

(2d) lateral 3-shot. Cut to:

(1) Deep 3-shot (racks focus from Steve to Peter to Annie). Cut to: (5a) fingers on glass. Pull out/tilt up to:

(5b) Lateral 3-shot. Glass shoots toward camera.

she continues her invitation. On her mention of Peter, there is a cut to a tight MCU of him, Annie in the background frame left (3a). There is a creaking sound, and as Annie pauses, Peter turns right to look behind him, motivating the camera to dolly rapidly left to right around him (3b). With Annie's renewed call to Charlie, Aster cuts back to her CU (2b), the camera tilting down to the glass on the table (2c) as she instructs the others to touch it, then it tilts up, pulls back, and booms up slightly to a 3-shot, the lens higher than the group (2d). When Peter speaks (*What the hell!*), there's a cut to a deep profile 3-shot favoring Steve, with Peter in the foreground, the focus racking first from Steve, on his reaction, to Peter for his line *Like, you don't feel the air flexing?*, then to Annie for her growing expression of discomfort (4). With the movement of the glass comes the cut to it (5a), the camera pulling back and tilting up to capture, in a lateral 3-shot, Steve, Annie, and Peter, while showing Annie's elation (5b).

Summary

When Annie invokes the ghost of Charlie, Peter feels "the air flexing," at which point the tumbler on the table moves of its own accord.

Questions

Audience: Will Annie succeed in raising Charlie? Does the flexing of the air mean she has?
Reader: Why the dolly around Peter? What effect does this have on our sense of where Charlie's spirit might be situated? What does it set up?

Commentary

The cut out of the long sequence shot to Steve's profile single comes with Annie's invocation of Charlie and emphasizes his alarm. For him, this marks a further step in her mental deterioration. Notice how, once Annie has called out Charlie's name, the clock stops ticking. Barely perceptible, the subliminal effect is profound, emphasizing as it does the following brief silence and its suspense. Steve's look right motivates the pan right to Annie's CU, a move given additional tension through the reintroduction of the score—Hitchcockian strings in a high register. Her line *Charlie, it's Mommy, and Daddy and Peter!* motivates the cut to Peter, who immediately turns to look behind him, his turn motivating the dollying camera. (Notice how camera and editing are closely connected to story, drama, staging, and performance. The term *coverage* barely describes such precision.)

The camera settles briefly on Peter's look behind him before Aster cuts back to the CU of Annie. The payoff to his look will come later in the scene, but for now the drama centers on the group and the tumbler on the table, the camera pulling back from Annie's single to the wider 3-shot, the fingers of the characters touching the tumbler according to her instruction.

When Annie calls for the spirit of Charlie to move the tumbler, nothing happens—the filmmaker has us wait for that particular frisson, instead shifting the locus of tension from the table to Peter, whose *What the hell! You don't feel that?*, together with the shift of angle on the group, has the effect of further unsettling us. Is Charlie's spirit to manifest itself through the tumbler or from some other area of the room—as was suggested by Peter's previous look behind, and before that, the high angle of the 3-shot?

Note how the focus is racked from Steve to Peter, then to Annie in the course of this new deep 3-shot. First we see Steve for his *What?*, his reaction to Peter's line, then we come to Peter for his answer, and finally, we come briefly to Annie for the distress she displays. The filmmaker privileges us with the sight of this new emotion, since Steve and Peter appear not to notice her change of state. The final racking of focus is not motivated by the interaction of the characters but by the filmmaker's duty to reveal vital information, knowledge that in this instance further feeds the scene's rising tension. This is given added force by the score's brief crescendo, which leads to the cut to the tumbler as it shoots toward camera. With this cut, Aster delivers the promise of the scene: the manifestation of a malevolent spirit, whether it might be Charlie's, Ellen's, or King Paimon's.

Annie's celebratory cry marks the end of the scene's third section as agency now shifts from her to the unseen presence. Had there not been that previous moment when Annie urged the spirit to move the tumbler, which remained in situ, the shock now afforded by its abrupt movement would not be as effective. The sudden shift from the oblique angle on Annie past Peter and before Steve back to the frontal angle on the tumbler on the table, meanwhile, intensifies the "jump scare." Dramatic narrative and visual language thus function together to create and convey visceral sensation.

Conclusion

Information: Annie assumes the power handed her by Joan. Peter is sensitive to the supernatural, while Steve remains untouched. A spirit is finally summoned.
Emotion: Exasperation (Steve). Impatience (Annie). Increasing apprehension (audience).
Visceral sensation: Shock (Steve, Peter, audience).
Vision: Our innate desire to invoke supernatural, dangerous forces, inherent in the horror genre.
This third section of the scene lasts under one minute. After the protracted take of the earlier sections, its intercutting marks an acceleration of pace to match the rise in tension.

Four: The Possession of Annie

The movement of the tumbler is followed by CUs of Steve, looking down to camera right (6), and Peter, looking down to camera left (7). As Annie opens the sketchpad,

(6) CU of Steve.

(7) CU of Peter.

(8a) 3-shot. Slow dolly right and pan left to:

(8b). Continue camera movement to:

(8c) Push in to:

(8d). Cut to:

(9) Insert: bookcase. Cut to whip pan:

(10a). Whip pan to:

(10b) Find 3-shot. Cut to:

(11). Cut to:

(12a) Steve looks under table. Boom up to:

(12b) Steve/Annie. Cut to:

(13) CU of Annie. Cut to:

(14) CU of Peter. Cut to: (6) Steve. Then comes a series of quick cuts to: (12b) Steve and Annie, to (14) Peter, to (6) Steve, back to (12b) Steve and Annie, then:

(15) Pan with Steve as he hurries out camera right. Cut to Annie (13), to Peter (14), to Annie (13), to:

(16a) 3-shot.

the film cuts to a deep 3-shot, right to left forward diagonal, favoring Steve, Peter closest to camera (8a), the camera dollying slowly left (8b) while panning right to give a left to right forward diagonal with Steve closest to camera (8c), then tilting down to the parents' hands fighting for the sketchpad and pen, then tilting back up, then pushing in to the tighter 3-shot (8d). The push-in has hardly settled when, with a crash of glass, Aster cuts for the briefest instant to the bookcase (9), then whip pans (10a) right to left to find the startled family from the back in a 3-shot (10b). As Annie turns to call to Charlie again, the film cuts to the frontal, lateral 3-shot (11), shortly after which the candle sends up a geyser of flame. As the family dog barks in the background, Steve leans down to examine the table's underside (12a). The camera booms up with him as he stares at Annie, now appearing possessed, for a Steve-Annie 2-shot (12b). Aster now cuts to a tight CU of Annie for her continued possession (13), then to a CU of Peter (14) for his reaction, to a CU of Steve for his (as per 6), then back to the Steve-Annie mid 2-shot (12b), to Peter's CU again (14) for his ongoing pleas for this to stop, back to the profile CU of Steve (as per 6), to the Steve-Annie 2-shot again (12b). As if she's become Charlie, the possessed Annie begins to scream that the others are scaring her, at which point Steve rushes out of the room to camera right, the camera panning with him (15). There are then cuts to a BCU of Annie, tightened from (13), for her prolonged scream, to Peter's CU for his resulting distress, the light in the room now turned on (by Steve), then to Annie's BCU again, which is interrupted when Steve throws water over her (16a).

Summary

Annie begs Charlie to draw on her sketchpad as Steve objects and Peter grows increasingly agitated. The spirit signals its presence. Annie becomes possessed. Steve puts a stop to the hysteria.

Questions

Audience: What is this spirit? Is it Charlie? What will it do? Will it repeat the act of supernatural drawing? What could this hysteria be leading to?

Reader: How does Aster make use of the tropes of the horror movie séance? How do editing, camera placement, shot selection, and sound work together to render this section so disturbing? Why is Annie's apparent possession, which could so easily have seemed ridiculous hokum, so effective?

Commentary

The stunned reactions of Steve and Peter in their individual CUs reinforce and prolong the shock of the tumbler moving of its own accord. (Dramatic events lacking reaction shots tend to have less of an impact than those followed by them.) The reactions of Steve and Peter mirror our own consternation, and the moment comes to life. Furthermore, the filmmaker is rigorous in returning to the story of each character, interweaving their perceptions, reactions, and flow of emotion throughout the scene and indeed the film. (In a frantic episode such as this, such an approach requires the acceleration of cuts that Aster later similarly employs as the events of the film move on to their climax.)

When Annie asks Charlie to repeat the act of supernatural drawing, this creates suspense, as we wonder what is going to happen and how the others might react to it. The tension is enhanced by the dollying camera of the 3-shot, with Annie the pivot, while Peter's fear, Annie's patient requests, and the insistent punctuation of the score invest the move with unease and energy. The interaction of the characters—Steve attempting to shut the sketchpad, Annie picking it up and opening it—is decisively contained and resonates emotionally within the framing. The inflection the camera imposes on the action through the diagonal geometry shifts as it dollies from the composition favoring the helpless Steve, deep in shot, to that favoring the increasingly terrified Peter, deep to frame right. There's a tilt down as both Steve and Annie reach for the sketchpad and pen, their hands flailing, that again focuses on the action, then a tilt back up and a push in as the couple continue to argue while Peter grows increasingly distraught. Although Steve and Annie argue, the move directs the pressure of the shot toward Peter so that the camera itself and thus our observation of him are rendered forces acting upon him.

The camera has barely settled when, with the sound of glass breaking, there's an abrupt cut to a shot of the bookcase at the back of the room that lasts less than a second before an invisible cut to a whip pan. Although we hear glass breaking, this is not shown—the brief insert of the bookcase and the whip pan plant the image on *the screen of the mind* so that we *think* we see the event—editing and camera movement prompt our perception of an incident never shown. The whip pan settles on the family, its suddenness and brevity leaving us as startled as the characters.

This frisson or *jump scare* is the payoff to (3a) and (3b) in which the camera dollied around Peter as he turned to look behind him; note how the filmmaker's use of camera placement throughout serves to heighten our unease. There are the shots to the front of the threesome, to the side of Peter, and the dolly and pan across the group to Steve's side, then the shots from behind. The combination creates uncertainty about the possible whereabouts of the spirit's entrance, suggesting its capricious nature. Here again, Aster utilizes the resources of the language of the moving image: staging expresses power play and agency; performances convey unease, fear, and friction; framing contains the moments and specific areas of drama; sound—or the lack of it—works on the audience with subliminal stealth; and camera placement and movement encircle and taunt the characters as if the camera were a presence itself—the spirit of Charlie, or one pretending to be her. How the audience is made to *perceive* the scene *heightens* the scene. This interaction—demonstrated here so clearly—of world and story, and our perception, emotion, and visceral sensation in reaction to it through the filmmaker's address to us, demonstrate the symbiosis of viewer and film that occurs when cinema is working on all levels.

When Annie turns to ask Charlie what might be wrong, Aster cuts to the frontal 3-shot again. We, however, retain the sense of a danger emanating from the back of the room. There's a second of stillness and silence before the candle on the table flares, its flame shooting up to obscure for an instant Annie's face. This jump scare is so effective because of the brief hiatus it interrupts so suddenly; because of the visual stasis that precedes the flame's abrupt movement; because of the sudden loud noise it makes; because of the previous shock of the glass breaking in a different place; because it follows that earlier scare before the audience has time to fully recover from it; and because of the tumbler that moved earlier, next to the candle, locating the spirit's presence here prior to its shift over to the bookcase. The spirit now seems ubiquitous, mischievous, and unpredictable, having seized control from Annie.

As the flame quickly subsides, Aster remains on the frontal 3-shot while the story continues. Steve and Peter puzzle over the candle, their reactions inserted to maintain our engagement with both and to underline the shock at what they and we have just witnessed. When Annie starts to show signs of possession, we know the spirit has settled in one place: within her. The candle simultaneously reignites of its own accord, prompting Steve to step forward to investigate. The story beats here are distinct despite the brevity of this last section of the shot, so that we miss nothing. There's now a cut to Steve as he looks under the table, a visual echo of Annie's similar peering under Joan's table during the earlier séance. As Annie was searching for rational explanations, so is Steve, while Annie herself has moved on to acceptance of supernatural phenomena, and indeed to be possessed.

With the rattle emitted from Annie's throat (very much a possession horror movie trope), Steve rises into a 2-shot, the focus racking to Annie in profile. The score's percussive thrum accompanies Annie's guttural susurrus, abruptly giving way to the Hitchcockian high register strings used throughout the film. The distant barking of the family dog is heard, then Annie speaks in the voice of a child. This tightly designed soundscape, making use of both diegetic and non-diegetic elements, each swiftly superseded by the next, signals the coming acceleration of pace as panic sets in, both for the spirit (or Annie?) and for Peter.

The following cut to a frontal CU of Annie comes after her child-voiced *Hello?* and with Peter's offscreen *Mom?*, which prompts her to turn to him immediately after the cut. She repeats the *Mom?* as if a child, then turns back, looking up and to camera left, and again cries *Mom?* Aster allows us no respite as the climax to the scene approaches. There's an immediate cut to Peter for his *Dad, I don't like this!*—a line that surely articulates our own reaction. Then, as Annie, again in the voice of a child we assume to be Charlie, questions what is going on, and there comes a series of quick cuts: to a CU of Steve; to the 2-shot of Steve and Annie as Annie calls again for mom; to Peter, who continues to beg her to stop; to Steve; then to the Steve-Annie 2-shot, at which point Steve rushes out, motivating the camera's pan to the right.

Throughout this crescendo of the drama, there's an insistence and building of the score, the high-pitched strings punctuated by ominous low chords. Like the new, fast rhythm of the editing, the rapid shifting of camera placement and angle, and the performances of the actors, this conveys a terror out of control. The patient opening to the scene now pays off. Aster, having stretched the spring of suspense to its limit, releases it. No ghost or demon is seen, yet a presence is palpable. Indeed, the scene is more effective for the *absence* of any apparition—a trope of the horror or ghost movie perhaps, but here crafted with mastery by Aster.

Also notable is the terror of the possessed Annie. It's as though the spirit is more afraid than the family, a reversal of our expectations to render the scene all the more frightening. A display of simple malevolence on the part of the visitor here would be less effective—and besides, this is to come in the film's denouement. Using it at this point would lessen the power of its currency later. (One could also argue that if this is Charlie speaking, she would indeed be petrified.) There's a general principle at work as well: a nervous, vulnerable assailant is often more unsettling (and credible) than a confident one. Fear is contagious, in horror movies, in thrillers, and in life. It is visceral, neural, and animal, and here the filmmaker makes use of this primordial force of cinema to the full—until this point the scene has evoked a subcutaneous chill, but here it delivers its promised explosion of comprehensive terror.

Returning to the editing of the scene, as the spirit's panic grows we see Annie's BCU again. There follows a cut to Peter's CU as he screams for his mother to stop. A light is turned on by Steve an instant after the cut, but the hysteria continues to ramp up as the score reinforces the cacophony of screams. There's a cut back to Annie for barely more than a second, then a cut to an earlier angle in which Steve, both literally and metaphorically, throws cold water over Annie. The splash appears to come toward and over the lens, creating a subjective experience for us—as if we ourselves undergo Annie's shock. Seen from the opposite angle, this would merely have *depicted* her experience. Shown as it is here, it *projects* it.

The climactic section of the scene is now complete.

Conclusion

Information: The spirit taunts the family, then manifests itself in Annie. It is now present in the home, taking over the family's territory. Steve is powerless to stop it until he throws cold water over Annie. Peter is helpless and terrified.
Emotion: Apprehension, bewilderment (Steve and Peter) Trauma (Peter). Fear (Charlie or the spirit). Bewilderment (Annie). A combination of all these (audience).
Visceral sensation: Adrenalin, shock, terror (Steve, Peter, Annie, audience).
Vision: The disintegration of the family unit. The power of the mother. The thrill of terror.

The filmmaker's deft modulation of ambiguity and uncertainty throughout this scene works in several ways. Our initial misgivings about the precise nature of Annie's intentions are followed by our doubts as to whether she might succeed and our fear that she could. Joan, apparently, could summon the dead, but will Annie prove capable of bringing back Charlie? We fear she might be, but at the same time we crave to see what happens if she does.

Five: The Resolution

The water throwing (16a) is followed by a cut to the reverse 3-shot for Annie's reaction (17a). The cut back to the initial angle (16b) shows Annie separate from Steve and Peter. Then comes a cut back to the 3-shot favoring Annie (17b), the scene's final shot.

Summary

Annie is released from her possession but does not know what happened. Peter remains distressed. Hostile to Annie, Steve comforts Peter.

(17a) Annie recoils. Cut to: (16b) Steve comforts Peter. Cut to:

(17b) Deep 3-shot.

Questions

Audience: How can Steve empathize with Annie? Will Peter recover? Has the spirit really gone away? When will it return? And how?
Reader: How does the scene resolve itself? How does its ending invite the next step in the story? Can such a brief, final section be effective? Is more needed?

Commentary

With the cut to Annie, the final section and punctuation of the scene begin. The score ceases abruptly, along with Annie's possessed mania, as the family dog continues to bark and Peter to sob—a spare soundscape that contrasts strongly with the preceding pandemonium. Annie appears utterly unaware of what has been transpiring, but Steve, rather than offering her comfort, glares at her as he consoles Peter. Both angles show Annie to be apart from the bonding of Steve and Peter, the final shot revealing her bewilderment. The configuration of characters—Steve and Peter versus Annie—is now consolidated. Annie seems incapable of caring for Peter—a task left to Steve—while her psychological collapse is set to deepen.

The coda is brief but essential, posing questions that drive the narrative onward. Will Annie understand what happened? Can Steve protect Peter?

Conclusion

Information: Annie is ignorant of her possession.
Emotion: Bewilderment, suspicion (characters). Wary relief (audience).
Visceral sensation: Exhaustion (Steve).
Vision: Parental division at the heart of the collapse of the family unit.

This final section yields a break in momentum and energy, allowing the events of the scene to resonate before the start of the film's next movement or act. Now there will come an even greater acceleration toward the collapse of the family unit as each of the three characters progresses toward their fate.

Screenplay versus Film

The order of scenes around this point in the screenplay is significantly different from that in the film. Some scenes in the screenplay are omitted from the film, while the brief vignettes that follow the family séance are not described in the screenplay.

Screenplay order:

1. The séance with Joan.
2. Annie, in her car, hears Charlie's click.
3. The family séance.
4. Annie wants to know what happened. Steve tells her she must see a therapist.
5. Annie's nightmare of ants and setting herself and Peter alight.
6. Peter in his bedroom at night.

Film order:

1. The séance with Joan.
2. Annie, in her car, hears Charlie's click.
5. Annie's nightmare of ants and setting herself and Peter alight.
3. The family séance.
   (There is no subsequent scene between Steve and Annie as in 4 in the preceding list.)
   Vignettes of the model house, of the model depicting the moments after Charlie's death, then the words on Charlie's bedroom wall. (None of these is specified in the screenplay.)
6. Peter in his bedroom at night.

Why did Aster alter the order of scenes?

The Joan séance leaves Annie distraught, her state of mind underlined by the incident of Charlie's click in the car. Tracing her emotional journey from there directly to her ordering of the séance would create psychological and emotional discontinuity. She needs longer to gather herself and find her agency again. Putting her nightmare *before* the family séance allows it to prompt her decision to attempt to invoke Charlie. Were she to act on Joan's instructions immediately upon returning home, as she does in the screenplay, she might appear too readily under Joan's spell—the story demands she has a little further to go before the demonic conspiracy influences her decisions completely.

Also, the interleaving of the various narratives is better served by separating the two séances. Do we really want to see a second so soon after the first? Then again, might we not understand Annie's intentions too early on, when she wakes Peter and Steve, were this to segue from the scene with Joan; isn't it more compelling for us to discover her plan along with the others? The nightmare picks up on Annie's comments during the Joan séance, meanwhile, so the scene's new placement is far from arbitrary. The reader might also reflect that the payoff to the episode with Joan—Annie summons a spirit herself, and in the Graham home, too—is better rendered latent and held in reserve, albeit for one sequence only, rather than being delivered immediately.

The screenplay's scene in which Steve looks back with Annie on her moment of possession seems superfluous. It offers no new information; suggests Steve has hopes Annie might be helped when what he has just witnessed was traumatic; and promises a scene with a new character, a therapist, one Dr. Stetson, which is omitted from the film. In the screenplay the Stetson scene comes later, interrupting Annie's increased disengagement from any rational influence. Though well written, it obstructs the relentless progression of story and character.

There are structural considerations at work here also. With the daughter's apparent reappearance through the possession of Annie, the movement that began after Charlie's funeral has now come full circle. After the crescendo and climax that the scene delivers there can be neither any adequate subsequent ramping up of tension nor any halfway measure in its place. There has to be punctuation and breath in story, rhythm, energy, and emotion, a new starting point from which these elements can again build.

Transition to the Following Sequence

The film's vignettes stated here reprise episodes in the narrative so far: a shot pushing in on the model of the house in Annie's workroom and one on her reconstruction of the moments after Charlie's decapitation.

Aster pushes in on Annie's model of the Grahams' house.

Aster's camera moves over the model of Peter in the car after Charlie's death before the shot dissolves to one of writing on the wall in Charlie's bedroom.

These shots provide the needed punctuation before the new movement or act in the story, one that traces Annie's deterioration, Peter's developing possession, and Steve's inability to cope, all as supernatural forces take ever firmer control. There can be no further family cooperation after the events of the séance. The scenes with Peter that follow return us to his narrative thread and yield new energy. It is only after this that the film returns to Annie when, while working on a model for the gallery, she gets a call from Steve alerting her to *his* call from the distressed Peter. New momentum now picks up.

Barry Jenkins

Moonlight

Jenkins's second feature, adapted from Tarell Alvin McCraney's stage play *In Moonlight Black Boys Look Blue*, met with comprehensive critical approval, was a box office success, and won Academy Awards for Best Picture and Best Adapted Screenplay.

Not only distinctive in its searing authenticity, the film also takes its protagonist through three stages of development: boyhood, youth, and early manhood. The filmmaker must therefore "announce" Chiron, played by three different actors, three times. (He also introduces Chiron's friend and eventual lover Kevin in each of the film's three acts.)

For the reader, this aspect of the film offers invaluable insight into some of the approaches and means by which the filmmaker might introduce (or announce) their main characters. The following chapters explore each of the relevant sequences through a shot-by-shot analysis that attempts to reveal Jenkins's filmmaking art. These preludes not only work in and of themselves but also form a developing architecture of connection. Jenkins realizes the moment, the scene, the act, and the complete film with a rigor that in no way impedes the individual energy or emotion of each—an object lesson in how the filmmaker draws on both the methodical and the intuitive in creating the fabric of their film.

With scenes set "on the block," in Black, working-class homes, in a high school, and in a diner late at night, the movie evokes an everyday world of compelling immediacy. The filmmaker's cinematic artifice, largely invisible to the audience, proves on close inspection to be meticulous; indeed, its effectiveness rests on its unobtrusive functioning. An art that largely conceals art, Jenkins's discourse also demonstrates notable *coups de cinema*—particular shots so precisely crafted that they take root in the audience's cumulative memory as it watches the film and so come to constitute memes in the filmmaker's visual storytelling. The agile aesthetics of Jenkins's movie are both practical and elegant, proof that a poetic sensibility vested in the visual can be both a functional element in a filmmaker's storytelling and a source of profound emotional resonance.

Differences between A24's published screenplay and the film usefully point to the filmmaker's creative process. Changes within a scene, the reordering of episodes, and

The Art of the Filmmaker. Peter Markham, Oxford University Press. © Oxford University Press 2023.
DOI: 10.1093/oso/9780197631522.003.0019

the introduction in the movie of episodes absent in the screenplay reveal Jenkins's ongoing engagement with his material while offering the reader principles of the creative process from conception to physical production to editing.

Aspect ratio: 2.40:1

Lenses: anamorphic

Moonlight

Announcing Little

The opening sequence to the film can be divided into two sections:

> One: Announcing Juan
> Two: Announcing Little

One: Announcing Juan

In a single take, Juan's car comes toward camera (1a), Juan steps out (1b), crosses to Terrence and Azu (1c), and greets Terrence (1d). The camera circles R-L (so the background shifts L-R), pivoting around Terrence and Juan, losing Azu (1e). Juan crosses R-L out of the shot, as Azu steps back into the shot (1f), the camera continuing the circular movement around him and Terrence to find Juan in the background (1g), then continuing as Azu points to Juan (1h), motivating a pan (R-L) to his single (1i). Juan crosses L-R as the camera moves R-L to lose him and find Azu and Terrence, circling them as Terrence sends Azu away (1j), continuing to circle as Juan steps back into the shot, until it settles on a 2-shot of Terrence and Juan (1k). Juan bids Terrence farewell, crosses L-R forward (1l) to find the boys crossing the foreground (1m). Juan then continues to cross forward, now R-L as the boys are again briefly seen, now in the background.

(1a) WS of Juan arriving. Pan to:

The Art of the Filmmaker. Peter Markham, Oxford University Press. © Oxford University Press 2023.
DOI: 10.1093/oso/9780197631522.003.0020

(1b) Juan steps out, crosses to:

(1c) Juan continues to:

(1d) R-L circular camera move (so background shifts L-R):

(1e) R-L circular movement (pivots around Terrence and Juan):

(1f) R-L circular movement:

(1g) Circular move, dolly left:

(1h) Pan left to:

(1i) Juan L-R crosses to:

(1j) Countermove, circle, pull out to:

(1k) To:

(1l) To:

(1m). (1l) Boys cross in the foreground. Juan walks forward R-L as they disappear in the background behind him.

Summary

Juan checks out Terrence's street deals. A group of boys run past.

Questions

Audience: Who is this man? Where are we? Who are the two men he approaches? What does one want from the other? What is the "business" that dark T-shirt is talking about? Does the other man want drugs from him? Why is dark T-shirt nervous of the man called Juan? Why does Juan constantly look around? Is he running this operation? Who are the boys? Where are they going? What is this film about? What is its story?

Reader: Why the single take? What does it achieve? Why introduce Juan and not protagonist Little/Chiron at the start of the film? How does the filmmaker connect us to a drug dealer without alienating us?

Commentary

Before the opening titles are finished, we hear the sound of ocean waves. Although this is quickly superseded by a song, Boris Gardiner's "Every N . . . Is a Star," it provides subliminal information, acculturating us to the ocean as an important motif in the film. The song meanwhile becomes diegetic—the music on Juan's car radio. Recorded in 1973, its inclusion gives a sense that the film is set some time in the not too distant past.

This single take scene that opens the movie warrants analysis composition by composition, fleeting as these frames often are given the fluid framing and energy of this Steadicam shot.

Juan's car comes toward camera until his face is clear. He takes time before he exits, allowing us a moment in which to register him. Juan is the first character we see in the film, and in this scene we will spend some time with him, as we do throughout the first act. From the very start, he provides a conduit into the story so that when he disappears from the film we share with Chiron the feeling of his loss. (There's a miniature crown on Juan's dashboard—not easily noticed on first viewing but seen again when Juan takes Little home with him—that will become significant with the "announcing" of Black in the third act.)

Juan's car is blue, a prominent color in the film's palette. The car in the background is a deep red. Juan's shirt has bands of both colors, which will prove significant as they are applied to Juan and Little/Chiron. The other significant color traced through the film is yellow—as the camera circles around Terrence and Azu, a yellow car can be seen in the distance.

Notice how the sounds of the neighborhood are introduced: a world of activity, of generations, of domesticity. Even though we see no passersby, at least until the group of boys rush through shot at the end of the scene, we get the sense of a community going about its business. The filmmaker's challenge here is to present a scene of surreptitious street drug deals, away from prying eyes, but also to give a sense of the world in which it takes place. Sound design conveys what the scene visually cannot. No cars pass, nobody walks by (apart from a customer of Terrence, seen fleetingly as he runs), but we get the sense of this being a lived-in, bustling locality. (Note how during the banter between Terrence and Azu we hear, subliminally, distant police sirens—a pointer to the illegality of the dealing on the block.)

As Juan steps out of his car, two figures appear on the other side of the street, and as he crosses toward them he motivates the forward movement of the camera, which follows him. (This initial setup is repeated when Juan returns to this street for the night scene with Paula. As a consequence, we instantly recognize where we are. There are the same camera placement, similar framing, same staging, and same camera movement—were these different, we might not recognize the location so readily.)

Juan is a character with whom we are on a journey, although we don't yet know his name. Already he is our conduit into a scene we are to discover is about him. His looks to either side as he crosses the road seem innocent at first—he's watching for traffic, we assume—but they become more frequent as the scene develops. As Juan approaches the two men Terrence and Azu, their febrile banter starts to motivate the energy of the camera.

Notice how the camera loses Azu to camera left and frames on the moment of bonding between Juan and Terrence, and how the latter, shorter than Juan (no doubt cast as such), has to look up at him.

While on this 2-shot, the camera begins to circle right to left, a movement it continues almost until the scene's conclusion. Juan exits the frame, and Azu steps back in, begging Terrence for drugs despite having no means to pay. These two minor characters (Azu is not seen again in the film) provide the pivot for the camera's swift, continuing encirclement, the neighborhood swirling in the background—an element of exposition that, much like the increments of information concerning Juan that this opening episode delivers, we barely notice consciously—although we take in all the filmmaker conveys.

As the shot progresses, we catch Juan in the background, the filmmaker ensuring we never miss his presence for too long. Even if we lose him for an instant as the camera pivots on around Terrence and Azu, he's soon brought back into the frame as Azu calls to him, motivating a pan left to his single as the bickering addict and street-dealing youth drop out of shot. Juan steps forward in this single, and Azu and Terrence now reappear from left of frame, moments after leaving the shot to the right! (As the camera pans to Juan, it also pushes toward him, then pulls out as it continues the pan and loses him, perhaps facilitating a short, unseen cross behind the camera from youth and addict, stepping into the shot from frame left—an example of actors and camera working together.) This deft sleight of hand, invisible to us, subliminally surprises us, serving to build our attention.

The dizzying, encircling camera presses on with its right to left movement, simultaneously panning left to right as Terrence sends Azu away and finds Juan again with him in the frame for their handshake. Coming around to the front of the two, Terrence nervously babbling on and Juan asking *Business good?*, the camera finally settles—static for the first time since the film's opening. Juan continually scans the street meanwhile, which Terrence does not. The older man, experienced, controlling, and alert, is evidently in charge, taking on the demeanor of a caring father figure when he shows concern for Terrence's mother. Note how what has been a fluid, destabilizing camera is here stabilized by Juan, a force of steadiness in the street dealings, an illustration of camera and dramatic narrative—perceiver and perceived—working together.

Terrence has served his purpose as a minor character, that of setting up the character of Juan. He now fades into the background—returning only for the previously mentioned scene with Paula. Juan now crosses forward, at which point a group of boys, barely glimpsed, hurry past between him and the camera. (Their cries help reveal their presence.) The camera pulls back and pans to the left with Juan as he continues to cross, revealing the group again as they run off in the background. Looking away from the boys as if he has no further interest in them and they are of little consequence to the story we are following, Juan continues to cross as the shot ends.

Conclusion

Information: Juan runs the neighborhood's drugs trade. He appears to be caring, however.
Emotion: Desperation (Azu). Nervousness (Terrence). Calm wariness (Juan).
Visceral sensation: A dizzy excitement (audience).
Vision: The energy of everyday life. Addicts and drug dealers as everyday people.

Within a duration of under two minutes, a single take has been packed with information delivered with high energy. If the life, the banter, and the kinetic visuals with which the filmmaker energizes the take intoxicate us, the shot is meticulously functional too. Its style *is* its substance. What we see is a slice of life, animated, fluid, and unpredictable, yet the filmmaker's choreography and its symbiosis with his camera is precise, exact to each instant and fit for purpose throughout. Story, staging, space, environment, performance, and camera all work together. The camera does not merely depict the action but is complicit in, informs, and generates the scene's energy. The style appears flamboyant but is actually calculated, the seemingly free-flowing staging and performances tightly geared to the dynamics of the camera. The sense of spontaneity the filmmaker conjures is achieved through the elegance of his aesthetic. Every element of craft serves every other element, while together they serve his storytelling.

Notice how Little/Chiron is not introduced at the start of the film. He is faintly glimpsed for the briefest instant as he runs past Juan, but it is not until the first shot of the next sequence that we see him—and then only from the back.

Screenplay versus Film

The SOUND of the ocean is specified at the beginning of the screenplay, but not the Boris Gardiner song. Such diegetic music is generally decided upon during production and postproduction.

The screenplay describes three boys rather than the twosome of Terrence and Azu. Terrence transpires to be one of these boys, while Azu arrives only after the dialogue between Juan and him about how business is going. Azu addresses Juan, not Terrence. He reluctantly offers Juan cash for drugs, but Juan insists he pay Terrence. An elaborate ritual of sale, involving the other two boys, then begins. Juan hears a yell from a *LITTLE BOY* and sees across the road a gang of young boys chasing Little/Chiron. Juan's exchange with Terrence about his mother is absent.

This is more complicated than the scene in the film and more complex to shoot. There's a danger that Juan may seem less sympathetic running three drug-dealing youths than one. It is simpler to find Terrence and Azu already mid-banter, to have Terrence handling a one-on-one altercation, with Juan stepping in only when necessary, and to have the conversation about how business is going after Azu has left. The additional two youths of the screenplay are unnecessary and indeed obtrusive in the scene. Jenkins loses them in the film. Adding Juan's inquiry about Terrence's mother ensures we see him, for all his illegal activities, as a sympathetic character.

While Juan sees the young boys chasing Little in the screenplay, in the film he seems oblivious to the nature of the pursuit. The latter option renders his late appearance in the next section a surprise—not the case were he seen to have shown interest in the chase.

Two: Announcing Little

Little and the Bullies

The camera follows Little as he runs, shaky in the frame (1). There's then a cut around 180 degrees to him hurrying forward below camera (2a), followed, after his exit from the shot, by another boy (2b). The camera pans left to find the fleeing Little and tilts up with him as he comes up to a row of apartments by stairs at the far end of walkway (2c) and enters one apartment, followed by the second boy, coming up the near stairs (2d), who tries but fails to follow Little into the apartment. Inside the house Little, in profile L-R, holds his hands over his ears as he hears the other boy knocking on the door (3a). The camera pans with him as he crosses to show him in profile R-L (3b).

(1) Little runs. Cut to:

(2a) Hold for:

(2b) Pan left, tilt up to:

(2c) Hold for:

(2d) Cut to:

(3a) Push in, pan right for:

(3b) Cut to:

(4a) Handheld pan left to:

(4b) Pan left with Little to:

(4c) Cut to next section.

Three boys throw stones at a window of the house (4a). The camera pans left to find the cowed Little watching (4b), then pans further left with him as he moves away from the window and sits, head down (4c).

Summary
Chased by other boys, Little seeks refuge in a condemned apartment.

Questions
Audience: Who is this boy? Why is he being chased? Will his pursuers get into the house too? Will they hurt their prey? What is this house?
Reader: How does the filmmaker announce the film's protagonist? Why now? How does he invite the audience to feel for him?

Commentary
The camera's shaky framing of Little, who appears blurry and is barely contained within the first shot, gives a sense of the boy's precarious flight—although we do not yet know he's attempting to escape his pursuers. We don't even realize that a chase is taking place. (Is the camera itself keeping up with him or chasing him?) The boys' voices and the thunder of their running let us know they are close, either in front or behind, but their precise distance from Little is not yet clear. His blue backpack connects him subliminally in our minds to Juan's car, seen in the opening shot of the film.

This is our first sight of Little, whose name we do not at this point know. The filmmaker does not yet allow us to see his face.

With the second shot of the section, after the second cut of the film—two minutes in—the nature of what we are witnessing is revealed. Little runs forward (a cut of contrast in that respect) and looking behind him drops out of shot to the bottom of the frame, to be followed by another boy with a *red* backpack. (Remember the red car to the back of the shot as Juan's blue car pulls up.) This boy, dressed in black top and shorts, as opposed to Little's white top and jeans, wields a stick, his intention obvious. We have still not been granted a clear view of Little's face. (Incidentally, the foreground pillar soft to the left of frame not only creates a frame within a frame but renders the camera a voyeur, spying, if only for an instant, on the characters. Soon it will become the very opposite—a means of placing us "with" Little.)

The barking of a neighborhood dog heightens our sense of alarm as the camera hastily pans, tilts up, and dollies left to find Little, who, having ascended some steps, dashes along a walkway toward the door of an apartment—one of a row. He fails to open the first and fails with the second but finally manages the third (the second closest to camera). Here is an example of what is known as the "rule of three." Little's first attempt is thwarted by the locked door but sets up in our minds his intention: to find refuge. His second action, resulting from the failure of his first, also fails, but his third is successful—the resolution to what might be called this *micro-story*. Notice how a toy Santa sits abandoned to the side. The irony of the uncared-for figure in a story of an uncared-for child is poignant. Many in the audience probably won't notice it, but the detail is there, an element in the rich fabric of story and world the filmmaker weaves.

When Little enters the apartment, he leaves the outer, wrought iron gate open. His pursuer enters the shot not from the end of the walkway like Little but runs into frame close to camera, hurrying away from us to Little's door. This surprises, perhaps startles us—we expected to see the second boy appear but assumed he would have chosen the same route as Little. We witness what we anticipated, but it happens in a way we did not foresee. This is a simple illustration of how storytelling can work—by meeting our anticipation so we are not disappointed but delivering it in an unexpected way. We feel abreast with the story but also find the storyteller keeping ahead of us.

With the gate left open, we think for a moment that the boy will simply enter. Little is destined for a beating, we imagine. Not so. He has apparently locked the inner door, we discover, and his would-be assailant is reduced to beating his stick on it.

The sound carries us across the cut to the interior, where its echoing has prompted Little to clap his hands over his ears. Jenkins places us closer to his protagonist now yet still doesn't show his face. The shot is cloaked in darkness, and we find ourselves in constricted space—a contrast to the expanse of the film's first scene. The noise of the stick hitting the door, meanwhile, is deafening, not only to Little but to us.

Note how the light over a boarded opening creates the sense of darkness. Without it we would see nothing. With it the darkness is evident. This is an instance of the principle that to show a particular condition it is helpful to also show its opposite: to show stasis, contrast it to movement and vice versa; to show isolation, contrast a single figure with a crowd; and to show a particular color or colors, set them against neutral tones (as with Juan's blue car and the red car at the film's opening).

Little crouches, and the rapping of stick on the door finally ceases, replaced by the sound of breaking glass as the film cuts to a view through a window of three boys tossing projectiles toward the apartment. (Notice that the backpacks of the other two boys are black, not blue or red.) The camera pans left to find Little, in a profile MCU, watching his tormentors. Now, finally, the filmmaker has shown us the face of his protagonist. The boy is terrified—he leans forward for a clearer view, then recoils as a stone hits the glass—and we, having experienced the racket and darkness of the previous shot and having faced the projectiles thrown toward us as they are directed at him, also feel his terror. (Note how we *hear* but do not *see* glass breaking—the sound alone creates the image of this on the screen of the mind.) The filmmaker has designed his shots, his cuts, his sound, and his storytelling to compel us to empathize with Little. Not only is the action *depicted*, but the emotions it unleashes are *conveyed*. Jenkins's camera has been *complicit* in one way or another throughout these opening minutes, not passively observing but interacting with what it shows. Now, in collaboration with the scene's editing, it is becoming predominantly subjective.

The cut and pan to Little is interesting also in the way it reveals that time has passed since the previous shot. There haven't been sufficient moments in the scene for the boy with the stick to join his friends below, nor have we seen Little cross to settle by the window. Those actions would likely not have proved dramatically significant. Time has moved on, and we accept this without a second thought. There is also the issue of the layout of the apartment and its surroundings. Where is the window? It doesn't appear to overlook the walkway. Indeed, we can't be certain of the geography here, the relationship of one space to another. Is that important for our following of the story, though? No. Indeed, it's the very lack of temporal and spatial information that, far from *confusing* us, *unsettles* us in a manner that helps us share in Little's fear.

The camera now pans left with Little as he shifts away from the window, tilting down as he sinks to the floor. Jenkins has the sound of the projectiles fade out, giving us, in the final moments of the shot, the chance to hear Little's distressed breathing and spend a few seconds with him in his exhaustion and loneliness. Having us share intimate moments with a character, especially a main character, brings us closer to them in terms of empathy and narrative POV. The filmmaker does not cut once Little is on his haunches, but waits, allowing us to take in his despair as it grows. The story pauses as the character breathes—figuratively as well, in this case, as literally.

Conclusion

Information: Little (we do not know his name yet) is persecuted by other boys.
Emotion: Fear (Little). Apprehension (audience).
Visceral sensation: Panic, terror, despair (Little).
Vision: Escape from bullies the path to loneliness.

The emotional world and physical environment of Little have been set up. He is bullied, afraid, and lonely. The economic status of his neighborhood is revealed by the decrepit, empty apartment. Little himself is introduced during moments of intense anxiety. He is the vulnerable opposite of the imposing Juan: at the mercy of others, physically slight, and a mere child with no control over his life.

Screenplay versus Film

The micro-story of how Little enters the apartment only after trying other locked doors, then leaving open the gate so that we anticipate the bully chasing him will also enter, is not described in the screenplay (nor is the Santa toy). On the page, there's a cut to the interior coinciding with Little's entry. In the film the camera remains outside to catch the action of his pursuer.

The screenplay version keeps us in Little's narrative POV—he motivates the cut from exterior to interior. The film removes us from his experience at this point but offers the suspense provided by the open gate and the locked door. Either option works, but in different ways: in the screenplay we share in Little's action and emotion, while in the film we are compelled by suspenseful events he does not witness.

When it comes to what the screenplay describes as *A window, the rear bedroom*, however, these approaches are reversed. On the page, the window is described before Little is in place to its side. He then *creeps into ... THE REAR BEDROOM* to see the *three badasses* below him. In the film, we discover that our view of the boys has been shared by Little. We are in his narrative POV and not privileged by the camera being in the rear bedroom prior to the character's arrival. The filmmaker shows us the bullies before we are *aware* that Little also sees them, while helpfully omitting to explain the geography of the apartment.

The screenplay's description on the page of the last moments of the scene could not be more effectively expressed on the screen: *As he clinches his eyes closed, breath cloistered up in his chest*—words translated perfectly into image.

Little and Juan

Little explores the apartment (1a), the sounds of his assailants no longer heard, and finds a glass pipe (1b). He reacts to a sudden knock (2a), sees hands appear over the top of a boarded-over window (1c), and watches the board being torn down (2a), to see not a bully but Juan appearing (1d). Juan steps into the room (1e), asking Little why he's there. Little says nothing (2b). Juan probes further (1e). Little backs away (2b). Juan reassures him (1e), inviting him for a bite to eat, but Little remains silent

(1a) Hold for:

(1b) Cut to:

(2a) Cut to:

(1c) Cut to:

(2b) Cut to:

(1d) Cut back to: Little (2b). Cut to:

Cut back to Little (2b)/Juan (1e)/Little (2b) pushing in Juan (1e), hold Little (2b), hold for:

(1f) Cut back to Little (2b). Cut to:

(3) Cut back to:

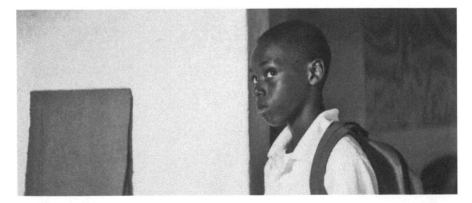

End on Little (2b).

(2b). Juan walks out the front door (1f), but Little does not follow (2b). In a tighter MS (3) Juan suggests Little accompany him. Little throws him a look (2b).

Summary
Juan arrives and offers to take Little for a bite to eat.

Questions
Audience: What's been going on in this place? Will the boys hurt their victim now that they are about to get in? (Oh, it's Juan, not the bullies!) Will the put-upon Little trust Juan? Should he trust a man we know to be a criminal? Will he go with him? What might that lead to?

Reader: How does the filmmaker create tension in the encounter between Juan and Little? How does this exchange, and indeed this scene, benefit from the chase just witnessed? How does the filmmaker end this scene in a way that compels us to continue watching the film? What does this section gain from following the opening episode? What are the contrasts between the characters, and how do they drive the narrative forward?

Commentary
There's another ellipsis in time between Little sitting on the floor in despair at the end of the previous section and his exploration of the abandoned apartment in the shot that follows (or is he—initially at least—seeking a way out?) This serves to reveal a new aspect of his character: left to his own devices, he becomes curious about his surroundings. He's not entirely passive then, which will prove integral to how the narrative is to move forward, particularly at the end of the first "Little" act and the second "Chiron" act.

Little motivates camera movement as he steps gingerly through the darkness, as sound design conveys the state of the floor on which he treads. (Note how the sounds of the neighborhood are absent; we are in this interior world along with the character.) He holds a glass pipe up to the light to see it more clearly and in so doing reveals it to us. There's a link to the first section of the film here—presumably this is where addicts such as Azu hang out once they have their supplies from Juan's business. (The pipe help up in the light from the gap over the board also draws our attention to the board.) Little points the pipe at himself, and as he examines it, there comes a loud knocking. Note how startling this is, not only to Little, preoccupied as he is with the pipe, but also to us, absorbed as we are by his fascination for it. (It seems he's innocent of knowledge of drug culture.) Without his curiosity and behavior and our worry, the knocking would seem less abrupt and less alarming.

The cut to Little's MCU, which both accentuates the shock of the knocks and reveals his apprehension, shows him in more light, as though from the gap over the boarded-up window. (His background meanwhile is partly a lit wall, partly a dark one.) The light on the wall at this point, before Juan has taken down the board, seems a "cheat" but is necessary to show Little's surprise clearly. With the hands seen clasping the top of the board, and as it's torn away, both Little and we the audience anticipate the re-appearance of the bullies. When Juan is revealed, we breathe a sigh of relief, quickly accepting events we did not witness: Juan's decision to follow the boys, his realization that one of them has hidden in the apartment, and his decision to come to Little's aid. (The opportune reintroduction of a character or element from an earlier scene is a dynamic of story that writers know well. We as an audience know it too, although as with other techniques of story construction and telling, *we are rarely consciously aware* that we know it.)

Juan's surprising appearance also exemplifies a key device of storytelling, namely that what appears at first as a problem reveals itself to be the solution. Little antic-ipates nemesis at the hands of the bullies but finds rescue at the hands of Juan. The negative transpires to be positive. The suspense of the imagined threat brings about the surprise of the rescue.

The stratagem relates to the challenge the writer faces at the movie's opening: how to bring Juan and Little together. They might simply encounter one another on the street, but that wouldn't be so dramatic, and besides, Juan's motives in engaging with the boy might seem suspect: Does he want to exploit him for his business, or might he have other, more dubious designs? Juan could have intervened in the chase, but then we wouldn't be privileged with our time alone with Little and so would not have come to know much about his character. Instead, the ongoing threat of the assailants not only presents Little with an objective (to find safety) but gives him an action (seeking refuge in the apartment), while creating suspense (the bullies are about to attack their prey), then a surprise (it's not the bullies who appear, but Juan.) The story thus moves economically from one step to the next, keeping us engaged as we wonder what might be about to happen.

Let's consider the *hierarchy of knowledge* once Juan has stepped over the sill into the room. We have a sense of Juan being a sympathetic character from his inquiries about Terrence's mother. Little, on the other hand, lacks any sense of him. (Only later in the first act does he realize what Juan does for a living.) *We* know Juan exerts power in the neighborhood to maintain equilibrium in his local drug trade. Little, by contrast, sees only his imposing physique and demeanor. He might fear that Juan, like his peers, could be about to mistreat him. When Juan attempts to get Little to trust him, there-fore, and while we might presume he's being genuine (unless we are familiar with such people, in which case we might see him as a threat to the boy), Little doesn't know whether he can safely accept Juan's overtures.

This dynamic informs camera placement and cutting as the new scene progresses. As the filmmaker intercuts between the MS of Juan, seen over Little's shoulder, to the MCU of the cautious Little, the height of the lens stays at the level of the boy's eyes. We look *up* at Juan along with Little, but we do not look *down* at Little along with Juan. We share in the perception of Little, but not of Juan—so we remain in the experi-ence, the narrative POV of Little. Note also how Little is present in the frame in both reverses, while Juan can be seen in his own shot but not in the reverse on the boy. The young protagonist has more screen time. We are "with" him for longer, although he never speaks—another element in Jenkins's introduction of his main character: the filmmaker makes us wait to hear a single word from Little until all of nine minutes into the film.

Knowing that Juan has a good heart and that Little is now probably safe, there's a danger of a lack of tension in the exchange, especially as the new arrival tries so hard to reassure the boy that his intentions are honorable. What lends the scene its compelling suspense is the uncertainty of Little's reaction and our uncertainty about what might be his best option. Will he accept the kindness of his savior, or will he not? If he doesn't, he's likely to fall into the hands of his persecutors. If he does, he could find himself at the mercy of a criminal with a dangerous career. There's also our desire to hear Little's voice. When will he answer Juan? Will he ever? The boy's position, backed against a wall and with Juan barring any means of escape, serves to further emphasize his vulnerability.

Juan suggests he take Little for something to eat, in the process opening the front door to the left of the frame and stepping out before turning back to the boy in a new shot, a closer MS. Why does he open the door and step out of it? Jenkins could have had him step over the sill and through the open window, but then he would have to help Little climb out, and physical contact at this point in the relationship is out of the question—we see that happen much later in the ocean swimming lesson. The window represents a previous story element and is already open; no need to return to it. Juan opening the door, on the other hand, not only offers a new element but also provides him with a physical action. The door is also a visual representation by the filmmaker that, like Juan's action, signals a fresh possibility for Little. An open door invites story and character to move on; a closed one might suggest the narrative can progress only within the established predicament and space.

The door is placed to the left of frame, the side generally considered the more stable, while the window is more to the right—which worked well when Little anticipated that the boys would break in and assault him. Juan's equilibrium, his avuncular reassurances, and his gentle manner are by contrast better suited to frame left. (This is a principle found in theater too, where stage right [camera left] is thought more stable and stage left [camera right] less so.)

After Juan's *Come on now! Can't be no worse out here*, the filmmaker cuts back to Little. If the boy still does not utter a word, his looks are eloquent. The first look at Juan shows he's heard his invitation. The second look down shows he's considering it. The third look at Juan indicates that he might have made a decision and is about to give his answer. (This is a *micro-story*.) We do not see or hear that answer, however. Jenkins cuts to black so that we are left wondering what Little will do. The scene ends not with an answer but a question, one that will be answered only when the following scene begins. A common fault of new screenwriters and directors is that they think a scene must conclude before the next can start. This can undercut tension, suspense, and narrative energy. An open ending, on the contrary, drives the narrative on.

Conclusion

Information: Juan is protective of Little. Little does not trust him.
Emotion: Apprehension (Little). Compassion (Juan).
Visceral sensation: Unease (Little, audience).
Vision: Vulnerability as motivator of empathy (central to the film).

This scene completes the prelude to the movie while presenting questions to carry the story forward. What is this boy's name? Who is he? Why is he bullied? Will he trust Juan; and if he does, what will be the consequences?

Screenplay versus Film

The screenplay describes an insert of a *glass pipe* at the top of the scene. In the film Little holds this up, and it catches the light. Perhaps Jenkins shot an insert, perhaps he didn't, but one is not needed, and any emphasis might give the wrong message: that the boy will become an addict. It might also give the right message: he will become a dealer—a future step in his journey that the filmmaker surely wants to come as a surprise.

On the page, Little puts the pipe down and *starts opening cabinets and drawers, just a kid exploring, when . . . .* Then come the knocks. This takes too long. And what would be in the drawers, if anything? The scene is not about the apartment or Little's exploration, of which we witness enough. Better to bring Juan in sooner.

The remainder of the scene as written is faithfully recreated on the screen, with one notable difference. Since Juan has all the dialogue and action, and Little reacts to him while failing to speak, it might appear on the page that the adult has the narrative POV. In the film this is with Little, articulated as it is through shot selection, camera height and placement, and cutting. Few screenplays stipulate camera angle or camera height, although some unobtrusive indication may be offered. The screenplay is not the film. It isn't even completely the blueprint for the film—assembled and shaped in this case by the writer-director according to his understanding of his script and how he sees its most effective representation on the screen. The evolution of a film from page to screen is exactly that: an evolution across different mediums.

Jenkins's final description, however, *Off Little . . .* , is exactly what he captures in his movie. The scene on the page, like that in the film, ends with a question.

Transition to the Following Sequence

The scene cuts to black, after which there appears in white lettering the legend: *i. Little.* (Now we know his name.)

There follows the first shot of this new act.

(1a) Tighten (zoom in) to:

(1b). Juan considers how to engage with Little (1a). The camera pushes in to the tighter 2-shot as he turns to the boy and leans in (1b).

Juan and Little have been in the same shot before, but here they are brought together in a 2-shot favoring Juan that shows them in a new environment and much closer to each other—an indication that their relationship has begun to develop. The composition invites the single on Little over Juan's shoulder that follows.

The score at this point takes on a notably warm tone, reflective of Little's new situation.

Moonlight

Announcing Chiron

The prelude to the Chiron act is comprised of two sections:

> One: Announcing Chiron
> Two: The Return of Kevin

One: Announcing Chiron

After the initial partial profile of a youth (1), there's a cut to a CU of Chiron (2a). The camera slowly dollies right, pulling out as it holds on Chiron (2b). A student is revealed foreground before the pan left to find an MS of Terrell (2c), who goads Chiron. Continuing the slow dolly out, there follows a pan right to Chiron, *two* students now in foreground, others in background (2d). There follow cuts to a CU of Terrell, his look close to the axis of the lens (3a), then to the CU of Chiron (4)—a repeat of the (2a) setup. A slightly looser CU of Terrell follows, angle as in (3a), the camera panning left with him as he rises to exit the classroom (3b). There's now a cut back to Chiron, framed again between the two amused students (2d), as the camera dollies left, pushing in while panning right to hold on Chiron until it finds his MCU (5).

Note: Most of this scene is covered by a master shot that begins with (2a) and runs throughout the scene. (3a, b) and (4) are inserted into this developing shot.

Without the shot settling, there's a cut to a high school hallway, students crossing toward and to the sides of camera. Chiron is revealed coming to center frame from behind a central pillar. Terrell appears from camera left and shoulder bumps him (6a), motivating the camera to pull out slowly. Terrell exits frame left, leaving Chiron to be bumped on his other shoulder by a second student. Chiron holds back, rocking gently from side to side as students stream past him, the camera continuing to dolly slowly back (6b).

Summary

Humiliated in class by Terrell to the amusement of his peers, Chiron is physically harassed by the bully afterward.

The Art of the Filmmaker. Peter Markham, Oxford University Press. © Oxford University Press 2023.
DOI: 10.1093/oso/9780197631522.003.0021

(1) Partial profile youth. Cut to:

(2a) CU of Chiron. Dolly right, pull out to:

(2b) Wider on Chiron and class. Pan left, pull back to:

(2c) MS of Terrell. Pan right, pull out to:

(2d) 3-shot of Chiron and foreground students, others in background. Cut to:

(3a) CU of Terrell. Cut to:

(4) CU of Chiron. Cut to:
(3a) CU of Terrell, looser framing. Pan to:

(3b) Pan left with MS of Terrell as he exits. Cut to:(2d) Repeat 3-shot, Chiron, foreground students, push in, dolly left to:

(5) MCU of Chiron. Cut to:

(6a) Wide on hallway, pull out to:

(6b) Wide on Chiron, center frame, and students.

Questions

Audience: Who is this youth? What does Little's interest in him signify? For that matter, is he indeed Little? Why is Terrell goading him, and for how long has this been going on? What's happened to Juan? Is he around to support Chiron?

Reader: When and how does the filmmaker "announce" the adolescent Little/Chiron? What impact on us does the eyeline of Terrell's CU have? How does the filmmaker emphasize Chiron's humiliation, then his isolation?

Commentary

A cut from a black screen, on which a blue light flashes, marks the beginning of the scene. As the score fades up, we see the partial rear profile of a youth. We know neither who this is nor where we are. With the cut to an MCU of another youth, the initial shot is revealed as his POV, and as a teacher's voice fades up and students are revealed in the background, we gather we are in a high school classroom.

This second youth's shirt is patterned with yellow—significantly so, as this prelude continues. (Perhaps the initial POV might be more readily understood if the youth in it were to be wearing a darker shirt in contrast to his observer's.)

The camera pulls out and dollies past a foreground student, obscuring, for a moment, the youth. During this move—and given the focus on a character we haven't seen before—we find ourselves suspecting that he is Little and that time has passed since the previous scene between Little, Juan, and Teresa, although there's been no title card. Once the youth is again visible, the teacher is heard clearing his throat to say *Chiron! You need something?*, to which the youth shakes his head. The filmmaker thus announces his protagonist, no longer known by his nickname but by his given name.

Note the process: Jenkins punctuates the transition from the previous act (the flashing blue light on the black screen [blue being one of the movie's two main colors]), he invites us to ask a question (Who is the youth we see watching the one shown in profile?), he provides the answer (he is Chiron), and he allows us to discover for ourselves the information that this scene is taking place some years after the Little "act."

Inviting us to do work in figuring out the youth's identity leads us to invest in and care about the character. We cared about Little as we got to know him, but there's a new actor playing the character now, so Jenkins has us *reinvest* immediately.

The insult from Terrell motivates the pan left to discover him. Note that he's wearing a *red* top. The filmmaker gives us time to register this new character before the bully's new homophobic slur—in which he refers to Chiron as Little, thus making doubly clear his victim's identity. Terrell's subsequent insult, greeted with approving laughter from other students, prompts the pan back to a wider shot of Chiron, framed now by two foreground female students also amused by the taunting. Several class members, meanwhile, apparently indifferent to Chiron's suffering, are seated around and behind him. (Note how the woman to the right wears a red/maroon top.) Just as the responses of the students around Terrell render his cruelty the more callous, so the entertained reactions of the foreground females highlight Chiron's humiliation. Note also that he's being picked upon by a male while other males are soon to be seen persecuting and assaulting him. Were the foreground students male, not female, we might think Chiron might muster support from females in the class—after all, he's found solace before in the caring Teresa. Now we see he has nowhere to turn, which will make Kevin's affable reappearance in the scene soon to come all the more significant.

The mise en scène of the WS—student, Chiron, student, with others behind him and to his side—visually traps him. He has no way out, just as he cannot escape his humiliation. Robbed of his red top from the previous act, he's powerless against those who now wear red.

The new cut to the CU of Terrell startles us. Coming after a long developing shot, it introduces a new angle, from Chiron's position. The new single comes with a narrow depth of field, and apart from someone on the edge of frame to camera right, we see nobody but the bully, center frame, with no headroom, looking *almost* into the lens and directly at us. The impact is visceral—we perceive what Chiron perceives and feel the brunt of the verbal attack he experiences.

The CU of Terrell motivates a cut to its reverse: a CU of Chiron, whom we feel receive the psychological blow from the bully's smear. Jenkins is keeping us close to his protagonist. Were he to have chosen to return to the frontal 3-shot and its angle, the narrative POV would have been third person. Were he to have gone to a wider shot of Chiron from Terrell's angle, the narrative POV might have been with Terrell, since we would have shared in his distance from Chiron. (The modulation of proximity and distance is an invaluable resource in the articulation of narrative POV.) Coming by contrast to a tight shot of Chiron maintains *his* narrative POV. The angle, from Terrell, allows the cut and camera to deliver the antagonist's barbs while ensuring—along with a perfectly judged performance by Ashton Sanders as Chiron—that we share in the put-upon character's experience. Indeed, the filmmaker holds on Chiron as the tormentor's threats grow uglier and the teacher breaks in to reprimand him and order him out of the room. Note that Jenkins does not cut to the teacher, whom we do not see. He is not "covering" the scene—shooting arbitrary setups to be assembled in the cutting room—but telling the story and telling it moreover from Chiron's point of view. Chiron does not look at the teacher meanwhile—he's too concerned with Terrell's insistent goading. A look at him, given the adherence to his *narrative POV*, might prompt an unnecessary cut to him.

The cut back to Terrell's CU comes with a slightly wider framing, presumably so that he can be held in the frame as he rises, the camera panning left to keep him in shot as he heads for the door. Terrell *has* to leave now, at least as regards the construction of the scene—his function in the episode served, he now needs to be removed. (We don't see him leave, only hear this, but Jenkins takes care to show the door through which he is about to leave. Were the filmmaker to show us the door closing, we would feel Terrell's absence. Jenkins, by contrast, wants to keep his threat present.)

Once Terrell has left, Jenkins gives us time with Chiron as his humiliation resonates. Note how he cuts not to the previous angle—from Terrell's chair—but to the front-on 3-shot, motivated by the bully's position as he's walking out. The axis of the drama remains between Chiron and Terrell. As we come to the shot, Chiron's eyeline is to the exiting bully. Were this not evident, our connection to him would have been severed—separated from his experience, we would be seeing him in the third-person omniscient, rather than what we have here, when we see him in a *third-person intimate* narrative POV. The wider shot also allows us to witness the two foreground students turning to him—which he registers—as if to accuse *him* of responsibility for the episode. Thus, guilt is transferred from predator to prey through two simple looks.

Those looks help motivate the camera's push in and dolly left as the movement of the earlier shot—from single to 3-shot—is reversed, with pressure being put on Chiron as the camera closes in on him to give his MCU, its angle identical to that of the earlier single. Note how he shoots a brief glance at Terrell's desk. With that look, we see his antagonist on the screen of the mind. No longer physically present, his persona lingers.

Ending with the single on Chiron should also be understood in the context of this opening sequence as a whole—the following scene, also a part of this "narrative unit," ends with him but in a wider composition.

The camera has not been allowed to settle on the scene's outgoing single before Jenkins cuts to a WS of the school hallway. There was once a dictum that one should not cut from a moving camera to a static camera. Like many such attempts at decorum (another being the prohibition of cuts from wide to close), this has, happily, long since faded into obscurity. The cut here works well because the *energy of the camera's movement* in the outgoing shot is transferred across the transition to the *energy of the action* in the incoming shot: the students coming toward the camera.

Chiron is not present as the shot begins but enters a couple of seconds in. (Note how he appears from behind a pillar so that he enters the frame in one distinct beat.) His brief absence is significant: when we are "with" a character, when we are in their narrative POV, and then when we lose them, we tend to want to be with them again— unless the character is repugnant to us, in which case we may dread rejoining them on their journey. Although we may find his journey painful, Chiron is hardly repugnant. Even if he's absent for only a couple of seconds, we experience, subliminally, the desire to see him again. No sooner have we been granted the privilege of rejoining him, however, than Terrell reappears from frame left, his red top drawing the eye. He bumps into his unsuspecting victim, comes to camera issuing more threats, and then exits frame left. The eye has barely had time to return to Chiron when another tormentor thuds into him from behind, colliding with his opposite shoulder. The manner in which the filmmaker times this staging, taking eye trace into account, works to take us by surprise so that we share in Chiron's shock. Note also how, because the second bully is dressed in black and gray, we don't notice him enter the shot before Terrell's exit. The wardrobe for the extras is also largely kept neutral, with bright colors generally avoided; we see only the story the filmmaker wants us to see while the world around—of which are always aware—gives it verisimilitude and life.

The camera continues to dolly back as the students stream past, while Chiron stays rooted to the spot, his stasis and lateral rocking contrasted with the forward vector of energy of the students. The shot works in other ways too; Chiron's isolation and loneliness in the face of his peers' indifference is powerfully rendered by the busy, populated frame. A closer single of him would not provide that visual contrast, nor would a distant, solitary Chiron in empty surroundings prove as effective. The quality of loneliness is conveyed by contrasting it with its opposite, the socializing of other students. Note also how the shot offers a contrast to the final shot of the previous scene, the tight MCU of Chiron. The filmmaker varies his visual language to show how, whether in a close or wide shot, Chiron's agony remains inescapable—either for him or for us. Repeating the same approach in every scene might result in visual monotony. Interweaving and interconnecting broader "linguistic" resources enriches both the visual fabric of the film and our engagement with it.

Finally, as the camera, and thus we the audience, moves away from Chiron, we experience what might be thought of as a "rubber band" effect of narrative POV. When a character we are "with" moves away from us, or we from them, and when we lose them—as we do at the start of the shot that begins the following episode—we wish to rejoin them.

Conclusion

Information: Little now calls himself Chiron. He is harassed by Terrell. Nobody in the class cares. Terrell has sidekicks in his bullying.
Emotion: Humiliation, loneliness (Chiron).
Visceral sensation: The stab of hopelessness (Chiron, audience).
Vision: Isolation within community (as opposed to Little's isolation in solitude seen at the film's opening).

The announcing of Chiron contrasts visually with that of Little. Chiron is present in the first scene of the new act. He's static, what's more, seated at his desk, whereas when we first saw Little, he was fleeing across open space. Little sought refuge but found himself trapped. Chiron is trapped from the start. Boy and youth are each persecuted in both preludes. There is a ramping up of the drama, though: Little is physically threatened by boys armed with sticks and stones, and is alone, while Chiron suffers the pain of humiliation in a packed classroom at the hands of Terrell, whose verbal brickbats inflict deep, psychological hurt. Little was met by a rescuer; will Chiron be so lucky?

Other filmmakers might have chosen to end Little's act with a shot of him, cutting next to a shot of similar size, framing, and angle of Chiron in order to make the link between them obvious. Jenkins's approach, in contrast, allows for the reverberations of Little's betrayal of Juan and of the latter's deep shame in the final scene of the film's first act. It also grants us the privilege of discovering Chiron at the start of the new act, both visually and through dialogue from the teacher and Terrell.

Screenplay versus Film

The transition from Juan at the end of the previous act and through the flashing blue light on the black screen is in the screenplay marked by *the sound of breathing, not labored or rushed but … proximal, right beside us.* We don't hear this in the film. Instead, Jenkins employs a suspenseful score that continues into Chiron's CU. This affects the tone the film communicates: with Juan's profile, the previous scene ends with his sense of deep shame. The score's melancholy yet tense nature picks up on that and with the introduction of Chiron transfers the resonance of the emotion to him. The breathing of the screenplay would surely have communicated urgency and intimacy useful for narrative drive but not so helpful for the flow of tone or rhythm. Nor would it serve to connect Juan and Chiron across the years. The screenplay connects the breathing to the lips of the youth in the incoming partial profile, but breath offers release, of which there can be none during the scene. On the contrary, Chiron's silence points to his helplessness in the face of Terrell's antagonism.

At the start of the classroom scene, the screenplay stipulates *From just the look of him, this is clearly the Little character from moments before aged to his teens.* In the event, Jenkins did not cast boy and youth with common looks or physicality in mind but instead chose remarkably capable actors, able to capture each stage of Chiron's development while at the same time manifesting the common essence of the protagonist. Rather than sacrifice casting options for similarity of looks, the filmmaker chose to sacrifice the latter for the option of choosing the best actors for Chiron's three ages. (Jenkins was more concerned about the *truth* of each actor's portrayal of the protagonist at his successive stages of development than with the *realism* of physical continuity.)

The teacher is described on the page as *MR. PIERCE (the biology teacher, late 20s, black).* In the episode in the film not only does he remain nameless, but he is not seen. (He appears later, in the scene in which Chiron takes revenge on Terrell.) Why not show him at this point? And what effect does this have? The filmmaker's shot design throughout the scene is entirely geared to conveying Chiron's story, emotions, and the sense of narrative POV that best serves them. He suggests the dimensions and geography of the classroom while never actually revealing their specificity. There's little opportunity to show the teacher—apart, perhaps, from in the panning shot of Terrell's exit. How might showing him inform our response to the scene, though? Wouldn't allowing us to see him send a message that Chiron might have his support? Might we expect a scene in which the youth tries talking to "Mr. Pierce"? Wouldn't this undercut the forthcoming reintroduction of Kevin, Chiron's sole hope of comfort, and subsequently lower the stakes of Kevin's later betrayal?

In the screenplay Terrell springs from his desk into *Chiron's face.* Not so in the film; the two aren't sitting close enough. Nor should they be. Proximity would lessen the impact of the bully's subsequent shoulder barge. Staging has been designed with a view not only to the drama of the scene but to the drama of the scene to come. Here is another interfunctionality then—not that of the various aspects of filmmaking craft, but that of the connectivity of its scenes. A *narrative unit* in a story is not merely a stand-alone element but finds its nature and representation in the context, and contrast or affinity with, other narrative units before and after it.

In the screenplay, Chiron ends the scene by staring at the door through which Terrell has exited. The movie's Chiron stares at Terrell's desk. On the page, the antagonist has left the scene. In the film, he's still present—in Chiron's mind and in ours.

Finally, Chiron on the page, unlike Chiron on the screen, does not suffer the second shoulder bump. Jenkins the director throws more rocks at his character than Jenkins the writer and that, for us, hurts, while inducing us to follow Chiron's journey through the film all the more intensely in the hope he might overcome the forces marshaled against him.

Two: The Return of Kevin

After a group shot through wire mesh of Kevin and the gang (1a), the camera racks focus to reveal the wire mesh in the foreground, then pans left to find Chiron peering down (1b). The camera tracks left and pans right to show Chiron in MS from behind (1c). (Note how the crossing of extras in front of Kevin's group helps motivate the camera move.) As Kevin's voice is heard, the film cuts to a 2-shot of him past Chiron (2a). The camera then holds their ongoing conversation and staging through fluid movement and framing that barely (intentionally) keeps both in the frame as Kevin circles Chiron.

Summary

While observing Terrell and gang, Chiron is greeted by Kevin. Kevin boasts of a sexual encounter with a female student as he attempts to bond with the reticent Chiron.

(1a) Wide, Kevin and gang. Pan left to:

(1b) Wide MCU of Chiron. Dolly left, pan right to:

(1c) Tight MS of Chiron. Cut to:

(2a) 2-shot of Kevin and Chiron. Hold and adjust, dollying, panning, circling as their conversation continues.

(2b)–(2i) Camera dollies left as Kevin circles Chiron. The shot ends on a single of Chiron. The single of Chiron is followed by a cut to a reverse MCU of Kevin, Chiron soft in the right foreground (3), then to the reverse OTS favoring Chiron (4):

(3) and (4). There follows a profile 2-shot in which the camera tilts down to Kevin's hand clapping Chiron's (5a), then, as he exits frame right, tilting up to an MCU of Chiron (5b):

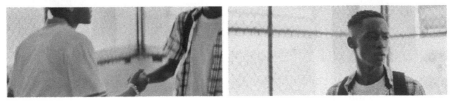

(5a) Tilt up to   (5b). Cut to:

Kevin exits (6). Cut to:

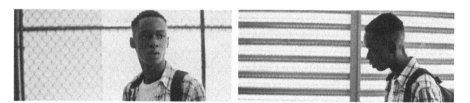

(7a) MCU of Chiron. Pan left with him to: (7b). *Note:* In (7a) Chiron's eyeline is closer to the axis of the lens than for (5b).

Questions

Audience: Who is this loudmouth? (Wait! It's Kevin!) Will Chiron accept his overtures? Will Kevin help protect Chiron against Terrell? Can he? What is the nature of this friendship, and what might it become?

Reader: Why not start on Chiron's profile, then discover he is looking down at Terrell and his gang? How do the framings in the shot that develops after Kevin's arrival serve the moment of contact between the two characters when it finally occurs? How does the filmmaker use color in the scene?

Commentary

The wire mesh, through which we see Terrell and his gang—before we are aware that Chiron is also seeing them—conveys a sense of entrapment common to Chiron's experience. Were we to see Chiron peering down before we see what he sees, that sense would not be so strong because we would know we were sharing in his perception rather than it initially being ours alone.

The shot echoes the moment in the first prelude in which we see Little's pursuers lobbing projectiles up at a window and the camera panning left to find the boy. While we might not consciously reflect on this, the repetition offers a subliminal meme that connects Chiron to Little.

As the camera dollies around Chiron, and we see him at his most vulnerable—with his back to us—we hear Kevin, although we don't yet know whose voice this is. It's a moment only, but his line takes us by surprise, and given the tension of the previous two scenes, unnerves us for an instant. With Kevin's arrival and the cut to the reverse of him past Chiron, there comes a change of energy. The melancholy score fades, and Kevin's lively banter prompts a new rhythm. Gone are the static shots and slow camera moves of the previous two episodes—the camera is now fast and fluid as it attempts to keep up with the newcomer's encircling while holding the two characters in the frame, which it barely manages. We want to see the two together, especially after witnessing and *feeling* Chiron's humiliation and loneliness. As if to tease us, the filmmaker allows us fleeting moments only, one or the other character shifting to the edge of frame. There's the briefest of handshakes as Kevin steps toward Chiron but no tilt down to show it. (Note how Kevin sports a stud in his left ear—a symbol of gayness.)

We probably gather that this is Chiron/Little's old friend Kevin, but if we don't, he mentions his name in the course of the "trick" he relates. Toward the end of the scene Chiron says, *Alright Kev!* So if we didn't know before, the information is clear to us before Kevin leaves.

Kevin's sexual boasts relate to the first act of the film, to the boyish eroticism of their wrestling and the episode in which the friends compared penises. Any early, faint hopes Chiron may have of reviving the relationship between them, of finding the love he so desperately needs, are cruelly dashed when Kevin brags about his encounter with a female student. Like the framing of the shot itself, as the camera appears to struggle to keep the youths in the frame—suggesting the precarity of their companionship—Kevin's affectionate badinage and what it might portend is rendered moot by his proclaimed sexual identity; no sooner has Kevin reappeared in the story than any comradeship, even perhaps romance, that Chiron might have anticipated is thrown into doubt.

Kevin is relentless in his attempt to rekindle their bond. He proceeds, as he vaunts his amorous escapade, to encircle Chiron, who in contrast to his volubility remains largely silent. The circling is the subtext—Kevin's story can also be seen as an oblique invitation to a sexual relationship between the two youths as he directs his proclaimed libido at Chiron, who cannot escape his courtship. Better he should be trapped by Kevin's affections, though, than by Terrell's bullying in a classroom—hence the protagonist's ambivalent reactions: turning away at one moment, looking down the next, and throwing Kevin a glance at another. (Kevin's related carnal encounter later provokes a dream Chiron will have—yet another element in the complex web of connection the filmmaker creates.)

The camera's moves and energy are largely motivated throughout this encounter by Kevin. It goes with him as he circles, panning to Chiron when he throws a question and returning to him as he re-enters the frame to lead the move onward further right or left. There are moments when Chiron's restless rocking from side to side claims the camera, however—this is a conversation, not a monologue, even if one interlocutor barely utters a word.

The cut out of the long take to the reverses comes within Kevin's lines *This stays between us, right?* [Cut.] *I know you can keep a secret.* Kevin's story is more than a mere boast. It is a means to an end, that end being a pact, a contract of secrecy to seal a friendship that is theirs and theirs alone. The cut emphasizes the moment when subtext becomes text, when the physical action of encirclement, verbalized, can be understood as psychological snare. Kevin's offer is one Chiron cannot refuse—or not without the prospect of betrayal. (Later in the act it isn't Chiron who betrays Kevin but Kevin who betrays Chiron—an irony Jenkins neatly sets up through Kevin's clever ploy.) Chiron says nothing but grunts quietly after the cut to this reverse. What can he say? By remaining silent, however, he concurs.

Barely noticeable at this point is the low drumbeat that fades in. Like a pulse, it takes us subliminally into the visceral experience of Chiron.

If the camera failed to catch Kevin's first quick handshake with Chiron earlier, there's now a deft tilt down from a 2-shot to show him slapping the hand of his bemused friend, an action that confirms his coercion of Chiron into the rekindling of their relationship. (The hand slap is later repeated after the intimacies of the later night scene on the beach.) At this point the scene is over (almost), all that remains being the exit first of Kevin, which we see when he walks through a significantly *open* door into the hallway beyond, and second of Chiron, which we do not see since the filmmaker cuts out of the scene before he leaves the frame. As the twosome part ways, Chiron says a final *alright Kev* while Kevin calls him *Black*, his nickname for him, so sealing his conquest.

Shortly after that Chiron, in the scene's final shot, pauses briefly, the camera coming to rest along with him. It is in this quiet, almost imperceptible instant, this second of understanding and reflection on Chiron's part, that the scene delivers its denouement: having taken onboard Kevin's advances, having understood his capture at his friend's hands, he ponders a future previously inconceivable. Unlike at the end of the prior two scenes, he is no longer alone emotionally, even though he is solitary in the shot. Performance (minimal, measured, delicate) and camera (patient, purposeful) come together for that eloquent second.

Note how the inner world of Chiron has already been given visual suggestion in the frames that begin this final shot, with the angle on him after Kevin exits closer to his eyeline than in his previous single. Why did the filmmaker take the trouble to move the camera, if only slightly? In the new single, Chiron's eyeline is very close to the axis of the lens, and consequently we feel more directly connected to him. Without this new eyeline, we would perceive his pause shortly afterward more as observers than as *experiencing* the moment with him. The filmmaker not only has us observe the moment but brings us *into* it.

Barry Jenkins's color control through production and costume design works alongside his other resources of visual language. We see a distant Terrell in his red top, but thereafter the color dominating the scene is blue. (There's a barely notice-able yellow caution tape tied to the corner of the mesh.) The blinds revealed when Kevin appears are blue and radiate a blue light, while there's a blue exit further along. Kevin has blue piping on the collar and pocket of his polo. The doorway through which Kevin exits (open and remaining open), and which we have seen moments before as background to the OTS on Chiron, is blue with a red sign—as though to remind us that the alternative to Kevin's courtship is Terrell's abuse. When Kevin exits, that red sign is framed out—the bully's power has been usurped by the lover's. Chiron and Kevin are together in a blue world from which all red has been removed. The filmmaker has finished his second prelude, and the second act of the movie can begin.

The blueness works on us subliminally. If we do not *think* about it, we *see* it. Here also, the yellow patterning of Chiron's shirt pays off. Neither red nor blue, it helps highlight his journey from one color to the other.

Finally, the soundscape throughout the scene functions to similar subliminal ef-fect. The gentle melancholy of the score that continues from the previous scene (and which counterpoints tonally the emotional brutality of Terrell) fades out with Kevin's greeting. Thereafter there's only the distant ambience of high school life—nothing we notice but enough to maintain the sense of a world around the characters—until those low heartbeat-like drums fade in. Toward the end of the scene, however, as Kevin exits and Chiron realizes the significance of what's just happened, we become aware of this new sonic element. Perhaps it's distant music, perhaps it's the thump of Chiron's heart, but either way it takes us, at a deep, visceral level, with him on his journey.

Conclusion

Information: Kevin wants to renew his friendship with Chiron. Despite his wariness, Chiron cannot reject Kevin's advances.
Emotion: Joy (Kevin). Wariness, relief (Chiron).
Visceral sensation: Dizziness. The stirrings of libido (Chiron).
Vision: Courtship as strategy, dance, ensnarement.

Here again Jenkins is master of the interfunctionality of the elements of the filmmak-er's art. Dramatic narrative, camera, production design, sound, editing, and perfor-mance work together to create a forcefully compelling *dramaturgy*: the interaction of dramatic narrative and its representation onscreen.

The filmmaker has successfully traversed several years and introduced a new version of Chiron, played by a new actor. The preludes to Acts One and Two each show Little/Chiron persecuted by bullies (an anonymous threesome in Little's case, a specific character in Chiron's), but whereas Little was rescued by a parental figure, Chiron is rescued—maybe—by a peer, a potential lover. The story is moving from the semblance of a family relationship to romance.

Screenplay versus Film

Kevin's entrance has less impact in the screenplay. On hearing his greeting, Chiron turns and sees *an admin type* moving away before he spots Kevin approaching. The film's version is quicker, more economical, and more energized.

The rest of the scene's dialogue remains more or less the same from script to screen, while on the page there is no indication of staging, although it may well have been forming in the mind of the filmmaker. Were it there, it might have inhibited the actors. Better to allow them to discover it, perhaps in rehearsal, more probably in the blocking on set.

Chiron's final beat in the screenplay, following Kevin's *Later, Black*, is the cryptic editing instruction *Off Chiron*. His cross left, his pause, and his heartbeat—all these elements are left to the set, the actor, the camera, and the editor. What's important in the screenplay is the instruction that Chiron should have the episode's final beat.

Transition to the Following Sequence

While he remains in the frame, the last shot of Chiron cuts abruptly to silence over a black screen. After less than a second the legend *ii. Chiron* appears in white lettering—identical to that introducing the previous Little act. Neighborhood ambience fades up, and as we hear a dog barking, we see in MCU, from the back, Chiron wearing the same shirt as in the prelude scenes. The depth of field is such that Chiron is sharp, the background soft. (The effect is created by the anamorphic lenses used for the film, which gives this quality, whereas the wider spherical lens needed for the same shot size would not give the same effect. See this back shot in Chapter 9.)

The camera follows Chiron, keeping his size as, after looking to the right, he turns and crosses to the left; throws a white and blue shirt over his shoulder (an echo of Kevin's polo); and then comes to the front door of his home, unlocks it, and enters. There's a cut to the interior as we continue to follow him as his mother tells him he can't stay the night because she has company.

Seen in an interior and in profile in the outgoing shot of the previous scene, Chiron's incoming shot shows him from behind, in an exterior. After sharing in his moment of realization immediately following his encounter with Kevin, we find him motivating the camera and taking us further into his story.

Moonlight

Announcing Black

Like the preludes to the previous acts, the one to Black's act is comprised of two sections:

> One: Announcing Black
> Two: Black's Business

One: Announcing Black

Paula backs out of her bedroom (1) and comes to camera. With her yell, there's a jump cut to her MCU (2). Black rises into a CU (3), sitting up in profile (4). The camera gently booms forward for an overhead single of Black (5), who then rises into a tight MCU (6).

Summary

Paula appears to Black in a nightmare. He wakes, reflects, and bathes his face in iced water.

(1) MS of Paula.

The Art of the Filmmaker. Peter Markham, Oxford University Press. © Oxford University Press 2023.
DOI: 10.1093/oso/9780197631522.003.0022

(2) MCU of Paula.

(3) CU of Black.

(4) Profile MCU of Black.

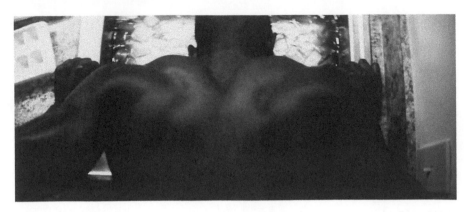

(5) Overhead on Black.

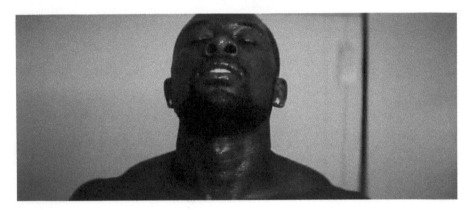

(6) Tight MCU of Black.

Questions

Audience: Who is this man? (It has to be Chiron, dreaming of his mother.) Why does Black wash in iced water?
Reader: What makes the shots of Paula so alarming? Why is the overhead shot so arresting? Of what are these echoes?

Commentary

The film's third prelude follows the transition from Chiron's arrest at the end of the second act. (Note: While the film comprises the three ages of Chiron, it does not follow any traditional three-act structure in terms of either the proportions of the acts or the modulation and rising of tension throughout them.) From the single of Chiron in a police car, there's a cut to a black screen, on which there are three red flashes, in contrast to the blue flashes that preceded the introduction of Chiron in the classroom.

The first shots we see—the appearance of Paula—repeat the shots, action, setup, composition, lighting, color, and framing of an episode that occurs toward the end of the Little act when Paula barks with (silent) fury at her son, then returns to her bedroom. That final MS of her is repeated here—except that whereas in the first version she crosses *into* her bedroom, here she backs *out*. (The shot is the same, simply reversed.) The composition is memorable, its horizontals and verticals, its lurid color palette, and the lighting on Paula's face decisively designed and so strong that we have remembered it. (Note also that she wears a red top.)

Paula's eyeline cleaves almost to the axis of the lens (perhaps a touch below) so that we feel her palpable contempt. With the use of a similar score—tense, arpeggiating strings with long, lower notes—the repeated shot is rendered all the more disturbing.

The cut to Paula's MCU comes as she screams, which alarms us—sudden, unexpected, and eliding a moment or two of her action. On the cut her mouth is already open, the jump in time startling us. Again, the shot is a repetition of the one in Little's episode, but whereas in that earlier moment the sound was muted under the score, this time the score drops out, and we hear Paula's screamed words *Don't look at me!*

While we may not recall exactly where in the film the first vignette occurred, it has remained in our memory. A meme such as this functions as an element of the connective tissue a film builds in order to bring about our cumulative emotional and cognitive engagement. Such an experience—as can be seen from this movie—is not necessarily dependent on "rising tension." The deepening enrichment of our emotional engagement is enough to satisfy us as we watch a movie. One that relies on little but rising tension—ramped up action, conflict, violence, physical stakes—may, on the contrary, in some cases prove less engaging.

The shock of the cut to Paula's MCU, Naomi Harris's harrowing delivery, and her scream bring us directly into Chiron/Black's narrative POV as the film cuts to a CU of him waking breathlessly. Putting us in the mind of a character as they are having a nightmare, then having them rise suddenly into the frame, has long been a trope common in cinema. There's consequently the danger in using it of resorting to cliché. *It was only a dream!* we think, after we've had that second scare—the character rising into the shot—upon which the drama evaporates. What makes the filmmaker's use of the trope so masterly here is that it's a repetition of the character's waking experience from childhood; that it links that first act with this final one; that it's used to "announce" ' Black, the third manifestation of Chiron, played by a third actor with whom we need to connect immediately, especially as he bears little physical resemblance to the protagonist's former manifestations; and that it relates to the nature and function of Chiron's previous introductions.

In the first introduction we find Little alone, fleeing from three unnamed, barely glimpsed bullies. In the second we discover Chiron trapped in class among classmates while a single, named bully torments him with verbal abuse and threats. Both forces of aggression are external. In the third introduction we find ourselves *in the mind* of

Black, his force of antagonism *internal*. Black has absorbed the painful experiences of his childhood and is in a place of emotional and psychological trauma from which there can be no escape, only denial—until he learns there may be relationships that need not be abusive. When Black rises into the shot, we know instantly that this is Little/Chiron/Black. (Note how Black wears a "do-rag" similar to Juan's—he now becomes Juan, running his own drug dealing business.)

In the earliest introduction, by taking us through the steps of his storytelling the filmmaker leads us to discover Little. In the second he teases us for a moment, inviting suspicion that the youth we see is Little, then lets us know he is. Now, in the third permutation, he has us realize at the very instant we first glimpse the new face that this has to be our protagonist.

Again, the filmmaker invites empathy with Chiron. This will prove especially important as the early scenes of this last act progress and we learn what he has become.

From the front-on CU of the panicked Chiron/Black there's a cut to a profile as he collects himself. Our brief glimpse of his muscular biceps and shoulders, then the fullness of his features, proclaims a very different Chiron from the slightness of the boy and the sallowness of the youth. Much about him has changed, and the profile CU marks a moment in which we realize this. Had the filmmaker merely prolonged the first CU, we would not so cleanly move from the information that what we've seen is a nightmare to our recognition of his newly robust physique. The fresh angle also offers a necessary beat between his shock at the nightmare and the action he takes in the following shot.

The impression of the strapping Black is reinforced by the cut to the overhead shot of him dipping his face into a sink full of ice, showing his musculature ripple as he rises toward the lens. The shot is suffused with a blue light—the color of his support systems (Juan, the ocean, Kevin). The act of ablution, meanwhile, echoes Juan's swimming lesson, Little climbing into the bath after Paula has sold their TV, and Chiron dipping his face into a washbasin full of ice after Kevin has punched him in the face. This latter was shown in an overhead shot of similar composition. As with the nightmare of Paula, the decisive design, the formal precision of both framings sparks our connection of one to the other, perhaps subliminally, perhaps consciously. Were this episode shot from a different angle, differently framed, less striking, and less defined, the memes would be less forceful, the connection less direct. (*Note:* the guiro-like sound in the score might be considered a sonic representation of ice cubes knocking together.)

Black rises into a new CU, takes a breath, and wipes his face with his hands as if to finish cleansing himself of his vulnerability and fear. His former self washed away—or so he imagines—he displays in the next shot and the scene it initiates the defenses he has constructed against the world's antagonism.

Conclusion

Information: Chiron remains haunted by his treatment at the hands of his mother. He believes he can cleanse himself of his inner demons.
Emotion: Terror. Denial of trauma (Black).

Visceral sensation: Shock. Numbness (Black).
Vision: Lurid color and heat as emotional pain. Coldness as self-distancing.

By beginning the third prelude with the nightmare, the filmmaker shows what follows to be the result of the defenses Black has constructed. Without the sense of his inner vulnerability, the later removal of this armor—physical but more importantly emotional—would not be organic to either the act or the movie. The character who as a boy takes refuge in a crack house, as a youth seeks relief in revenge, and as a man hopes for safety within the edifice of physical strength and neighborhood power finally discovers the truth of himself through surrender to his emotions and needs. As the nightmare shows, it is his inner world he needs to recognize, accept, and deal with. Once he can achieve this, his true goal, his *super objective*, his outer forces of antagonism fade to insignificance.

Screenplay versus Film

There is no nightmare shown at the opening of this sequence in the screenplay. Black wakes from one we don't see. After Chiron looks to Kevin from inside the police car at the end of the previous act, there's a cut to a black screen, the sound of breathing, and then Black awakes. The connection here is to his relationship with Kevin. This transition implies it is Kevin's betrayal that haunts him. As we are to learn, the incident did indeed affect him profoundly, but it is the underlying primal trauma of maternal betrayal that constitutes his deepest malaise. This is the childhood experience that sets off his journey and prompts him in manhood to adopt the persona and defensive posture of Black. Were his suffering at the hands of Kevin the cause of his nightmares, he would hardly be likely to call himself by the name his betrayer gave him. The screenplay's version of this opening makes little sense, then. What follows in the script further exacerbates that dysfunction, while what comes after in the film builds its architecture of connectivity.

It would seem that Barry Jenkins decided to construct the new nightmare from the two shots of Paula verbally abusing Little as a new means of beginning the film's third prelude. That he may not initially have planned this in no way suggests shortcomings as a filmmaker. Filmmaking is an evolutionary process; the cutting room is central to the cumulative reach toward a movie's functioning and identity. A film is a work in progress until its release. Using available footage to create a new scene, one not conceived at its writing stage, is not only a valid but an invaluable facet of the filmmaking process. (Not that actor Trevante Rhodes would in his performance have been reacting to the memory of Kevin's betrayal, as is the case in the screenplay. Even so, the new version works. We understand that Black's shocked awakening is prompted by his nightmare. This is an example of how montage creates and communicates narrative independently of the actor.)

It's been remarked that the screenwriter composes while the director assembles. To the extent that this might be true (and it isn't, entirely—articulation of narrative POV and modulation of tone are just two examples of composing), this is an example of the assembly function.

Two: Black's Business

The sequence begins with a cut from Black's hands wiping his face to an ECU of his gold "fronts" (2a), after which the camera pulls back to reveal his CU (2b) before cutting to the insert of a crown on his dashboard (3) as the vehicle moves right to left. The cut to Black's profile MCU shows him driving left to right (4a). The camera holds this frame as Black pulls up and Travis is revealed in the background. Travis crosses around the car's trunk, but the camera pans left to him only as he opens the passenger door, panning right as he climbs in (4b). The camera holds on the resulting OTS 2-shot favoring Black. The following cut is to a WS of Travis dealing "on the block" (5), revealed as the POV of Black, seen in MCU (6a). The camera tilts down to show Black taking out a revolver (6b), then tilts up back to his MCU (6a).

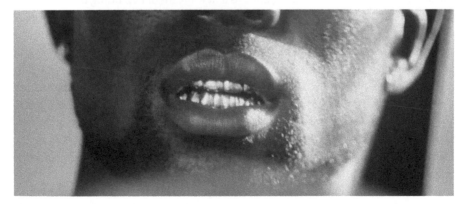

(1).

(2a) ECU of Black's gold "fronts." Pull out to:

(2b) CU of Black.

(3) Insert: crown.

(4a) Profile MCU of Black, Travis appears in the background. The camera pans left as Travis crosses to open the passenger door, pans right as he climbs in:

(4b) OTS Travis on Black.

(5) Wide: Travis deals.

(6a) MCU of Black. Tilt down:

(6b) Hand on gun, tilt up to (6a). Cut to black screen.

Summary

Black drives Travis, his subordinate, to deal drugs for him.

Questions

Audience: Whose gold teeth are those? What is Black doing? Who is this new youth? Is this gun going to be fired? To what fate is Chiron/Black heading?
Reader: How does this sequence benefit from being placed after Black's nightmare and face washing? How is the moment of Travis closing the car door achieved?

Commentary

The reveal of the gold "fronts" makes for an elegant transition from the previous CU. As Black's hands wipe downward over his face, it is as though they reveal his teeth. In terms of space and time, they don't. In terms of cinematic language, they do.

Once the camera has pulled back to reveal Black's CU, there is a cut to the car's windshield from outside, with a miniature crown prominent on the dashboard. Like Black's do-rag seen previously, the object reveals that he has assumed the dealings and status of former mentor Juan, who had a similar crown: the symbol of rule. The source music continued from the overhead shot, Goodie Mab's "Cell Therapy"—strident, assertive, and confident—sets the tone for Black's working day.

The cut to his profile as he makes a left turn to pull up reveals two parked red vehicles—the filmmaker again reminding us, if only subliminally, of his film's color palette. As Black brings the car to a halt, Travis appears in the background to walk around the trunk of the vehicle and make for the passenger door. The way in which he is shot closing it bears scrutiny, since we never see the door. On close inspection, the camera mount appears to have been attached to the door! How else could the shot have been achieved? The shot is held for the ensuing OTS shot of Travis and Black. Shooting characters getting in and out of vehicles can present problems. It may take up valuable screen time, can require additional setups that take inordinate hours to shoot, and is usually of little dramatic interest. Jenkins's elegant solution shows the importance of practicality in the approach of the filmmaker. He manages to tell the micro-story of Travis appearing and getting into the car, and without a cut continues with their conversation, losing nothing in the process.

Travis and Black discuss a woman, Black appearing to enjoy the banter and hiding from Travis—and himself—his true sexual orientation.

The subsequent cut to the WS of Travis making a deal lacks context until the following cut reveals Black watching, at which point we come to understand this has been his POV. Given the same angle, and the sudden disappearance from the frame of Travis, a cut to the single of Black beforehand would be both awkward and confusing. In addition, time moves on swiftly from the 2-shot, and the intervening events—the arrival, Travis stepping out to meet the clients—are not depicted. The ellipsis delivers the impact of the episode too: Black is working in the same fashion as Juan, with Travis as his Terrence, although there's a difference—unlike Juan before him, he chooses to remain in his vehicle, his fear surpassing Juan's wariness.

Black looks around before the camera tilts down to show him reaching for a gun. The weapon looks exactly like the revolver carried by Juan when he peeks through the curtains to check who is knocking at his front door in the final scene of the film's first act. Were it different, the connection between mentor and pupil would be weaker. It *has* to be an identical model so that we understand that Little/Black has become what his teacher was.

Having revealed the gun, the camera tilts back up to Black. The shot is barely held before there's a cut to a black screen. A person appears for the briefest moment in the background to frame left, which surely necessitated the shot's foreshortening before we notice them, but the timing seems right in any case and accentuates the shock of seeing the protagonist armed, which reverberates into the opening of the new act.

Conclusion

Information: Chiron controls a neighborhood drugs trade as Juan did. The activity is dangerous, and he is fearful.
Emotion: Suppressed (Black).
Visceral sensation: Fear (Black). Shock (audience).
Vision: The mentor's unintended influences on the student.

Jenkins's third prelude sets up the film's last act with economy. The introduction of Little takes some time over several steps as we are induced to know and care about him. The introduction of Chiron is quicker, that of Black quicker still, but shocking too over several beats: his nightmare, his terror, his denial, his defenses, his business, and his gun.

Screenplay versus Film

The two are notably different. In the screenplay, this sequence is placed much later, after Black has received the call from Kevin telling him where he works and just before Black sets off to find him. The prelude in the screenplay is comprised of the waking from a nightmare we don't see, the face washing in iced water, and then the visit to Paula that in the movie does not occur until after Kevin's phone call.

Why the radical reordering? The architecture of connection in each of the two versions is markedly different. In the screenplay, the waking up in terror follows from Kevin's betrayal of Chiron. Black then goes to see his mother, the juxtaposition implying that despite her abusive parenting, he still regards her as a source of support for an emotional crisis rooted in his friendship with Kevin. Indeed, at the end of this scene with Paula there is a moment of reconciliation between the two. In the film, it is his mother, not Kevin, who is the source of his malaise, against which he defends himself by building himself up physically (an activity shown later when, as we hear Paula's voice in a call, we witness Black working out with weights) and by assuming the characteristics of Juan. The movie's prelude is thus shorter than the screenplay's, its thread of connection more assured.

Black's relationship with his mother is primal, her abuse inflicting deep damage. His relationship with Kevin, on the other hand evolves throughout the film. It is *this* connection that offers him his chance of self-realization. Only after Kevin has called him and the two speak for the first time since his arrest after his assault on Terrell does Black summon the strength to visit his mother.

A detail at the end of the Black-Travis sequence also differs. In the film this episode ends when Black reaches for the gun. In the screenplay (in which this moment does not occur in the prelude but later in Black's act) he steps out of his car with it and makes his way to Travis and the two clients. There the scene ends. What are we to imagine is to happen next? Whether intended or not, there's the suggestion of violence, if not in this encounter then at some point to come. There are two guns in the film, Juan's and Black's (although alike, presumably they are not the same weapon), and neither is fired. Bearing in mind Anton Chekhov's frequently quoted comment on the nature of guns in dramatic narrative (not always to be taken literally) to the effect that if one is seen early in a story it should be fired later, there's a danger that we might anticipate Black using his weapon. In a different film in another genre that might be appropriate, but *Moonlight* is not that kind of film. Better not to suggest it might be, then. Having Black keep the weapon at his side as a precaution renders it an element in the introduction of his developing character, not the seed for subsequent action. Black doesn't carry it into the world but puts it down, its function in the story complete and his emotional journey set to continue.

A Note on the Transition to the Next Sequence

After the legend *(iii) Black* has appeared on a black screen, the story of Black and Travis continues. Time has passed, and the new episode takes place in the evening when Black visits his underling.

(1a) View through windshield, continue and pull out to (1b) Black arrives at Travis's home. The miniature crown is center frame as Black slows and turns left then right to meet Travis.

The story of Black and Travis then continues with the cut into the youthful accomplice's apartment. There, Black accuses Travis of stealing from the proceeds of his sales, only to reveal he is taunting him. Such gratuitous cruelty, an echo of Terrell's bullying, is the low point in Chiron's journey. Coming after the previous episode of the deal rather than Black's visit to Paula—as is the case in the screenplay—the scene drives the story forward. The reconciliation of son and mother needs to be "earned," as it is when placed after Kevin's phone call. Moving from Black's unearned reconciliation with Paula to his act of bullying makes little sense. The simple rearranging of the order in the film rectifies the problem and gives the flow of story and character consistency and logic.

Chloe Zhao

Nomadland

Based on *Nomadland: Surviving America in the Twenty-First Century*, a nonfiction book by Jessica Bruder, Chloe Zhao's Academy Award–winning film takes nonfictional material, and by interweaving it with the fictional story of invented character Fern creates a metafictional discourse very different from the story making and storytelling of feature films in general. Part dramatic narrative, part flaneurial reflection, Zhao's deftly executed hybrid is articulated by an agile and shifting aesthetic best explored not only by working shot by shot through specific scenes but also by taking examples of her approaches from the film's various narrative threads.

That these contrasts are interwoven to such effect and avoid affectation or incongruity is testament to an organic creative vision on the part of the filmmaker. Faces, details, vistas (of nature, of artificial structures), orchestrated sequence shots, personal stories related by nonactors in documentary fashion, staged scenes between accomplished actors, sequences of lament, and vignettes of solitude or absence together constitute an innovative language. Indeed, Zhao's film conveys a sensibility of both quiet individualism (Fern the lone flaneur far from the Hollywood archetype of the adversarial protagonist) and generous mutuality (the communities of the "unhoused" and the place they assume alongside nature), a creative insight that encompasses a metaphysical vision of the human soul in a universe accorded representation by the filmmaker's practical aesthetics.

The following chapters offer examples of the filmmaker's choice of visual language for the film's particular narrative threads. Instead of adopting the format of chapters as in the previous case studies, the last two examples here follow an approach tailored to the manner of the film's visual and narrative discourse.

A note on the screenplay: the script available online at https://deadline.com/wp-content/uploads/2021/02/Nomadland-Screenplay.pdf (dated January 12, 2019) appears to be a transcription of an earlier cut of the film. Improvised, true-life accounts given in the movie by nonactors are offered word for word—evidently an impossibility for any screenplay written before the shoot. Also included are several scenes absent in the film, such as Fern's visit to Swankie's son and her exchange with the caretaker of Empire's abandoned gypsum plant. As is surely the case with those scenes in the screenplay that are more extensive than their counterparts on the screen, it would seem that these elements were found through the editing process to be superfluous.

The Art of the Filmmaker. Peter Markham, Oxford University Press. © Oxford University Press 2023.
DOI: 10.1093/oso/9780197631522.003.0023

For the reader watching the film and comparing it to this screenplay, these discrepancies reveal the importance of pruning a narrative. Only when director and editor—one and the same in Chloe Zhao's case—can see the entirety of an assembly might these excisions become fully apparent. Although *Nomadland* is a singular film, this principle is common to the filmmaking process. Finding what is not needed is as essential as seeing what is. Zhao's distinctive approach to the making of her film, then, to an extent revealed by the available screenplay, paradoxically offers an insight into the filmmaker's art in general. This innovative filmmaker thus shows herself to be also a classical one—the spectrum of her skills is evident in the film's passages explored in the following chapters.

Aspect ratio: 2:40

Lenses: spherical

Nomadland

Empire—Opening and Ending

Nomadland begins and ends with a lament for the city of Empire in Nevada following upon the demise of its gypsum works. As the story starts, Fern sorts through her belongings before taking a few things with her as she leaves town. At the end of the film, she returns to let go of them and pay one last visit to her former home before returning—now for good—to her life on the road. This narrative symmetry is reflected in the repetition of places and the framings of them.

Opening

A title card reads:
On January 31, 2011, due to a reduced demand in sheetrock, US Gypsum shut down its plant in Empire, Nevada after 88 years.
By July, the Empire zip code, 89405 was discontinued.

Then follows the first image.

The Art of the Filmmaker. Peter Markham, Oxford University Press. © Oxford University Press 2023.
DOI: 10.1093/oso/9780197631522.003.0024

Fern is revealed in a wide MS (1). She takes a box of plates (2a) and places them in a vehicle (2b). She returns to her belongings, picking out a jacket (2c).

Wide on the storage units and distant gypsum plant (3). Profile 2-shot, Fern and storage unit owner (4). Fern sets out on the road (5).

Summary

Fern opens a storage unit door, takes plates out of a box, puts them in a van, holds her deceased husband's work jacket close, places the box of clothes she's found in the vehicle, pays the storage unit owner, and leaves town.

Questions

Audience: Who is this woman? Who was the owner of the jacket? Where is this woman going, and why?

Reader: What is the information the filmmaker is imparting by simple action, simple objects, and nuanced performance? How does she use the depiction of space to communicate inner emotion?

Commentary

The concise title card tells us the setting and circumstances of the film's opening episode.

The "announcing" of Fern, revealed as the storage unit door opens, is immediate, as is the snowbound terrain behind her. The next shot holds as she puts a box of plates into her van and returns to pick out a work jacket from a carton of male clothing. From her reaction as she holds it to her face, we assume it belonged to a man she loved who is no longer alive—her husband probably. The storytelling is simple and economical, the sense of grief poignant.

There follows a cut to a wide vista in which we see Fern place the box of clothes into her van, which is parked in front a row of storage units. In the background stands an industrial plant. The light is dim and somber, the colors subdued—gray and blue, with the barely perceptible reds of an American flag on signage to the right of frame. There is no score, and with little ambient sound all we hear are Fern's footsteps on the snow.

The sense of desolation and emptiness in this shot is palpable. The sudden shift of perspective from the previous frame that revealed Fern holding a jacket in a moment of deep emotion to this wide, distanced view, in which a blank, gray sky dominates the frame, rendering Fern tiny by comparison, startles us. Note that the effect on the big screen will be considerably greater than on a smaller one—the gypsum plant clearer, the sky more oppressive, Fern's action more easily seen. (This dynamic of shot size is true of the vistas throughout and true also of the contrasts in scale that the filmmaker employs.)

The sequence's final shot of the van traveling along the road through a vast snow-flecked plain toward distant hills (Where is she headed?) is given similar force by its contrast to the previous 2-shot in which Fern pays the owner of the storage units, hugging him before he departs. The cut from the instance of warm affection to this vast, icy, indifferent landscape chills us and invites our wish for a return to a more human scenario. The direction of the road, which winds from the left of frame to the less stable right, renders such a return distinctly uncertain.

Conclusion

Information: Place and circumstances. Fern leaves her life behind and with a few mementos, sets out on the road.
Emotion: Grief, affection, resolve (Fern).
Visceral sensation: Chill (audience).
Vision: The ephemerality of the human-made world versus the permanence of the natural world.

In a little over a minute and a half, the filmmaker has introduced a character, a world, a milieu, an economy, a backstory, strong emotion, and a sense of scale (a face, two vistas), and has posed a question: To where is this woman heading, and why?

Screenplay versus Film

In the available screenplay, the film begins with the following montage:

Music. Title sequence:
Archival black and white photos of Empire—One of America's longest-running mine and company towns in the Black Rock desert of Northern Nevada.
The factory. Workers. Meetings in board rooms. White piles of gypsum against black mountains.
Families playing at the pool. People leaving church. Grand opening of a grocery store. Faces smiling. Children playing in the yard of a grammar school. A community flourishing.
Proud townsfolk posing outside the factory. Young lovers getting married. A man mowing his lawn. A young woman standing in front of her house, looking at the camera. She is FERN.
Title sequence ends.

Although the contrast to the storage unit scene described next, which begins the movie, would have afforded the episode considerable power, the screenplay's opening surely would have acculturated the audience to a different film. *Nomadland* is in many respects a road movie in which a character deals with grief, the demise of a city in Nevada, and the loss felt in consequence of this. (The screenplay's opening might have the effect of suggesting the film is specifically *about* the city's decline, not the story of Fern, whereas the concise, informative title card of the movie provides the information needed but offers no life, no tone, and no imagery.) While it may be a lament, Chloe Zhao's film is also a conjuring of idyll—shifting, often fragile, but above all life affirming. By starting with the vignettes of Empire in its halcyon days, the existence in communities of the "houseless" subsequently depicted would be denuded of its defiant felicity. The two worlds—the regular, stable way of life previously offered by the city and the transient, independent situations of Fern's fellow travelers—would be in conflict, to the possible detriment of the milieu explored in both book and film.

There is also the question of tone. The bright optimism, the energy, the activity, and the colorful dailiness described on the page would surely seem incongruous.

Zhao comes to know her film as she comes to make it. The screenplay's Empire montage has no part in her vision, but it seems that she discovered this to be the case in the course of production and postproduction. Knowing the identity of the film one is making presents the filmmaker with a substantial challenge—namely, to have a strong sense of the movie that is to be composed, assembled, and unified but at the same time to be open to the journey of realization afforded by the creative process and to allow that unpredictable path to inform each stage of the filmmaking. The DNA exists, so to speak, but the evolution is facilitated. Certainty without uncertainty threatens lifelessness in the finished film. Uncertainty without certainty invites chaos.

Ending

This section is comprised of three narrative units:

> One: Fern Lets Go Her Possessions
> Two: The Gypsum Plant
> Three: Fern Leaves Empire

One: Fern Lets Go Her Possessions

Summary
Fern returns to Empire to dispose of her possessions.

Fern returns to the storage units (1). Cut to her MCU as she talks to the owner (2). The owner loads her belongings into his pickup (3). OTS Fern on owner and son (4). Cut back to Fern (1).

Questions

Audience: Have we come to the end of the movie?

Reader: How does the filmmaker tell the story so economically and effectively?

Commentary

After a shot of Fern's van traveling through the icy vista—framed as it was in the film's opening sequence—comes a view through its windshield of the storage units, the abandoned gypsum plant prominent behind. We know immediately that the protagonist is returning to Empire. The reappearance of the owner of the units, who has loaded Fern's possessions onto his pickup, reinforces the film's narrative symmetry, while the sight of a man closing Fern's unit's door offers us the information that this marks the end of her connection to the town.

Before the cut to the next sequence, the filmmaker returns to the CU of Fern as she reflects on what she must now do. The temptation here is to "cut to the chase" and go directly to the gypsum plant. The cut back to Fern as the owner "wipes frame" (crosses in the foreground) to leave her alone, and the holding on the shot as she looks at him, to frame left, then turns to look frame right, is essential, however, in that it both punctuates the end of the sequence and shows the micro-story of her shifting thoughts.

Composer Ludovico Einaudi's melancholy piano theme accompanies the sequence, continuing into the following episode. The filmmaker's control of tone—a pathos avoiding sentimentality—is sure-footed. Together with the faithfulness of Joshua James Richards's cinematography and Frances McDormand's facility for the most delicate nuancing of performance, Zhao's navigation of the storytelling at this crucial point, through both direction and editing, remains masterly.

Conclusion

Information: Fern is about to finally leave Empire behind.

Emotion: Tentative acceptance (Fern).

Visceral sensation: Coldness (Fern, audience).

Vision: The return to a significant place for final resolution.

With similar simplicity and economy to the opening sequence, in just four setups— the view of the units, Fern's CU, the owner and his pickup truck, and a reverse from Fern on him and his son—the story is told.

Screenplay versus Film

The conversation between Fern and the owner of the units is far wordier in the screenplay. The owner's son is present, as he is in the film (shutting up the unit), and Fern talks to him. The owner has more dialogue, but in the film there is only his final, ironic comment, *We'll see you later.* (We know she will not be returning.)

The screenplay is dated after the shoot, and given that the life stories of various of Fern's fellow travelers, included in its pages, were not prescripted but improvised as the camera rolled, it may well be that the screenplay's version of this scene was shot. What exists on the page, like the former dialogue, is the transcript of it. Why then is it not in the film?

The brief, pithy, economical exchange seen on screen is surely more effective than its screenplay counterpart. Looks, pauses, and a lack of the portentousness the screenplay suggests are appropriate to both the circumstances and the flow of story at this point. Reflection on the backstory and current circumstances is the prerogative of Fern alone—if her thread is to be highlighted. Once others join her lament, the power of her acceptance is diminished. We might think her realization has been spurred by the contemplative commentary of the unit owner rather than her personal experience.

The meaning of this final series of sequences lies in imagery rather than dialogue. This is not to make any sweeping statement invalidating dialogue as a resource of storytelling—it certainly delivers considerable rewards elsewhere in this movie—but wrongly placed, words can detract from the eloquence of the image. Spoken laments tell us what the film is about, while silence, setting, and what we *see* allow us to arrive at realization for ourselves. (Words that explain images tend to be extraneous. Words that counterpoint or contradict an image or in some way add a layering to the discourse may on the other hand prove telling.)

The owner's last line on the page, *Times have changed*, seems such an obvious insight that the entirety of what follows would be rendered banal.

Two: The Gypsum Plant

Summary
Fern visits the abandoned gypsum plant and reflects on the past.

Wide on Fern approaching the gypsum plant (1). Wide interior of plant; Fern crossing toward camera (2). Wide on office; Fern enters (3).

Insert: Fern's fingers wiping dust (4). Insert: empty office (5). Insert: mug (6). Insert: hard hat (7). CU of Fern (8).

Questions
Audience: Can Fern get over this?
Reader: How does the filmmaker show the past? How does she modulate the passage of time?

Commentary
The gypsum plant has been seen previously as a component in the shot of the line of storage units. The story of Fern and the units completed, the plant now fills the frame in the first shot of the new sequence. Fern is seen from the back, small in the shot as she approaches the structure walking from right to left—and in screen language returning to the past. When the camera remains static and a character we are "with" walks away from us, as Fern does here, we naturally want to see them from the front, preferably in a closer shot. The next cut—to a dark, empty, and cavernous interior— reveals a distant Fern silhouetted by a backlight as she walks toward camera. We find her even smaller in the frame—our wish to come closer to her grows stronger as the camera places us farther away and as we feel the desolation the filmmaker conveys through darkness and space, through depth, and through the sound of Fern's footsteps, muffled in the silence.

The filmmaker cuts to a gloomy meeting room as Fern enters frame left. Like the previous shot, the light source (a window) is center frame, providing an element of affinity to connect the two shots even as their spaces contrast strongly. A bare table captures the light while Fern, in a profile LS, remains in darkness—we are kept from her still. The positioning of two empty chairs to frame right accentuates the sense of absence—an example of the principle that *to show an absence, one must show a presence.* (We imagine two people sitting on these chairs.) The placing of the chairs also serves to direct the eye and the energy of the frame toward Fern. Situated to frame right, their past-ness is perhaps rendered more present, more "alive" than it might seem on frame left.

The next cut reveals Fern's fingers leaving a trail as she wipes dust from the table. From the vista of the gypsum plant to the immense chasm of its interior to this enclosed room, then to the detail of this insert, the filmmaker moves from macro- to micro-, bringing us into Fern's tactile experience. Indeed, as her fingers sweep away the dust, and as we hear the faintest *swish* of fingertips on the table, we *feel* her sensation. We have been taken from observing Fern from a distance to an intimacy with her, while the quiet intensity of this simple shot suggests the passage of time since the plant shut down.

With the almost imperceptible sound of the swish and the end of Fern's action, Einaudi's plangent score and ambient sound fade out. The following three images are shown in an absolute silence of which we are only subliminally aware. As with the lack of human presence, this absence of sound renders this montage haunting yet strangely tense. Without knowing it, we crave an ambience, which the filmmaker denies us until its reintroduction will be at its most effective.

The pronounced diagonals of the following shot of a deserted office serve to accentuate the impression of lifelessness the filmmaker creates. This is further evoked by stillness and silence. Fern is absent. There's no kinetic energy. Time does not pass, and the room seems trapped in a frozen instant. The effect is chilling.

Unconstrained by Andrei Tarkovsky's stricture that cinema works not by montage, as posited by Sergei Eisenstein, but by the passing of time in a shot, Zhao cuts to a second defiantly static, silent frame of a mug on which we see the ironic letters *US.* Again, the diagonals in the composition are strong, along with the absence of passing time, while there is contrast in the space depicted in the respective images.

From the mug to the right of frame we now find a shot of a hardhat to the left, diagonals continuing to be prominent, stasis and silence continuing. While the dirtied white hardhat *contrasts* with the dark mug, the close detail of two inanimate artifacts bears an *affinity*—and as always, these two aspects combined make for a crisp cut.

What are these three timeless, soundless shots in which Fern is absent? Are they her POVs? Is she present, off camera? (No hand reaches in, nor do we hear her footsteps or breath, while no shadow passes across any surface.) Are they selective impressions to which we are granted witness? Are they symbols of grief—for a lost population and more specifically for Fern's lost husband? Is this a journey through various rooms that we share with Fern, or are we ourselves taking a tour alone? There is no answer to these questions. The shots function as all of these things at once, both economical documentation and visual poetry of the everyday, replete with meaning yet somehow beyond analysis. While the shots may appear merely to depict their subjects, they *immerse* us in their poignancy.

A further observation regarding these static frames is the importance of rhythm in editing that they demonstrate. Without kinetic energy (although framing, composition, mise en scène, lighting, shape, and line create visual energy within the individual shots) and without sound, the drive of the discourse relies on cutting alone. The time it takes for us to see and understand a frame determines that rhythm. Too little time and we fail to take in information. Too much and we grow bored. Just the right amount and we are left wanting more yet ready for the next image.

Only now, after three shots of inanimate furniture and objects and after a sequence that has denied us a clear view of Fern's face, does the filmmaker reveal her—and in a CU, too. Without being consciously aware of it, we hear the faintest ambience. At last, time moves on. At last, we connect to a living, human presence. At last, the filmmaker presents us with human emotion in the performance of McDormand, whose consummate sense of how to modulate expression in a CU demonstrates the craft of the actor as filmmaker *in front* of the lens.

Fern's sense of loss is palpable. The sequence delivers its impact—emotion finally released through her subdued tears. It is at this point that thanks to the journey she has taken she can finally express the grief bottled up inside her. In her solitude, in the quietness of a CU in which the soft-focus background is barely perceptible, we the audience are privileged by the filmmaker to share in the most intimate of her feelings. It is often said that in drama, inner consciousness must find expression through outer conflict. Here though, Zhao reveals the deepest stirrings of a character with a pathos even a novelist, blessed with the flexibility of description afforded by prose, would be hard-pressed to emulate.

Conclusion
Information: This place is frozen in past time.
Emotion: Grief (Fern). Melancholy (audience).
Visceral sensation: Emptiness, the tingle of fingers wiping a dusty surface (Fern, audience).
Vision: The eloquence of modulated space and time.

This simple sequence exemplifies many aspects of cinematic language: composition, mise en scène, setting, space, light, movement, stasis, presence, absence, passage of time, sound, silence, the articulation of narrative POV, and performance. In conception, execution, and realization it provides a lesson in the art of moving and static images. It tells the story of Fern's visit, evokes the backstory of her loss and a community's demise, and finally—through her look—suggests the story is about to move on to the next episode. Its imagery is at once functional and poetic, realistic and mysterious. Through simplicity if offers complexity, through economy resonance.

The episode now complete, the film's final sequence may begin.

Screenplay versus Film

As with the scene between Fern and the storage unit owner, so the screenplay version of this scene begins—once Fern has entered the gypsum plant—with a wordy exchange. Here it's between Fern and a caretaker, present with his wife, who gives her access to the interior. The two scenes with this character, the sight of two llamas *munching on lawn weeds*, and vignettes of the neighborhood—of places described as being *frozen in time*—form the narrative up to the point when Fern returns to her former home. The caretaker called Albert describes his job and how the company has been keeping the weeds down with goats and llamas, and gives an account of the plant's last working day.

This is superfluous. The filmmaker's haunting montage of rooms and objects "frozen in time" offers visual poetry rather than verbal explanation. As with the earlier scene by the storage units, we escape the lecture delivered in the screenplay.

Might one suggest that the filmmaker "got it wrong" and had to rectify her mistakes? No. That would be to misunderstand the nature of the filmmaker's creative process and Zhao's distinctive approach in particular, which embraces revision, evolution, reassembly and, indeed, reconceptualization.

Her gathering of material for *Nomadland* in part took the form of a documentary approach by which she facilitated the telling of nonfictional personal stories by nonfictional people, which are interwoven with the fictional story of Fern. The accounts of several individuals are included in the finished film. Others, it would seem from the example of the storage unit owner and the caretaker, are not. Even so, the act of filming them seems to have informed the movie. For example, the screenplay describes how *Albert wipes off the dust on a red button on a control panel*. Surely this action informed the insert of Fern wiping dust from the surface of the table in the meeting room. Similarly, Albert's lines about his experience of being in the factory immediately after his switching off of its power inspired the montage that replaces his scene: *It was quiet in here. Too quiet. The last thing you want to hear in a factory is silence.*

Instead of having Albert tell us about this, the filmmaker has us *experience* it. Far from rectifying "mistakes," she builds on the foundations she permits herself to discover.

Three: Fern Leaves Empire

Summary
Fern pays one last visit to her former home before setting out on her new life.

(1) WS behind Fern.

(2) MCU of Fern as she slows.

(2) WS of Fern as she approaches home.

(4) Fern enters home. Pan with her to

(4a) Fern looking into bedroom.

(5) Fern in bedroom.

(6) Fern in kitchen.

(7) CU of Fern reflecting.

(8) WS of Fern leaving home.

(9) WS: of Fern setting out on the road. Note the compositional similarity to shot (1) and the contrast in terms of distance and vista.

Questions:

Audience: Where is Fern going? Do I feel saddened or satisfied she is visiting her former home? Will I be left here, now she is leaving? Will Fern's life on the road work out?

Reader: How does the filmmaker tell the story visually, suggesting the flow of interior emotions and thoughts without voice-over? How does she conclude her film with both an end and a beginning?

Commentary

Fern's CU at the end of the gypsum plant sequence is followed by three vistas of the environs of Empire. When we find her again, we see her from the back in a WS, the camera following her at a distance. The composition employs a single-point perspective that suggests inevitability—Fern is walking toward her destiny. The narrowing perspective of her path is accentuated by diagonals that the snow accentuates to either side of the road and by those suggested by the treetops. (The diagonals converge in low center frame.) The shot's bleakness is conveyed by trees barren against a gray sky and single-story homes devoid of any sign of life. There is no score and little sound apart from a quiet ambience and Fern's steady trudge.

From this shot there's a cut to an MCU of her as she hesitates very slightly, obviously looking at something off-screen to camera right, before continuing her walk. The camera, meanwhile, continues to track with her. Without any change of her sad but composed expression and with only the slightest blink, McDormand's Fern offers us no indication of what is to follow.

Her look motivates the cut to a house. Now the frame is static, the camera fixed. The diagonals of the previous two shots have been replaced by horizontals and verticals as we see the house flat-on. These contrasts afford the new image an impact that suggests this is a house of some significance, and if we don't realize immediately that it's Fern's former home, we surely know it is when, less than a couple of seconds in, she appears in the shot to frame right, approaching it. (Again, there is the suggestion of a return to the past with this right to left vector of energy.)

Note how, while the shot at first seems to be her POV—the cut to it was motivated by her look—she walks into the frame. Not only is this economical in terms of shots (there's no cut back to her from what she sees, no pan or track with her as she walks toward the house), but it energizes the storytelling through a compression of the passage of time: when we see Fern in the new shot, she's already farther from the camera and closer to the house than we could anticipate. Although the filmmaker is in no rush to end her film, pacing the sequence with deliberatively measured control, she uses the change in the function of the shot to keep one step ahead of us; what we initially understand in one context we instantly grasp in another without the slightest jolt of disengagement. Note also how we have again come from the frontal CU of Fern at the gypsum plant to seeing her from behind walking down the road, to a frontal MCU of her as she sees her former home, to seeing her from behind again as she approaches it. This oscillation serves to keep us engaged with the character as we both *share* in her journey and *observe* her on it.

There's a slight, imperceptible jump in time as the filmmaker cuts to the house interior for Fern's entrance. She has barely reached the porch before—from the interior— we see the front door open as she enters. We lose her for a fraction of a second only, whereas if this were to have been depicted in real time, there would have been an interval between Fern reaching the porch, stepping up to the door and turning the handle, and her entry seen from the interior. To avoid negative time, her journey is truncated so that there's no break in our engagement. (Compare this to the scene early in *Hereditary* in which we have to wait to see the Graham family enter their home.)

We saw Fern from behind in the shot of the house and now see her from the front as she enters. A sense of desolation and emptiness is immediate, but what is it that accentuates this? A completely empty room would make less of an impression than the one here with sparse detritus scattered across the floor. Not only does this prevent any perception this might be a pristine, yet-to-be occupied environment, but its presence amplifies our sense of absence.

As Fern crosses toward camera, she motivates it to push gently in, bringing her almost into an MCU. As she turns into the hall, the camera pans, and again we see her from the back, moving away from us. Her look into an open doorway to camera left motivates the cut to the interior of a bedroom. The wardrobe is empty, but again this absence is reinforced by the presence of a carpet and by a grill leaning against the wall.

Fern turns and looks to frame right and so, in the next cut to the kitchen, she enters the shot from frame right, the flow of energy maintained over the cut. (Even in such a quiet, gently paced, almost meditative sequence, there is a clear flow of energy.) Note how the pronounced diagonals of the bedroom give way to the horizontals and verticals of the kitchen, and how its windows reveal the exterior vista that beckons Fern. Indeed, no sooner has she settled, *her back to us again*, than there's a cut to the kitchen door, seen from outside as she opens it to step into a CU.

Now we see the masterly skill of an actor working with the camera. McDormand offers a lingering look to frame right. She takes a breath and after a few potent beats looks—barely perceptively—down. Again, the look lingers before, with precise delicacy, her jaw ever so slightly tightens and she gives the faintest smile. This shot tells its micro-story and reveals the actor as a storyteller. What though, is the micro-story she tells?

1. Fern opens the door and steps out.
2. She settles.
3. She scans the vista.
4. She absorbs what she sees.
5. She reflects upon it.
6. She makes a decision.

Once her decision is made, there's a cut to Fern's MS from the back, the world before her. We hear intimations of birdsong, and she steps out. As she walks away from us, the camera booms down and pushes gently forward through the open door. The gate beyond is open, and as Fern steps through it, we hear the poignant strains of composer Einaudi's piano. Note that the gate is already open. Fern has made her decision and is walking toward the life that she's discovered is for her the true one. Having already opened her existential portal, she has no need to open a new, physical one.

As the camera continues its measured move forward toward the snow-strewn landscape and hills beyond, Fern crosses to camera left, to exit the frame, the resulting empty shot held for four resonant seconds. Her move to the stable left of frame as opposed to the less stable right is significant. The left of frame is now no longer suggestive of the past but of a new stability. She is about to embark on a "houseless" life on the road, yet the subliminal sense offered by her exit is one of her heading for her true home. For Fern, the film suggests, this is not any physical edifice but a state of mind.

The shot that follows, as the score picks up, tracks from left to right, as if to balance that stability with a vector toward the unstable right—articulating visually the thematic paradox of permanence found in transience. We at first imagine this to be Fern's POV but discover her white van coming into shot from frame right, heading, as the road gradually bends, toward the shot's final single-point perspective, the camera following at a respectful distance.

Fern now heads neither to the left of frame nor to the right but directly away from us, toward her destiny. The filmmaker has expressed this through camera, cutting, performance, and finally the fundamental geometry of the screen, understood by us at the most profound, primal level. After this, there comes only the film's final cut to black.

Note how, once Zhao has cut to Fern's backshot, we never again see Fern's face. We may want to, but our wish is not granted. Other filmmakers might have cut to her profile as she drives contentedly along. That would have been a mistake. It would offer a sense of completion, not continuation. The film would be over, not only on the screen, but in the mind. Zhao's film, by contrast, may end on the physical screen but, as we desire to see Fern again, lives on into that last black screen, through the credits that follow, and beyond. The end of the film is the end of her connection to Empire, her previous life, but also the beginning of her new life.

Conclusion

Information: Fern takes her final decision to set out for a life on the road.
Emotion: Conflicting melancholy and resolve (Fern). Catharsis (audience).
Visceral Sensation: A calming.
Vision: The cycle of memory and expectation. Acceptance as freedom.

The extraordinarily agile discourse of *Nomadland* finds in its final episode a denouement of immaculate, classical style. Not a word is spoken after the storage unit owner's fanciful *Well, we'll see you later*, yet the eloquence of the visual language says everything. There's no character but Fern, whose journey we continue to share, taken as we are by the filmmaker into her innermost thoughts and emotions. There's silence for much of the sequence, yet every slight sound counts for more than a wash of score. There's little color in the monochrome palette, and the light is generally flat, yet the images are vibrant. The story is simple, the stakes hardly climactic, yet the episode compels and satisfies us, revealing the film's protagonist at the moment of her greatest epiphany—one she could not have attained without the journey she has taken through the film.

Screenplay versus Film

In the screenplay this last scene warrants only the briefest paragraph, which does not describe the action in detail but gives an invaluable impression of what we see in the film. (Was it written before the scene had been edited, perhaps?) The following lines, however, connect significantly with Fern's final CU: *Fern is unable to move, not forward nor back. She allows herself, for a moment longer, to be lost in time.* How perfectly Zhao captures that moment on the screen, and with what mastery McDormand realizes it.

Finally, the last shot of Fern's white van heading toward the distant hills is not described in the screenplay, only the empty landscape seen after she has walked out of shot. The filmmaker evidently chose to give the sense of Fern's presence and journey until the very last frame, depriving us of it only by cutting to black.

It can be challenging to conceive of the precise opening and closing images of a film at the stage of the screenplay, so it would seem legitimate to discover them in the processes of shooting and editing. What is pre-planned should not obstruct what is discovered along the way. Once seen, images speak to the filmmaker as they may not when described on the page. Nor is the precise nature and flow of a film's connective tissue apparent until the work on assembly and early cuts. Zhao evidently embraced this unpredictable process, engaging with it as she navigated her film toward its final form.

Nomadland

Storytelling from Life and by the Filmmaker; Resonance from Nature

Storytelling from Life

Fern's fictional journey serves as narrative spine and accompanying heart for the stories drawn from life that are related, unscripted, by several of the people from the *Nomadland* book. These vignettes are shot very simply, in CUs and undoubtedly in circumstances the filmmaker ensured were conducive to the speakers' sense of emotional safety as they delivered their often painful accounts: minimal crew, minimal equipment, absolute quiet, lack of distractions, absence of time pressure, eschewal of notions of performance, and an invitation to spontaneity. Trust between filmmaker, actor, and nonactor would have been developed beforehand, with other less personal moments and scenes perhaps shot first.

The following illustrations show CUs on Swankie, Linda May, Bob Wells, and Fern as she listens to Swankie. (There are similar reverses on Fern for the other vignettes.)

Simple storytelling from characters in single shots as Fern listens.

These heartfelt accounts serve to illustrate how effective simple vocal storytelling on the screen can be and begs the question as to when, in more conventional cinema, flashbacks might or might not be needed as a character relates a past episode. As

The Art of the Filmmaker. Peter Markham, Oxford University Press. © Oxford University Press 2023.
DOI: 10.1093/oso/9780197631522.003.0025

Swankie, Linda May, and Bob Wells speak, fleeting images from their stories play out on the screen of the mind. Nuances of expression, turns of the head, and looks on the part of the speaker animate the physical screen.

Bolstering this sense of primal storytelling is a sequence set around a fire at night, when various houseless" people in the encampment, known as the RTR (Rubber Tramp Rendezvous), who do not appear elsewhere in the film relate their individual experiences to the rapt attention of Fern and others.

Fireside storytelling rendered in CUs of tertiary characters.

These vignettes are interspersed with shots of Fern and other listeners, including the fictional Dave, played by David Strathearn.

Fern and others listen.

So far so good, but were the filmmaker to rely on separate singles throughout, on speakers on the one hand and Fern on the other, a sense of disconnection might arise. This Chloe Zhao avoids by at other moments including both in the frame. The following illustrations show an example from an episode involving Fern and Swankie during which they patch the paintwork on Swankie's van. After an initial shot on the hands of both as they prepare by wetting sandpaper, there follow four shots, key moments of which are shown here.

A 2-shot of Swankie and Fern is held as their scene progresses.

The shooting is simple so that the nonactor need not be aware of the camera. Swankie has a simple and practical objective, too: to teach Fern how to patch paintwork on a van, something she herself has been doing on a regular basis and nothing she needs to "act."

Zhao shows herself adept at working with nonactors. She finds scenes that do not involve "performance," that avoid complex camera moves that might constrain and intimidate a nonactor. She aims for spontaneity rather than artifice, employs fluid framing, lets her footage prompt her cutting, and utilizes the steadying hand of accomplished actor McDormand— with whom, it appears, nonactors could feel comfortable. None of this would have been possible without a considerable degree of "people skills" on the part of the filmmaker, who creates the space and environment for those in front of the camera to work without impediment and allows the nature of her process to facilitate her aesthetic.

Storytelling by the Filmmaker

Elsewhere, Zhao adopts a more precise approach to shooting. Placed between Fern's first exchange with Bob Wells and an instructive gathering of the community, the episode of Fern's morning walk evokes a sense of the activities, scope, and setting of her new world. This shot punctuates the narrative, offers a contrast to the CUs and editing of the scenes before and after, and provides a sense of the passage of time. Prompted by Wells's line *I think connecting to nature and to a real true community and tribe will make all the difference for you*, the shot shows Fern reflecting on his words as she wanders through the very entities he has described.

Fern walks from right to left. Taking into consideration the generally accepted nature of frame right as suggestive of instability and frame left of stability, we might— subliminally—see her as heading homeward. If she were to head in the opposite direction, our sense of her journey might not be to a new rootedness and instead of building on Wells's words in the previous scene, might have the effect of undercutting them.

As Fern takes a walk through the RTR, the filmmaker maintains the energy through the single take, evidently achieved as the sun was rising over the distant hills. Camera, pacing, and staging are meticulously coordinated, background action integral to the shot's quiet elegance.

Contrasting with Fern's walk, the groups she encounters are static, while the first cyclist crosses left to right and in the opposite direction to her walk. The second cyclist crosses from right to left before the first reappears, moving again from left to right, motivating the camera as it continues to track with Fern, panning right to find the t'ai chi group. Immediately after this, Fern calls out *Good morning!* to someone out of frame left, thus directing the energy again to that side. Finally, distant lights reveal ATVs traveling left to right.

This directional oscillation is deliberate, the aesthetic classical and an approach that contrasts to Zhao's filmmaking in the episodes to either side. Because it is prompted by Wells's comment that invites Fern, and indeed invites us, the audience, to take a look at the world of community and nature he defines, and because McDormand's art conceals itself behind her effortlessly naturalistic performance, the effect is not incongruous.

The scene is described very simply in the screenplay: *Fern takes a long walk through the camp. People going through their morning routines, cleaning, washing, cooking, a few gathered by the bonfire.* Linda May's line is there, then *a Roll of ATV speed by.* However, as one would expect, there is no indication of the complex orchestration of the shot. This the filmmaker leaves it to herself to design as director, using the building blocks of actor, the groups of people, additional extras, and the layout of the location.

Resonance from Nature

Nature, as Bob Wells states, is intrinsic to this world, and along with this deft sequence shot, it finds its imagery in the film both in close inserts that contrast with the human CUs and in expansive vistas. These form an essential element of the film's discourse even if they do not "move the story on." Cinema is an experiential medium, and images on the "big screen" can impart a sense of wonder (or horror) that a description on the page may find hard to match.

Following the nighttime storytelling around the fire, prompted by the last speaker's words *My sailboat's out here in the desert*, and prior to the Fern and Bob Wells scene is a brief montage to mark the passage of time and offer a contrast in terms of both light and subject matter: night to morning, the human face to images of nature. There is a visual poetry to these images that mesmerizes. They invite a moment of reflection on our part that serves to enrich our empathy for Fern and give breath to the narrative. (The second Bob Wells exchange is preceded by similar images.)

Vignettes of nature announce a new day.

The term *dramatic narrative* tends to suggest an ongoing sequence of episodes of friction. *Nomadland*, while it contains such scenes, particularly in the case of Fern and Dave, eschews the canards of "rising tension" and unremitting antagonism. Fern and Lina May, Fern and Swankie, Bob Wells, and Derek the storage unit owner never for a moment fall out, never quarrel, never seek to win out over one another, yet the film is engaging, compelling, and indeed deeply moving. The mesmeric quality of the filmmaker's imagery forms an aspect of her cinematic address to us that punctuates and informs the human interchanges she traces throughout her film. Equally striking images appear elsewhere:

Zhao tells a simple story of Fern's exploration of the Badlands through a sequence of simple but striking images culminating in her POV though a hole in a stone.

The filmmaker's cinema becomes cosmic in Fern's POV, through a telescope, of Jupiter.

Spectacle has long played a part in the power of the moving image. There are filmmakers and films that forswear it, and there are those that revel in it. Neither is superior to the other. What is important is for the filmmaker to work with their voice and to be able to find and convey the identity of their film. With *Nomadland*, Zhao excels in both respects.

It is worth considering also how a filmmaker's cultural foundations might inform their sensibility. The adversarial individualism accepted in the United States tends to prompt ongoing conflict in cinematic narrative, which at its best constitutes movies of immersive suspense and action. Zhao, by contrast, offers a vision of individual and community as part of the universe. That vision is reflected in her imagery—from CUs of the human face to vistas of desert, snowy landscapes, seascapes, or ancient woodland. Her depiction of space in these panoramas, whether unpopulated or peopled only by the tiny figure of Fern, may be an indication of the sense of a universe not defined, still less driven, by human presence. The frozen vignettes of details in the gypsum plant (see p. 286.), which appear outside the passing of time as we experience it, seem similarly to intimate a realm beyond human experience, conveying an impression of the mystical rarely found in an American cinema rooted in the struggles of the individual in a social environment of one kind or another. Even when a protagonist is found pitted against natural forces in this cinema, the drama tends to be founded in combat with nature. In Zhao's vision, on the contrary, the individual exists alongside nature, seeking neither to defeat it nor even to entirely understand it, yet dependent on it in some spiritual way, even if nature itself, one might imagine, has no need of us.

Nomadland

Fern and Dave—Invitation and Departure

Invitation

This scene—one that might be described as an *obligatory* scene between the film's two main characters—begins a sequence in the home of Dave's son in which Fern is presented with an offer of domesticity, family, and the stability of a permanent home. Although both Frances McDormand and David Strathearn are exemplars of their film acting craft, it is simply shot and consistent stylistically with the approach to scenes involving nonactors.

The fictional characters Fern and Dave and their fictional story are not taken from the film's source material, Jessica Bruder's book. Because of how Chloe Zhao handles the shooting and cutting of their scenes and how the actors modulate their performances, however, episodes between them never seem out of place within the film's discourse.

Five setups are used in this scene. Following are the frames that, even without the scene's dialogue, tell its story.

The scene begins with an establishing 3-shot of Dave, his grandchild, and Fern. That same frame is repeated toward the end of the scene as Fern is left, quite literally, holding the baby. Note how the diagonals of the bed to frame left and the crib to frame right, and Fern's placement at the apex of the room's corner, direct the eye to Fern and (as the shot is repeated) to her with the baby, exerting visual pressure through the shot's geometry—Zhao's organization of composition and mise en scène is unassuming but deft.

The CU of Fern is earlier intercut with an OTS of the infant and Dave and a 2-shot of them that becomes a single on Dave once he has lowered the child. This coverage and its editing—which heightens Dave's importuning—also has the effect of putting pressure on Fern, strengthening as it does the force of his offer to her of residence in his son's guest house.

The filmmaker has Dave hand the child to Fern and leave them alone in order that we will see her reflect on the choice she faces—to stay or go. The WS would not be right for the scene's end, as our seeing Fern in the space the room affords would preempt the sight of her out in the world, her place at the film's end. It might also suggest she could be indifferent to the child. The insert of the baby's hand placed in Fern's prevents such an impression, and as Fern's fingers begin to gently enfold the child's, we infer she is a caring person. There is also the implication that she might be drawn to Dave's offer.

The Art of the Filmmaker. Peter Markham, Oxford University Press. © Oxford University Press 2023.
DOI: 10.1093/oso/9780197631522.003.0026

Dave invites Fern to settle in his family's home.

The return to Fern's CU at the end of the scene reinforces this. Her look to frame left implies a pondering and, followed briefly by a look down to the child, clearly suggests she is weighing her decision.

Screenplay versus Film

The screenplay describes Fern folding laundry, whereas in the film she has no "business" but simply sits listening to Dave. This static staging emphasizes the importance of the episode for Fern, one that leads to her final decision. The script also lacks the end of the scene in the film, in which Fern sits alone with the baby. Her pondering of her decision is absent on the page but very much needed on the screen.

Departure

The following scenes—Fern and Dave with the family's horses, dog, and chickens, then a family Thanksgiving dinner—suggest she might indeed have been swayed by

Dave's invitation. Emily, Dave's daughter-in-law, confides in Fern that Dave *likes you a lot*. (The last section of the scene in the screenplay in which they discuss Empire is cut from the film—once Emily has revealed Dave's feelings, the episode has served its purpose.) Fern then watches Dave and his son James play piano.

Having had Fern digest the attractions of Dave's proposal, the filmmaker takes her back to her own journey as we see her alone, taking the decision to leave. The following images clearly tell that story:

Fern weighs whether to stay with Dave and his family or leave for the open road.

The sequence begins with a WS to give context: Fern on the unstable right of the screen, the home of Dave's family to the stable left, the one in opposition to the other. There is no score, only the ambience of the wind and the suggestion of far-off thunder. In a CU, Fern looks to camera left. The filmmaker cuts to her POV of the home, a shot *into which Fern herself walks* (seen from the back as she heads toward the back steps). As we hear the faint neighing of a family horse and the crowing of a chicken—a subliminal reminder of the earlier scene with Dave—then again the distant thunder, Fern treads quietly through the living room. The camera tilts down to reveal a child's toys on the rug—a reminder of the shot in which Fern holds the baby—then up to find her picking out a couple of notes on the keys of the piano (a connection here to her sight of Dave and James playing it together). In the subsequent WS she settles by the far corner. (The composition of diagonal line mirrors that of the Fern-Dave-baby scene.) There follow static, empty vignettes of an empty kitchen and a child's highchair. Fern then reappears, silhouetted in the dining room by light from its double window. She rises to exit, leaving the last frames of the shot empty.

Note how the elements that constitute this sequence work in and of themselves but also connect to the scenes we have just witnessed in Dave's family home, a clear instance of how cumulative memory informs the process of storytelling and story watching. The reader might also compare these static vignettes with those in the gypsum plant sequence: frozen images that stand outside of time's passage.

Never again do we see Fern in a settled domestic environment. In the next shots, she is by contrast already out on the road, driving through a rainstorm:

Fern drives from human settlement to coastal wilderness, from the heart of a home to the edge of a continent—a physical journey conveyed by precise imagery that reflects the path of the character's consciousness.

It is often suggested that the interior worlds of a character are the stuff of novels and that in film characters reveal themselves through action. Is that necessarily true, though? If F. Scott Fitzgerald, a novelist, said *Character is action*, here, as in the previous sequence, a filmmaker shows the inner mind of a character through a succession of images. All that Fern does is walk through a couple of rooms, leave one, and drive away in her van through a rainstorm toward the coast. It's not so much her actions as the filmmaker's shots and their assembly that take us into the workings of her mind as she makes the decision to forego settled life. Nor does Zhao rely entirely on performance alone (outstanding as McDormand's skills are), but rather utilizes visual language and practical aesthetics honed to the needs of her storytelling to convey information and emotion. Indeed, the simple descriptions of this section in the screenplay are poignantly realized through these atmospheric images.

Conclusion

The art of the filmmaker incorporates both the practical and the imaginative. It is an art of the functional and the mischievous, the precise and the fluid. It adheres to universal principles, which it nevertheless subverts as and when opportune. It is common to humanity, yet informed by specific cultures and generations, founded on the primal nature of our perception but enriched by our familiarity with its evolved complexities. Shared by the community of filmmakers, it also serves the sensibility of the individual cineaste. It is both simple and sophisticated, crafted and discovered, unchanging and changing. An amalgam of elements from other narrative forms, it is also singular, self-assertive, a distinctive art the equal of its peers. Relatively recent in history, it harkens back to the earliest visual storytelling to be found on the walls of the darkest cave chambers. Perennial yet constantly reinvented, it offers both provenance and contemporaneity. Agile, grounded, impatient, stealthy and quiet, transgressive and bold, invisible, self-aware, measured, rebellious, reverential—the filmmaker's art is as protean as it is constant, robust as it is fragile, modest as it is spectacular. It renders the fictional the living, the unknown the known, the known the seen, and the ineffable soul the image visible on the screen.

The aesthetics of the screen are the primary resource of the art of the filmmaker, who utilizes them not as embellishment, as a measure of decorum, or as "style" independent of "substance," but as a practical resource integral to their film's address to the audience. These aesthetics inform a cinematic language in which meaning is in part inherent and in part found through use.

Cinema's visual language cannot be adequately understood in terms of abstract rhetoric or grammar alone but needs to be considered in the context of the realms in which a film comes to life: in the fictional world "beyond" the screen; on the planarity of the screen; on the "screen of the mind"; in the hearts, minds, and guts of the audience; and in the memories of that audience.

The tasks of the filmmaker can be recognized as the communication of information; emotion; visceral/tactile/neural sensation; some manner of vision that relates to theme; thematic question, and a sense of meaning, perhaps paradoxical, related to the human condition.

These tasks and the address that facilitates them serve the filmmaker's overarching duty as storyteller—engaging their audience whether by prompting its constant anticipation and riveted attention or by utilizing a measured stealth to reward its patience as the film progresses.

The Art of the Filmmaker. Peter Markham, Oxford University Press. © Oxford University Press 2023.
DOI: 10.1093/oso/9780197631522.003.0027

Composition—the arrangement of *ikones* such as space, depth, shape, line, light, and color—and *mise en scène*—the placement of characters, objects, and setting in the frame—together comprise the broad concepts through which the screen's practical aesthetics can be understood.

The shot forms the building block of the progression of images, its selection, subject matter, size, and precise purpose given significance both by its discrete nature and by its context—in the scene and in the broader framework of a sequence, act or movement, and in the attributes of the visual discourse of a complete film.

The framing of the shot serves to modulate the tension it conveys and to define the information it imparts, and it relates to frames before and after; its use is fundamental to its import.

The various ways in which the camera relates to action, whether observing, complicit or participatory, critical, passive, or dynamic, will affect the audience's relationship to the action on the screen.

Camera angle—frontal, half-profile, profile, back, raking, overhead—also determines the nature of our connection, as does camera movement, either steady or unsteady, which may be motivated by the energy in the frame, may run counter to it, or may be unmotivated and orchestrated instead by the filmmaker. Lateral (x-axis), vertical (y-axis), and deep (z-axis) moves (or a combination of two or three) have a profound impact on the audience's relation to the action on the screen; these moves are at times descriptive (panning/dollying without guiding eye trace), at others narrative (allowing the eye to register one image after another), or "editing in camera" (as in the process of the camera's movement it frames up on a succession of images). Lenses and their effects further determine the nature of the image and its impact on the viewer.

The editorial process involves the detail of cuts within a scene; transitions between narrative units; and the flow of emotion, narrative, rhythm, and tone throughout an entire film. Time and space are modulated through cuts, as are physical movement and the flow of energy. The lack of a cut or cuts in a scene can be as significant as their inclusion.

The visual elements of successful transitions may contrast from an outgoing shot to the one incoming, may bear elements of affinity, or may encompass both aspects.

Sound is integral to the language of cinema; is interior to the audience (while image might be considered exterior); and may serve verisimilitude, send a message either directly or subliminally to create an image on the screen of the mind, direct the eye across the screen, prompt emotional or visceral reaction, or present an immersive soundscape. Sound may reinforce the impact of an image or action or offer a dissonant emotion or tone.

Music, which may be diegetic or non-diegetic, score or source, also functions in these ways. It may be of the time in which a film is set or be anachronistic, may take on the emotion of an episode or counter it, either bolstering the action or offering a comment on it. A movie may eschew music, while moments in a scene or sequence may be shown in a silence more potent than volume.

While these aspects of the filmmaker's art remain of constant significance and reflect an understanding and embrace of decades of cinematic practice, the language of cinema is continuously evolving as sensibilities shift and change over time. New cultural influences and depths, new and diverse filmmakers, fresh stories, new worlds, and material previously ignored or excluded bring about the ongoing invention and agility that renders cinema a living universe.

Whatever the conditions of the industry, the nature of a film's presentation, or the platforms on which it is watched, whatever the technology by which a movie is manufactured, the art of the filmmaker offers a conduit to our common humanity, its puzzles, paradoxes, horrors, joys, enduring mystery, and heart.

Glossary of Shot Abbreviations

BCU big close-up

CU close-up

ECU extreme close-up

EWS extreme wide shot

LS long shot

MCU medium close-up

MS medium or mid-shot

OTS over-the-shoulder shot

WS wide shot

Bibliography

Case Study Screenplays

Hereditary, A24 Films LLC (2020)
Moonlight, A24 Films LLC (3rd ed. 2020)
Nomadland, https://deadline.com/wp-content/uploads/2021/02/Nomadland-Screenplay.pdf

Always Crashing in the Same Car: On Art, Crisis, and Los Angeles, California. Matthew Specktor. Tin House Books (July 27, 2021).
"Are Rereadings Better Readings." Nathaniel Stein. *The New Yorker* (November 1, 2011). https://www.theparisreview.org/interviews/1791/the-art-of-fiction-no-137-alice-munro.
The Art of Dramatic Writing: Its Basis in the Creative Interpretation of Human Motives. Lajos Egri Touchstone, revised edition (February 15, 1972).
"The Art of Fiction No. 137." Alice Munro. *Paris Review*, no. 131 (Summer 1994).
The Art of Pure Cinema: Hitchcock and His Imitators. Bruce Isaacs. Oxford University Press (April 1, 2020).
The Basic Works of Aristotle. Modern Library, reprint edition (September 11, 2001).
"A Birthday Tribute to Alfred Hitchcock." Richard Brody. *The New Yorker* (August 13, 2013).
Hitchcock by Francois Truffaut. Simon & Schuster, revised edition (October 2, 1985).
In the Blink of an Eye: A Perspective on Film Editing. Walter Murch. Silman-James Press, 2nd edition (August 1, 2001).
Lessons with Kiarostami. Ed. Paul Cronin. Foreword Mike Leigh. Sticking Place Books (May 29, 2020).
Nomadland: Surviving America in the Twenty-First Century. Jessica Bruder. W. W. Norton & Company, 1st edition (September 4, 2018).
Notes on the Cinematograph. Robert Bresson. NYRB Classics, main edition (November 15, 2016).
On Film-making: An Introduction to the Craft of the Director. Alexander Mackendrick. Farrar, Straus and Giroux, 1st edition (August 31, 2005).
A Personal Journey with Martin Scorsese through American Movies. Martin Scorsese. Miramax Books, 1st edition (December 2, 1997).
Philosophical Aesthetics: An Introduction. Ed. Oswald Hanfling. Blackwell/The Open University (April 8, 1992).
Philosophical Investigations. Ludwig Wittgenstein. Ed. Joachim Schulte. Trans. P. M. S. Hacker. Wiley-Blackwell, 4th edition (October 12, 2009).
Sculpting in Time: Tarkovsky The Great Russian Filmmaker Discusses His Art. University of Texas Press, illustrated edition (April 1, 1989).
The Secret Language of Film. Jean-Claude Carriere. Trans. Jeremy Leggatt. Pantheon, 1st edition (September 20, 1994).
Transcendental Style in Film: Ozu, Bresson, Dreyer. Paul Schrader. University of California Press, 1st edition, with a new introduction (May 18, 2018).
The Visual Story: Creating the Visual Structure of Film, TV, and Digital Media. Bruce Block. Routledge (August 5, 2020).
Zama. Antonio Di Benedetto. New York Review Books Classics (August 23, 2016).

Online Resources

Abbas Kiarostami: 24 Frames. The Culturium (October 13, 2019). https://www.theculturium. com/abbas-kiarostami-24-frames/

"Cinema is a matter of what's in the frame and what's out." Martin Scorsese. Facebook (July 8, 2013). https://m.facebook.com/scorsese/photos/a.490754917661162/499327946803859/.

Krzysztof Kieslowski Was a Giant of the Cinema and a Crusader for Humanity. Sven Mikulec. Cinephilia & Beyond (n.d.). https://cinephiliabeyond.org/krzysztof-kieslowski-giant-cin ema-crusader-humanity/.

Krzysztof Kieslowski: A Masterclass for Young Directors. Cinephilia & Beyond (n.d.). https:// cinephiliabeyond.org/krzysztof-kieslowski-masterclass-young-directors/.

"Make the Audience Suffer as Much as Possible." Alfred Hitchcock. *Time*, no. 12 (March 20, 1939). https://time.com/vault/issue/1939-03-20/page/54/.

Martin Scorsese Directed Movies: Interviews and Quotes on His Filmmaking Techniques. S. C. Lannom (February 27, 2020). https://www.studiobinder.com/blog/martin-scorsese-style-of-filmmaking/.

Moonlight. Setdecor (n.d.). https://www.setdecorators.org/?art=setdecor_awards_det ail&SHOW=SetDecor_Film_MOONLIGHT.

"Philosophy of Film." *Stanford Encyclopedia of Philosophy* (first published August 18, 2004; substantive revision July 30, 2015). https://plato.stanford.edu/entries/film/.

A Rare Recording of Stanley Kubrick's Most Revealing Interview. The Marginalian (November 27, 1965). https://www.themarginalian.org/2013/11/27/jeremy-bernstein-stanley-kubrick-interview/.

What Is an Anamorphic Lens? How to Get That Cinematic Look. Leon Barnard. (November 14, 2021). https://www.studiobinder.com/blog/what-is-an-anamorphic-lens-definition/.

Filmography

Aftersun, Charlotte Wells (2022)
Amarcord, Federico Fellini (1973)
American Honey, Andrea Arnold (2016)
Another Year, Mike Leigh (2010)
An Autumn Afternoon, Yazujiro Ozu (1962)
Capernaum, Nadine Labaki (2018)
Chinatown, Roman Polanski (1974)
Citizen Kane, Orson Welles (1941)
Come and See, Elem Klimov (1985)
Dark Passage, Delmer Daves (1947)
Down by Law, Jim Jarmusch (1986)
The English Patient, Anthony Minghella (1996)
The Fabelmans, Steven Spielberg (2022)
The Farewell, Lulu Wang (2019)
Flowers of Shanghai, Hou Hsiao-hsien (1998)
The 400 Blows, Francois Truffaut (1959)
Funny Games, Michael Haneke (1997)
Gangs of New York, Martin Scorsese (2002)
Hereditary, Ari Aster (2018)
I Vitelloni, Federico Fellini (1953)
Ida, Paweł Pawlikowski (2013)
If Beale Street Could Talk, Barry Jenkins (2018)
The Insider, Michael Mann (1999)
Marie Antoinette, Sofia Coppola (2006)
Midsommar, Ari Aster (2019)
Moonlight, Barry Jenkins (2016)
Napoleon, Abel Gance (1927)
Nomadland, Chloe Zhao (2020)
Notorious, Alfred Hitchcock (1946)
On the Waterfront, Elia Kazan (1954)
Once Upon a Time in Hollywood, Quentin Tarantino (2019)
Pain and Glory, Pedro Almodóvar (2019)
Parasite, Bong Joon-ho (2019)
Passing, Rebecca Hall (2021)
The Piano, Jane Campion (1993)
Pickpocket, Robert Bresson (1959)
Le Plaisir, Max Ophuls (1952)

Ratcatcher, Lynne Ramsay (1999)
Rear Window, Alfred Hitchcock (1954)
The Rider, Chloe Zhao (2017)
Roma, Alfonso Cuaron (2018)
Roundhay Garden Footage, Louis le Prince (1888)
Stagecoach, John Ford (1939)
The Third Man, Carol Reed (1949)
Three Colors Blue, Krzysztof Kieślowski (1993)
Three Colors Red, Krzysztof Kieślowski (1994)
Throne of Blood, Akira Kurosawa (1957)
Tokyo Story, Yazujiro Ozu (1953)
2001, Stanley Kubrick (1968)
West Side Story, Steven Spielberg (2021)
The Wrong Man, Alfred Hitchcock (1956)

Index

For the benefit of digital users, indexed terms that span two pages (e.g., 52–53) may, on occasion, appear on only one of those pages.

Figures are indicated by *f* following the page number.

wonder, as category of cinematic resource, 4, 34–35, 68, 300

world of the film, 1–2, 4, 10–11, 15, 16, 26, 31, 35–36, 39–41, 42, 43–44, 49, 50, 52, 57, 64, 74, 92, 99, 101, 121, 132, 133, 134, 137, 138, 144–45, 146–47, 155, 158, 162, 197, 203, 218, 225, 226, 234, 239, 251, 259–60, 281, 308

Wrong Man, The, 108, 108*f*, 137–38, 147

x-axis, 124, 127, 309. *See also* lateral axis

y-axis, 106, 124, 309. *See also* vertical axis

Yun, Grace, 43–44, 91

z-axis, 124, 126–27. *See also* deep axis

Zhao, Chloe, 1, 4, 17, 23, 26, 31, 34–35, 37, 43–44, 46–47, 53, 148, 153, 275–76, 282

zoom, 125, 126, 243*f*